Achieving IT Service Quality

The Opposite of LUCK

Achieving IT Service Quality

The Opposite of LUCK

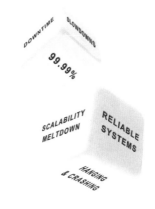

Chris Oleson   Mike Hagan   Christophe DeMoss

Synergy Books

Achieving IT Service Quality: The Opposite of Luck
Published by Synergy Books
PO Box 80107
Austin, TX 78758

For more information about our books, please write to us, call 512.478.2028, or visit our website at www.synergybooks.net.

Publisher's Cataloging-in-Publication
(Provided by Quality Books, Inc.)

Oleson, Chris.
    Achieving IT service quality : the opposite of luck /
Chris Oleson, Mike Hagan, Christophe DeMoss.
    p. cm.
    LCCN 2009901736
    ISBN-13: 978-0-9823140-2-9
    ISBN-10: 0-9823140-2-7

    1. Information technology--Management.
    2. Information resources management.   I. Hagan, Mike.
    II. DeMoss, Christophe. III. Title.

T58.64.O44 2009   658.4'038
                         QBI09-600010

10 9 8 7 6 5 4 3 2 1

Table of Contents

The Time Machine

Back in July 2000, I was working on a custom Customer Relationship Management (CRM) system for one of the nation's largest telecommunications companies. We were adding customers at a rapid clip, with no signs of slowing. I had worked on the system in various capacities for a number of years. The system kept record of every customer of the company, and if a customer wanted to change any aspect of their account, it had to come through the system. Change a phone number? CRM. Change address? CRM. Add a feature? CRM. Ask a billing question? CRM. There were 10,000 representatives who used the software every day.

The problem? It wasn't working, and hadn't for several weeks. The system was partitioned by geography, and the largest partition (New York), which held 20% of the system's customers, would cease to function under peak load—meaning weekdays from 9 a.m. to 7 p.m., Eastern time.

This was particularly surprising because up until then, things had seemed to be working fine. One of our technicians was concerned about some statistical anomalies he was seeing, and we had occasional flare-ups in the database that would resolve themselves. But the business, by and large, was working fine.

The main technical symptom was that the primary database server would start to exhibit contention, where different processes would be fighting for control of the same resources. So some of the processes would have to wait, which increased CPU consumption until there was none left, which would make everything slower, causing the problems to snowball until all processes were at a standstill.

At the time, I had only been in IT for six years and was in a state of panic. I was the manager of a team intended to optimize availability and performance. We had made modest improvements in a few parts of the system but were not prepared to tackle this. Yet somehow we had to.

My routine was to come in early, around five a.m., and manually monitor the system. It would break down in pretty much the same fashion every weekday at around nine. Throughout the day, we would try to minimize the impact by curtailing nonessential activities on the system, and we'd get a daily tongue-lashing (most of it in a stern New York accent) from the business, which was utterly and understandably frustrated. In the afternoon, we'd plot what changes to make to the system to improve things, and after the system was brought down at night, we'd apply those changes and hope for the best. I usually stuck around to see if the changes went in as planned.

Personally, I was not faring well through all of this, not that anyone was. In addition to managing a team that was positioned to help fix things, I felt doubly on the hook because I had helped to create the system in the first place. I felt like a failure. To say I was stressing out was an understatement—despite being extremely tired, I wasn't sleeping well, and I was having stomach problems to boot. (I noticed more than a few people chewing on antacids those days.) And I wasn't a lot of fun to be around, either.

> ### The Business
>
> Your IT department likely doesn't exist for its own sake. It's there to support some business objective. We often refer to the people in your company who are not in IT, yet who are trying to achieve business goals, as "**the business**."

Throughout this iterative process of monitoring and making changes, I was grasping for answers. I figured there had to be a better way, not only to resolve this problem, but also to stay out of this type of situation in the first place. I asked the experts brought in to help us. I asked my management. I searched the web. I went to the bookstore and looked for something relevant. And largely I came up empty and disappointed.

After several more weeks, and after making dozens, if not hundreds, of changes (both technical and procedural) to resolve the problem, we got back slightly above water (though it took nearly two years to get everything fully stabilized). At first, we kept searching for the one thing that was busted and could be fixed to bring things immediately back to normal. Unfortunately, this silver bullet didn't exist, and, as it turns out, it rarely does. The turnaround in this case required a lot of trial and error, and crazy amounts of heroism from folks throughout the enterprise.

Despite everyone's best efforts, a lot of damage had been done to the company as well. It cost the company hundreds of thousands of "hard dollars," from overstaffing and overtime in the call centers, as well as incalculable "soft dollars," such as the opportunity costs of not having the IT teams focus on more valuable initiatives, low employee morale, and damage to the brand through poor customer experiences.

Does this seem like a freak occurrence—something that could never happen to you? Unfortunately, these events are not all that uncommon. It would be easy to dismiss this type of thing as the perfect storm, but all you have to do is search the Internet for news stories about massive systems failures, and you will see numerous examples.

In the end, we had all learned the hard way how to do some things properly and, conversely, how not to do some other things. I mused that if I could have traveled back in time to give myself some advice in early July 2000, or better yet earlier that year, things would likely have gone much, much better. And I vowed at that time to do two things:

1. Not to let it ever happen again.

2. To help out anyone else as much as possible if they were in the same predicament.

That is the impetus for this book. I cannot create a legitimate time machine. But I have learned a lot working in this field the last six years. My coauthors, Mike and Christophe, have built up a lot of quality experience as well, based, in part, on similar crises. Combined, we have worked on dozens of different applications of different types, and over time, learned how to reliably keep IT services in a healthy state so that they rarely suffer crises. Time and again, platform to platform, business to business, there are certain methods that just work. We call this book "The Opposite of Luck" because the only way to effectively manage IT service quality is to utilize a systematic and comprehensive approach. Anything else is just a well-intentioned roll of the dice.

If I'd received that advice from my future self back in July 2000, I would have known that no matter how dire the circumstances, good crisis management techniques (as described in chapter 1) can help you make the best of a bad situation, and at minimum avoid making a bad

> ## IT Service? Application? System?
>
> Throughout the book we will use these terms according to context. In general, the content is aimed at improving the quality of **IT Services**, which has to do more with the overall experience of the users and value obtained by the business than with the underlying technologies. At times, however, content will relate to these underlying technologies. In these cases we will use terms with the following meanings:
>
> - **Application**: a business software program
>
> - **System**: either a host server or a combination of hardware and software

situation worse. I would have known what the four cornerstones of production quality are (chapter 2) and what key measurements I should have been collecting (chapter 3) to avoid being caught by surprise when I least expected it. I would have also known how to turn my problems into opportunities (chapter 4), and how to quickly find the root cause of my ailing system's problems (chapter 5). Even more importantly, I would have been able to avoid these problems if I had known about some fundamental rules of prevention (chapter 6). I would have also greatly benefited from better ways of envisioning information (chapter 7) and innovative ways of greatly expanding my influence to make organization forces work for me (chapter 8). I would have known the power of "the invisible hand of IT" (chapter 9), and how a new way of organizing my team (chapter 10) could have turned this monumental task into business as usual. I'd even have known how to prioritize all of the above to make the best use of my limited free time (chapter 11).

These techniques work for us, and they can work for you, too. Most of the advice is versatile, for anyone from a junior IT manager up to the CIO of a large shop. It ranges from tactical to strategic, technical to managerial, and throws in a healthy dose of organizational and political as well. Many of our observations are IT-specific, while others may apply more broadly to other aspects of management. You might find some of the insights to be obvious, while others may open your eyes for the first time. Those are the most fun.

Bottom line: we want to help you learn techniques that will prevent your business from feeling the same pain that ours did. I suppose it's a time machine substitute ("I can't believe it's not a time machine!"). I wish you well and hope that this helps you get on the path to making your own luck.

Chris Oleson, March 2009

Acknowledgments

We dedicate this book to our wives, Jennifer, Lisa, and Laurence, for their eternal patience!

Many thanks to veteran author Steve McConnell for providing quality advice and optimism.

And also our able (volunteer) review staff:

- JJ Ecker
- Brendan Gan
- Shawn Hammer
- Kim Hanson
- Will Howe
- Bob McKown
- Robert Miles
- Ingvar Petursson
- Tony Rapp
- Tim Sattelmeier
- Kirsten Simonitsch
- Roland Strolis
- Jeff Yee

And last but not least, we salute the multitude of dedicated and effective IT folks who served in the DRES trenches with us, helping to make IT better. Thank you all!

Less Firefighting, More Business Value

Some Like It Hot

When we think about a residential building on fire, the mental image we immediately get is of professional firefighters rolling up in fire trucks and dousing the flames with water. Obviously, this is an important action, which saves lives and property on a regular basis.

But does the act of firefighting itself, even when done extremely well, prevent fires from happening in the first place? No. Would we be happy if our homes caught fire on a regular basis, but help came quickly every time to minimize the damage? Of course not.

The fire departments around the world know this, too. They undertake a variety of programs to manage fire on all fronts, from crisis management to prevention. IT production quality management is similar to the business of minimizing damage from fires. Even though IT production crews should strive for excellent response to incidents, the greatest way they can serve their customers is by taking actions that will, at a minimum, reduce the impacts of incidents when they happen and, at best, eliminate them altogether.

Firefighting

Firefighting is the act of managing a specific kind of crisis: fire.[1] This includes the acts of receiving a 911 call or an automatic alarm and responding by driving to the site of the fire. Once there, the firefighters simultaneously try to save anything of value (including people) and put out the fire.

---

1 If you happen to be an actual firefighter, first of all, thank you, and second, this is only an analogy, so please don't be too critical of the details!

It may sound easy, but this is an area with many moving parts, and key decisions must be made quickly. While the predominant focus of this book is prevention, we do start with a chapter on crisis management (chapter 1). Good crisis management capabilities are a necessity, and it takes a select breed of individual to do this well.

However, firefighting doesn't prevent fires.

Getting the 411 on Your 911s

Implementing prevention measures intuitively makes sense. But until you know how you are faring today, it is difficult to know just how much improvement is needed or if certain preventive measures worked or not.

Every major city carefully tracks a core set of metrics related to fires that gives them an accurate assessment of how good or bad things are, such as how many calls the fire department responded to in a given month or year. Does your IT department track *all* its incidents? Cities know how many lives were lost and how many dollars of damage were done. Do you understand the business impact of all your incidents? For each incident, cities record how long it took to respond and try very hard to determine the root cause of each fire. Are you rigorously doing the same for your IT services? They also know how many firefighters they have, how many ambulances, how many fire engines, and how many fire stations. Does your organization know exactly how many resources are dedicated to incident response?

By tracking all of this data over time, cities can tell if things are getting better or worse. Applying the same approach to IT incidents can create a great foundation for prevention and improvement. In chapter 2, we uncover what the key metrics are for measuring production quality, and in chapter 3, we delve into how they can be measured.

Cities and government agencies also use this data, combined with investigative techniques, to understand causes of fires. In chapters 4 and 5, we uncover approaches to problem solving that leverage this data to put you in control of the situation and better equip you to take preventive measures.

Prevention

When firefighters aren't actively working an incident, what do they do? How do cities try to prevent fires from happening in the first place?

There are literally hundreds of fire prevention techniques in use today. Smoke detectors are commonplace. Household goods are made from fire-resistant materials. Building codes and building inspectors make sure that all new construction utilizes the latest and greatest methods to avoid accidental fires. Cigarette lighters often have childproof ignition systems. In IT, we can learn a lot from those practices. If we begin to think about each breach in service quality as equivalent to an incident the fire department responds to, and about what we can do to emulate all the prevention steps that go into fire prevention, we can leverage decades of best practices. Chapter 6 shows just how important prevention is for IT production quality.

In addition to taking preventive measures, fire departments and other organizations sift through all of the collected data to look for trends. A certain type of building material may be more prone to catch fire. Perhaps a certain model of kitchen appliance has caused an unusually high number of fires. There are a great many aspects of fire to consider.

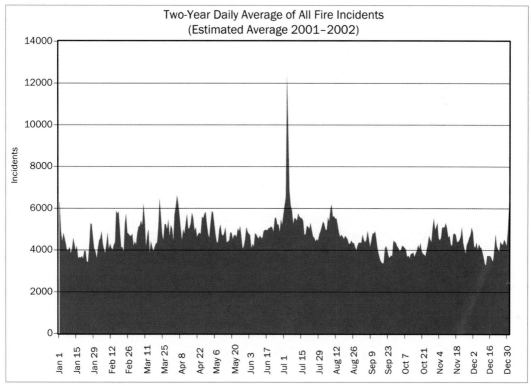

Source: "The seasonal nature of fires" U.S. Fire Administration, January 2005
figure 0.1. Fourth of July fires

As an interesting example, a study by the U.S. Fire Administration has shown that more fires get started on the Fourth of July than on any other day (fig. 0.1). Armed with this data, officials can implement more targeted prevention programs. This kind of analysis applied to IT can help spot relevant problems. Once you know the trends, then you can act.

Knowledge Is Power

To be sure, a fire department could be successful by putting out fires quickly, recording its progress, and implementing any high-value prevention techniques they can think of. But there's still more they can do.

For one, they can formally document their findings. If, for instance, they put their key findings about the past year into a 10-page document, they can send it to the city council and the mayor's office to request additional budget for staff or particular equipment. If you've ever had to justify a request for funds or headcount, you know how much easier this is when your request is backed by solid data.

Fire departments can take that same document and circulate it to other fire departments as well, for the greater good. Neighboring cities and towns may very well benefit from learning about the challenges faced by another city's fire department and how they approached the problems. Similarly, all the various teams in your organization can learn from each other through knowledge sharing.

Similarly, some fire departments publish a newsletter to the communities that they serve with tips on fire extinguisher use, smoke detector battery replacement, and fire drills. In this way, they are able to approach fire prevention from another direction.

Lastly, fire departments benefit from diagramming any complex parts of their industry. They can chart the location of all fire stations by what capabilities they have. They can chart the location of fire hydrants by what water flow they are able to provide. They can detail the contents of each one of their vehicles. All of the diagrams serve to make key information easier to access so that many more people can leverage it to do their jobs better.

In our experience, diagrams and charts are underutilized communication tools that can help an IT organization build and run better-quality products. We cover this in more detail in chapter 7. We also have found that the right information published to the right audience at the right time can greatly enhance success. We discuss how in chapter 8.

The Culture of Self-Sustaining Momentum

The fire marshal can steer a great number of these activities. From his office, he can dictate that fire hoses be dried out a particular way, statistics be kept, reports be published, and make various other directives. If he makes the right decisions and gets his personnel to consistently perform in an effective manner, he will get better results than if he let everyone do their own thing.

But he can't make every single decision at every level. Nor can he make decisions while on vacation,[2] nor after he retires. What he can do is create a culture of constant

---

2 Unfortunately, the BlackBerry may have changed this somewhat.

improvement. He can ensure that his people know that it is paramount to cut average response times from seven minutes to five minutes, and that no building in the city should be more than 75 yards from a fire hydrant. Then everyone on staff can make decisions about their work accordingly. By fostering such an environment, the fire marshal is leveraging the energy of his full organization instead of getting results through his own efforts only. This can be extremely powerful when used in any organization.

In chapters 9 and 10, we demonstrate how IT leaders can tap into the great pool of energy available to them throughout their IT department, and produce extraordinary results. In chapter 11 we share strategies for effectively putting this all into practice, even when the task seems insurmountable.

The Fire-Resistant Pyramid

Fire departments are not successful by just putting out fires quickly. As evidenced above, they must do a great number of activities in complementary areas to make a difference. Operating production IT systems effectively requires the same approach.

In this book, we show you how to undertake quality improvement activities that will make you better at crisis management (firefighting) and incident avoidance (prevention). We know that the more of these tactics and strategies you implement, the better your chances are to have stable, productive, and profitable production IT systems.

The advice starts off fairly straightforward, such as how best to resolve an incident quickly, what quality metrics are the most important, and what attributes to monitor on your servers. But tactics such as these, while powerful, will only get you so far.

In later chapters, the counsel becomes more strategic: we unlock the secrets of making your production systems run predictably to help your business see you as an enabler rather than just a cost center or order taker. We let you in on secrets such as how to detect and fix problems before they happen, how to get the most out of other departments, how to find the perfect person for your key operations roles, how to focus the central leadership message of your department, and how to leverage organizational design to get the most out of your own department.

To help organize all of this information, we utilize a hierarchical model represented by a pyramid (fig. 0.2). We like to think of this pyramid as fire resistant, because it acknowledges that fires do and will exist, but that doesn't mean you have to get burned. The pyramid is a depiction of the Production Maturity Model, or PMM. In the following pages, we will start with the foundation and work our way up.

The more tactical tips for success start at the bottom of the pyramid: In Level 1 (Crisis Management, a.k.a. firefighting), we focus on how to resolve a crisis quickly and efficiently. In Level 2 (Defining Quality), we uncover the four cornerstones of production quality, how to measure them, and how to use the power of data to improve quality.

As you progress along, the more strategic material is located near the top of the pyramid. There you'll find Levels 3, 4, and 5. Level 3 (Prevention), focuses on activities that will minimize your chances of having to visit Level 1. Level 4 (Information Promotion), shows how documenting and broadcasting information in certain ways can take your results to a higher level. Level 5 (Perpetual Motion), discusses how you can direct organizational forces toward your quality objectives, effectively harnessing energy beyond your own.

figure 0.2. The Production Maturity Model

The levels are not hard-and-fast rules about the order in which things must be done—though in many cases it would be difficult to proceed out of order (for instance, setting specific system quality goals without knowing the current state of the system). In many cases, though, it's entirely possible to selectively perform activities in the higher levels while simultaneously taking action in the lower levels. The primary value of this pyramid is just as a framework for organizing hundreds of key thoughts and best practices. It is also an interesting way to do a rough assessment of your current situation. If you feel like your department has levels 1 to 3 covered, but it doesn't do much in levels 4 and 5, then you have a fairly good idea of where you stand.

One last piece of advice about digesting this material: while there are many tips here, you are probably already doing a lot of these things (and you should continue to do them!). And incrementally, over time, you can pick and choose what you like best to add value to your department, buffet-style.

Only you can prevent forest fires.

Crisis Management

From a management perspective, this is the best way we know to get out of the hole you're currently in.

Chapter 1: In Case of Emergency, Break Glass

Level 1
Crisis Management

In Case of Emergency, Break Glass

How to Manage a Crisis in IT

Chapter Overview

If your IT service or solution is not working and is impacting the business in an extremely negative manner, it's in crisis. The service or solution must be stabilized before you can begin to implement the proactive quality improvements needed to avoid crises in the first place. Right now, you're dealing with an emergency, and you're sounding the alarm.

This chapter will show you what actions to take in order to resolve crises as quickly as possible. We'll let you know how to assemble the appropriate team and explain highly effective ways to get them properly focused. We'll also talk about how to have them work quickly yet methodically, how to monitor your progress, and how to know when you've reached the desired end state. This chapter provides guidance on the fundamentals of crisis management so you can achieve the stability necessary to begin transforming your organizations to produce the quality results you desire.

Clear the Smoke

This book isn't really about crisis management. It's about running your IT applications and services in such a manner so as to avoid crises in the first place. That being said, if you are currently in crisis mode, or inherit a system in poor shape, you must achieve some form of acceptable stability before you can move on to activities that will benefit you greatly in the long term. As with any emergency situation, the right reactions can make the difference between a catastrophe and a near miss. So here's how to get out of the jam.

Definition of a Crisis

The nature of a particular systems crisis can vary from implementation to implementation. Often a crisis will be a stability/availability problem (possibly due to an underlying scalability problem from either poor planning or poor software implementation). Ultimately, though, if your business is clearly unable to achieve its business objectives on a regular basis due to IT failures in a particular system, it's a crisis. Crises can last for days, weeks, or even months.

These crises, depending on the size of the enterprise and the type of the problematic system or service, cost your company anywhere from thousands to millions of dollars per week. This includes both direct costs, in terms of lost sales and extra manpower needed to perform the work, and indirect costs, in terms of customer and employee confidence and satisfaction. You must act fast and decisively to get things back on track.

Leadership

The first and most critical step in resolving such a crisis is to make sure you have the right people in charge of resolving it. It is critical to choose one to two leaders to spearhead this effort. The leadership needs to be both technically and managerially skilled, and also be empowered to make decisions about how the crisis will be resolved; they must also have the appropriate authority or sponsorship to implement what needs to be done without bureaucratic impediments. The idea of authority is important and can't be emphasized enough. Whoever is in charge must have the backing and support from leadership to implement what needs to be done to get things working again. If the crisis leader or leaders don't have the pull required to do (or authorize) what needs to be done, then they aren't set up for success and will likely fail.

Countless volumes have been written about what leadership is, and we won't attempt to recreate them here, but suffice it to say that your leaders must have the right stuff to get the job done. Judgment, poise, demeanor, intellect, enthusiasm, focus, and vision are only some of the qualities needed for this role. The crisis leaders also need to be respected, voracious learners who continuously probe those around them for new ideas and fresh insights. Putting the right person or people in charge is the most important decision of all.

> **Factoid**
>
> SWAT, originally a police term, stands for "special weapons and tactics."

Once leadership is chosen, a virtual team must be drafted to put out the fire. Often this is called a SWAT team or task force. If the problem is big enough, it makes sense not only to have production personnel involved (system administrators [SAs], database administrators [DBAs], etc.), but also senior architects, developers, and any other relevant technical troubleshooters available in IT.

It also makes sense to colocate your SWAT resources as much as possible. Put them in a big room (sometimes referred to as a war room) so that they can collaborate as easily as possible. Initially, they will groan about this, and certainly working in close quarters presents challenges (you'll need more recycling bins for Red Bull cans), but in this case the ends justify the means, and you'll progress much more quickly. It also lets everyone know how serious you are. If you leave everyone in their old seats, they may be tempted to do their regular jobs and work on this crisis in the margins, which is not what you want at all.

Vendor Assistance

If the problem has anything to do with third-party software or hardware, relevant vendor experts should be brought on to the team as well. In terms of vendor support, don't settle for occasional phone support. Especially if your enterprise is big, demand to have the vendor provide one or more experts on-site full-time. If you're already paying for maintenance and support, you should insist on this at no additional charge. Situations like this will often reveal just how dedicated your support vendors are to your success—like they always say they are during the sales process for their products.

If you must pay extra for vendor support for your SWAT team, don't pinch pennies foolishly. Consider the cost to the business if the crisis continues. If your vendor seems not to understand the urgency of your issue, make sure to explain the severity of the business problem to them. If that doesn't work, enlist the help of your CIO to get them properly motivated. If you are an important customer to those vendors (in terms of revenue or a strategic relationship), you should not hesitate to apply pressure. If your vendor is being unnecessarily difficult, feel free to ask them if they'd like to appear in the Wall Street Journal as a key contributor to your crisis, and watch them turn flush. Spending time with your supplier's competitors to consider alternative technologies will also help get their attention.

If you don't think the problem lies with your vendors, but you're not sure, at a minimum you should call your vendors to put them on alert. Let them know what the situation is and that you may be calling on them for expert support in the near future, depending on how things go.

Once you've assembled your virtual team, lead a kickoff meeting to get everybody rallied behind a common goal: to resolve the crisis. Establish a sense of urgency and criticality—make sure everyone has a true understanding of the impact of the crisis on the bottom line and the reputation of the firm. Be specific. Develop a detailed plan of attack capturing who's responsible for what action by when and the expected result. Establish daily status meetings with the SWAT team, as well as daily executive status communications. Agree with the team on a set of objectives that will define a successful exit from the crisis or the finish line. This is very important. If you don't define where the finish line is, people will behave in one of two typical ways, both of which are negative:

1. The go-getters will assume the finish line is closer than it really is, and they'll sprint until they burn out and collapse, which is bad for both them and the SWAT team effort.

2. The rest will proceed at a slow pace, assuming the finish line is so far out in the distance that they must overly conserve energy to ensure they make it to the end.

Once the objectives are defined, it's important to track them in a highly visible place like a whiteboard in the war room where all will see them. Refer to them constantly to keep the team aligned and focused.

First-Aid Kit Essential: Workarounds

If things are truly dire, you need to approach the problem from multiple angles at the same time. One of these angles that can be particularly effective over the short term, especially for scalability issues, is to implement *workarounds*. A workaround is a suboptimal way to temporarily accomplish the same business goal as the service that is not performing well; a contingency plan is the same thing, except it is prepared in advance. Either one will often require sacrifice on the part of the business, IT, or both. The following are a few examples of workarounds:

- Stop all nonessential business activity on the system in trouble. This could be certain types of reports, queries, extracts, or other activity. It can be a lot of work to track all of these activities down, so dedicate one of your less-technical people, perhaps a project manager, to inventory them.

- Move as much processing as possible to off-hours or weekends—whenever your system is typically at low load. This includes rescheduling some types of maintenance, batch processing, backups, and even rescheduling human processing where possible. An extreme example of this would be taking customer orders on paper and rekeying them in the evening. While extreme, if it takes hiring temps to make it work, it may still be worth it to keep the business running until IT issues can be fixed.

- Shift the work to a different yet similar system already in place within your company. We once worked at a company that had seven separate systems to take orders. Yes, they were all somewhat customized for specific types of orders, but when one system went down for several days, we utilized one of the other systems to help fill the gap.

Monitor the Situation

SWAT teams rarely storm into a critical situation without understanding as much as they can about it first. After your team has been assembled, one of the first things you need it to do is monitor the various aspects of the problem, including how well the application is performing from a business perspective. You need to do this for the following reasons:

1. You need to be able to tell how bad it is.

2. You need this information to come up with specific ideas about how to make it better.

3. You need to tell if the changes you make are helping or hurting, and by how much.

There are two main categories of monitoring during crisis management, which are complementary and should be executed in parallel: end-user experience monitoring and infrastructure monitoring.

Understanding the End-User Experience

For a large crisis with a user-based system, you'll need to get a few IT people out in the field to ascertain exactly what the end users are experiencing. Is it slowness? On what functions? What times of day? Having an end-user monitoring system will greatly help in this task, but if you are in a crisis situation, nothing will replace having people in the field. A field presence from IT provides the following benefits:

- It provides your technical team with specific, expert descriptions of the problem. We have seen countless situations in which the IT team is trying to resolve an issue they don't understand because they are working off of unsubstantiated information relayed from the field through indirect channels. The team in the field should maintain and share a historical log with all of their findings, including specific dates, times, and locations.

- It establishes local technical support. Your folks will have the ability to look at local log files, export them to the technicians back at IT, and, in the event of a client-related problem or client-related workaround, make any adjustments to the client system or even recommend any business process changes as necessary.

- It demonstrates to the business that you understand, care, are engaged, and are trying to solve the problem. This is often overlooked—maintaining morale and support of the business is a huge benefit to the SWAT team effort.

They will be more patient if they are actively engaged in the process and understand directly the difficulties and challenges you are facing.

- It helps facilitate the successful application of workarounds mentioned in the previous section. Often field personnel will know or help develop the best workarounds.

- It provides confirmation that your technical monitoring is providing accurate results. Your field technicians might need to perform manual stopwatch timings and put the results in a spreadsheet by hand if it is a performance problem and no automated monitoring solution exists.

Infrastructure Monitoring

In addition to providing field support, it is important to acquire, save, and trend as much technical data as possible regarding your problem. Here is a list of what you'll need:

- All physical hardware metrics, database performance metrics, network statistics, storage statistics, and client statistics.

- Every log file you can get your hands on, including those for the server-side applications and the middleware.

- The exact version numbers of all of the above, down to the patch level. Not just 12.6, but 12.6.4.13 r3.

- The value of every configurable setting for all of the above.

- The volume of transactions the system is handling, and how many users are on the system.

- The change control log for every change made starting several days (or, in some cases, weeks or months) before the problem started, up through the current day.

The utilization and throughput data should be collected on a very short interval (e.g., every five minutes). This is because if you choose a relatively large interval, like thirty minutes, and the problem only occurs in spikes of three minutes, then the problem could be hidden in the average. The only caution is, if you make the interval too small, e.g., 20 seconds, it may end up taxing the system so much that the monitoring itself ends up degrading system performance.

Once you have this data, make it readily available to all members of your task force. They will be able to analyze it from the following perspectives:

1. Is any of the data out of industry norms? For instance, does a key machine in your architecture run at 100% CPU (or high load averages for UNIX systems) during peak load?

2. Does anything jump out that is different than when the system is running smoothly? Correlate the data to the problem periods to find out.

3. What has changed since before the problem started? Do any of the changes correlate to the problem?

This will give your think tank plenty of things to chew on, as well as ways to prove or disprove their various hypotheses.

Note that most of this data should be collected regularly, even when there is not a crisis! But if you don't have it, you need to get it. Furthermore, not having it might be part of the reason you're in the crisis in the first place.

Methodical Triage

Okay, you have the team in place and you've captured all the relevant data you need to come up with solutions. Your team is energized and has come up with a dozen changes of various sizes they are eager to implement. So what do you do now? Virtually the rest of this chapter deals with how to safely implement these changes. It follows some of the principles emergency rooms follow to triage patients, or decide what aid to administer to them. It may be counterintuitive to slow down when you're in a crisis, but here we go.

It is likely you will be under enormous pressure to fix things quickly. The business will want to know that changes are being made, to give them hope that things will get better soon. Senior management will want the same.

This is all fine and good, but here is a key piece of advice: resist the temptation to guess. Some technical folks will assert that a change should be made just because they think so. Or that they guess that the problem is X, therefore the solution must be Y. Do not fall for this, unless you feel very lucky, or the change is a snap to undo, or the system is already 100% down so there is nothing to lose. Many such changes end up causing more harm than good, taking additional effort to back out and impairing your ability to introduce good changes later.

It is far saner to only allow changes that have some basis in fact to be implemented. "We have seen this specific problem in the logs, and the vendor says to increase parameter Z to alleviate it. We tried it in a test bed, and it worked without harming anything else." That is a solid rationale.

Part two of this advice is that it is unlikely that a single change is going to make everything better. We see this on occasion, where some parameter was at a very suboptimal setting, but it's rare. If there was a silver bullet, then chances are it wasn't a major crisis to begin with. Much more likely, you'll have to make large numbers of total changes in concert to get to the point where all is functioning normally. So set expectations that it's a long road and you're looking for measured progress from day to day.

One Change at a Time

Earlier in this chapter, we prescribed attacking the problem from many angles and doing a great many things in parallel to save time. But a production environment is one area where making multiple changes simultaneously is not a good idea. When you make more than one change at a time, you don't know if the benefit (or detriment) caused by the changes was a result of change A or change B. It is important to isolate each change as much as possible. One exception would be if two changes are in very different subsystems (for instance, a change in your disk array, partnered with a change to a handful of client systems). So other than that, limit your changes to one at a time. Usually this means once per day at most, since most changes have to be done during the maintenance window or during the lowest-volume time of the day if the system does not have a regular maintenance window. If that doesn't apply to your change or your system, then you might be able to make multiple changes per day.

> **TIP**
>
> Don't make a bunch of changes all at once. Doubling your bet to get even is a recipe for going broke. It's the behavior of gambling addicts, not IT professionals.

We can't stress enough the importance of sticking to this principle rigorously. It is very tempting during a crisis to accelerate the rate of change in order to improve the situation quickly. But we have seen this approach backfire and prolong the state of instability. Consider this example:

The SFA Double Take

A sales force automation system (SFA) performs so poorly for remote users that they prefer to manage the sales process with spreadsheets rather than with the designated system. To improve system performance, the IT team decides to take advantage of an upcoming maintenance release (MR) to install a firmware patch to a network compression device. The MR also has some code improvements targeted at improving the situation for the same user group. The following Monday everyone claims success as performance is indeed improved, and some of the users who had given up on the system now start using it again. But then something unexpected happens. On Friday, the busiest day of the week (thanks to roaming sales personnel coming back to the office to update their accounts' information in the system), performance becomes even worse than before. The higher system usage is the only observable difference from previous weekdays. Immediate troubleshooting doesn't reveal the cause of the problem, and nobody knows whether the MR, the device patch, or some new scalability bottleneck is to blame. By the time Friday's peak hour is over, too little data has been collected to allow finding root cause. The following week, the investigation continues, and the performance testing team tries to reproduce the situation to no avail.

Week two goes by, and the same situation happens again on the second Friday after the changes were made. What puzzles everybody is that while usage is higher than it had been recently, it has not yet reached the extreme volumes seen just before the close of the previous fiscal quarter, during which performance did not degrade under load. So the cause must lie with a change made recently to the system.

The vendor of the compression device argues that the patch has been thoroughly tested and can't conceivably cause performance to be any different during high load as it is during low load. The only other change that had been made to the system is the MR. The decision is therefore made to roll it back during the upcoming weekend. On the Monday after the rollback, users complain about old performance problems coming back. This confirms that while the MR was suspected to cause the problem on Fridays, it did contain some performance improvements. In the meantime, the development and test teams put everything else on hold to investigate the problem with the code. But Friday comes around, and to everyone's surprise, the system hits the same bottleneck as the two previous Fridays. Simultaneously, the network compression device vendor puts out an advisory about a scalability limitation in its latest patch based on feedback from other customers. You decide to roll back the patch, bringing the system back to its original state three weeks ago. At this time, you can't re-implement the MR because you're still not 100% sure it didn't have something to do with the issue. So you go into another week of poor system health but finally get through a Friday without any sign of the scalability bottleneck. But then you look at your usage volume for the day and realize that it is lower than usual because of a nationwide sales force convention in your company.

By now your performance test team has been able to reproduce the issue with the patch and confirm the defect, and your development team has stopped looking for an issue in the MR. You think it's probably safe to reinstall the MR, but the sales organization needs to sign off on the change, and you are out of time for the coming weekend. Additionally, some decision makers have lost all confidence in the MR and want one more pass of performance testing before giving it the okay. On the bright side, you look forward to the opportunity to go through at least one high-volume Friday to make sure the patch was truly the cause of the problem. Finally, on the fifth weekend after the original rollout, you put the MR back in, and wait yet another week to confirm that all is fine.

And you are not done. You still need to wait for the vendor's revised patch, take it through testing, and roll it out, because your users in remote locations are still complaining about performance issues.

Comparative timelines of the scenario and a more conservative approach.		
Week 1	Implement MR and firmware patch	Implement MR
Week 2	Troubleshooting	Implement firmware patch
Week 3	Roll back MR	Roll back firmware patch
Week 4	Roll back firmware patch	
Week 5	Re-performance test MR	
Week 6	Re-implement MR	

While this example may seem far-fetched, it really isn't. We have seen this type of scenario happen at multiple companies. In trying to save time by combining changes, you can actually delay the introduction of a valid fix and cause disruptions to ongoing work (pulling development, test, and other resources away from what they were doing to work on the crisis), thus prolonging the crisis.

As illustrated by this example, when multiple changes are introduced within a very short time interval, with no ability to validate the success of a change before putting the next one in, it is almost impossible to know with certainty that any one change didn't have an adverse effect. And if it did, it could take days, weeks, or even months before you realize it and correct the situation.

The best methodology for choosing changes is to have your team keep a list of all changes that they'd like to make, along with their anticipated benefit, anticipated risk, amount of testing performed, and duration of the change itself. Have a meeting every evening to decide which change will be performed that night. Perhaps some changes look very promising but just aren't ready yet. Perhaps a particular change would be perfect but conflicts with some mandatory database maintenance, so be on the lookout for conflicts with various jobs as well (if you have a formal change control process, you'd probably want to invite a representative from the change control team to your meeting as well, or use this meeting to prepare for what change requests you will bring to the change control board). Then have a follow-up meeting the next day to ascertain how well or poorly your change went.

Testing

Some changes can easily be tested. However, when it comes to these production quality issues, due to limitations in testing infrastructure, some changes cannot (or can only partially) be tested. If this is a prolonged problem, it is in your best interest to make sure the SWAT team has its own test bed, where they can tinker. And have them test every proposed change as much as they can. Because with testing, you might reduce your change fail rate from 30% to 10%. If 3 out of 10 of your changes make things worse, you will have little credibility and not be able to get things done. Conversely, if 9 out of 10 changes make things better, you will have all the credibility you need. So test. And even if you can't verify that the change will yield the expected benefit, test to verify it won't introduce some unforeseen negative consequence.

Types of Changes

The changes will generally fall into one of five categories:

- tuning

- maintenance

- vendor patches

- specific bug fixes

- hardware upgrades

If you aren't actively investigating all five categories as areas of opportunity, assign a different person from the team to each underrepresented area to investigate.

Timing

There are a few points about timing that will make your implementation of changes much more successful. While you should strive for excellence in the changes that you make, assume 10% of them are going to fail with bad effects. Each change should have a back-out plan, although usually those disrupt the business as well.

Perform an honest risk assessment for each change, and time the changes accordingly. For instance, let's say that your business is extremely busy on Monday, fairly busy Tuesday through Friday, slow on Saturday, and opens late and is extremely slow on Sunday. When would you want to do your riskiest changes? Saturday night (Yes, we know this won't be popular with the troops). When is the best time to do the least risky changes? Tuesday through Thursday nights. When is the best time to give your team a rest from making any changes? Sunday night.

Now don't go make these rules and assumptions up on your own. Nobody knows the potential pain better than the business. Engage the business leadership in your timing decisions. They don't need to know every little detail, but they should have a say in the big decisions; the last thing you want to do is blindside them at their busiest hour. Also, getting the business on your side will grant you more flexibility—if a change is so complex you need more time to implement it, perhaps they will agree to close for business an hour early to buy you some wiggle room.

Resolution

Congratulations. Once you have iteratively made enough quality changes to get things back to normal, it will be tempting to disband the task force and send everyone back to their normal jobs, where no doubt they are behind on some important work. But before you do, there are a few key things you need to see to. You may be able to gradually roll off some key people early, but keep some around until the following is complete.

The first thing is to thank the SWAT team for their efforts and reward them appropriately. At the same time, tactfully remind everyone that the true heroes are the ones who avoid crises in the first place.

Secondly, make sure that the good results of your work are not lost. Get a few people to gather all of the relevant information into an archive, so if a similar problem happens again in the future you don't have to start at square one. A well-executed lessons-learned meeting can help cement the factual lessons. Record relevant details of how the problem happened, what the symptoms were, and how it was solved. Consider putting this data into an intranet wiki for easy retrieval and updating by the staff. Deliver this information to the development, design, and architecture teams so they ensure future systems don't face the same problems.

Finally, take action to make certain the circumstances that allowed you to get into such a problem state in the first place are not allowed to recur. In addition to the knowledge gained, you have a limited window to leverage emotion—people will listen to you. Use the pain felt during the crisis and the capital you built up by solving it to launch the institutional changes needed to avoid a future meltdown. Seize the day! Implement the lessons learned (perhaps via a formal program) and also follow the principles covered in the upcoming chapters.

The Culture of Heroism

This SWAT team approach can be very powerful. With it, you can assemble a very effective force to tackle huge issues. Some IT shops even get very good at it—perhaps too good. If you're assembling a SWAT team at regular intervals, even if they are very effective, something is wrong. It is critical that much more effort is spent keeping your business out of trouble than bailing it out once it gets there. Furthermore, task forces lose their effectiveness over time. If you succeed with one task force, people will be energized. If you need to call four task forces within nine months, your people will be demoralized because you can't seem to get anything right and they can't get their normal work done. So don't become dependent on them as part of your core methodology.

Does your IT department value a culture of heroism over a culture of prevention? If, at the annual holiday party, you lavish awards and attention on your key firefighters, but neglect the folks who methodically run a tight ship, you are probably sending the wrong signals to your staff. If so, it's time for a change.

Summary Checklist

✓ **Recognize a crisis**: If your solution or service is impacting the business in a highly negative way for an extended period of time, it's in crisis.

✓ **Deal with the crisis**: The purpose of this book is to avoid crises altogether, but when they do happen, you must stabilize your service or solution before you can start building a culture of quality.

✓ **SWAT Teams**: Create a SWAT team to resolve crises.

  ○ **Leadership in times of crisis**: It's critical to assign the appropriate leader or leaders of the SWAT team effort. The leader must be both sufficiently skilled and empowered to take the actions needed to resolve problems.

  ○ **The right SWAT team**: Your SWAT team must consist of skilled resources from all key teams, including vendor and business representation.

  ○ **SWAT team location**: The SWAT team is ideally colocated in a single room whenever possible.

✓ **Exit criteria**: Set objective quality targets that define what stability means and when the SWAT team effort ends.

  ○ Use technical monitoring to assess progress.

  ○ Understand the end-user experience to ensure technical improvements are translating into the needed business benefits.

✓ **Change management**: Use disciplined change management to effectively balance the risk of changes against the intended rewards and to understand the specific impacts of changes.

  ○ Make one change at a time whenever possible.

✓ **Too much of a good thing**: It's important to be good at crisis management, but it's dangerous and costly to become exclusively reliant on it. The best IT organizations do crisis management very well but very infrequently.

Defining Quality

In production IT, it's not that difficult to figure out if you're doing a good job or not. You just need to know what to look for. Once you know, you'll likely approach things…differently.

Level 2
Defining Quality

Level 1
Crisis Management

The Four Cornerstones of Production Quality

Introduction to DRES

Chapter Overview

For every mission-critical system or service, it is important to monitor and measure downtime, response times, error rates, and scalability. Collectively, we call these DRES. If you spend all of your focus on some of these areas, yet ignore others, your system is at risk of critical failures.

For downtime, it is insufficient to just measure availability, because it is easily possible for availability figures to be misleading. This can be remedied by computing an index that takes into account business impact, and providing the result along with any availability percentages.

This chapter provides an introduction to what DRES means and why it's important. Details on how to leverage the DRES framework are provided in subsequent chapters.

Vital Signs

In this book, we espouse a philosophy and methodology to achieve production excellence with large enterprise IT systems. Essential to this is defining and understanding exactly what system quality is.

Production quality in a large enterprise IT system can be elusive due to the sheer magnitude and complexity of it all. These systems can be incredibly intricate, complex, and multifaceted, much like the workings of the human body. As with your own physical well-being, no single metric tells the whole story when trying to understand and assess the overall health of an entire IT system. You have to measure multiple dimensions from multiple angles to tell the full story. If your blood glucose level is outstanding, is it safe to say you're healthy? Not if your body mass index is too high. How about if your blood glucose and BMI are excellent? Are you healthy then? Not if your bad cholesterol is 350—a heart attack may be in your near future. With large systems, not measuring one of the key facets creates the potential for overlooking critical flaws or problems. You also have to put data in perspective and assess it against historical figures to truly understand overall IT system health.

The bigger the environment, the more relevant this is. When you have thousands of concurrent users and tens of thousands of daily transactions, thousands of machines or other devices, dozens of servers, scores of network connections, and more, you must focus on key quality indicators to ensure optimum system health. Emergency room trauma doctors have evolved their diagnostic techniques to focus on what they have appropriately named "vital signs." Anyone who has watched the television show *ER* knows that these vital signs are heart rate, blood pressure, body temperature, and respiration. These aren't the only indicators of physical health, but, by definition, they are the most basic and most essential measures of immediate health. A competent doctor checks these first before diving down into more specific health indicators. Do you know what the corresponding vital signs of system health are for your large system? Are you a competent system doctor, or are you one high-profile problem away from a justified malpractice suit? If the overall health of your system took a turn for the worse, would you know before it was too late?

> ## Definition
>
> **OLTP** stands for "online transaction processing," where humans are manually interacting with a system to perform business transactions.

Our experience managing systems has taught us that the vital signs of system health are:

- **Downtime** (often referred to as *availability*)

- **Response times** (of user interfaces and transactions for OLTP systems, a.k.a. *job performance* for batch-processing-oriented systems)

- **Error rates**

- **Scalability**

Collectively, we refer to these as DRES. Unmanaged, any one of these areas has the potential to impact your users, take down your business, and send you personally to the unemployment line. In other words, if you aren't monitoring, measuring, trending, and actively working vital indicators in each of these four families, you leave yourself exposed to a potential problem that can turn out your lights.

Are there other areas to be concerned about? Absolutely. For instance, usability (the functional design of your applications) can seriously impact your business, but that is outside the scope of this book. Security is a large area that we will lightly touch on later, though it is not the focus of this book.

Downtime

> **Definition**
>
> **DRES—"Downtime, Response times, Error rates, and Scalability"**—forms a useful mini-framework for examining production quality. We leverage this concept extensively throughout the book.

Downtime is probably the most well-known and often used of the four system health vital signs. Availability, as it is typically defined, is a percentage measure of system uptime. Is the system up when it's supposed to be? One hundred percent availability indicates zero downtime. Availability is essential, since a down system cannot be used to accomplish its defined business purposes. Availability is the most fundamental of all quality metrics, yet the time has come for it to evolve to better show the true business impact of downtime.

Calculating system availability only as a straight percentage may not tell the full story of the business impact of system downtime and create a possible disconnect with the business customer. The reason? Not all outages are created equal. If your system availability is 99.9%, how do you know that some or all of your 0.1% percent downtime isn't having significant or even devastating negative impacts upon your business? Say you only have 10 hours of downtime for an entire year, but 5 of those hours come at the most critical time to your business and result in tremendously higher impact than the other 5 hours of downtime. Consider this: If you were running an airline, and were tasked with reporting on the availability of your aircraft fleet, would you treat 60 minutes of downtime for a commuter plane grounded at a small regional airport, late at night, during the off season the same way you would treat an hour of downtime for a jumbo jet grounded at your biggest hub airport at noon on the busiest travel day of the year? Is your IT organization treating all outages equally, or is it dedicating more focus to the ones causing the most business pain?

Do you even know which outages cause the most business pain? Think about it. Is an ERP outage more critical when you are trying to close out the books for a quarter or for the year than, say, an outage on a regular business day? Is a sales system outage for a retailer of electronics more critical on Black Friday[3] than on an unusually slow sales day some other time of the year? Are certain components of system functionality more critical than others? Was the system downtime impacting some users but not others?

> **Definition**
>
> **Enterprise resource planning, or ERP, systems** typically combine software to manage the disciplines of supply chain, manufacturing, financials, human resources, and possibly other areas of the business into a unified application suite. Example products in this space are SAP and Oracle.

---

3 Black Friday: the day following U.S. Thanksgiving Day, one of the busiest shopping days of the year.

The simple percentage availability measurements often do not and cannot take into consideration these factors. Imagine being a CIO, sitting in your boss's staff meeting, and feeling highly confident because you know you are meeting your availability goals, and then hearing the VP of Sales announce that his department won't be making its quarterly sales goal because of a system outage that came at the worst possible time for them. What will your response be? "That outage isn't a big deal. We're still hitting our availability goal." Or perhaps worse: "I wasn't aware that particular outage caused so much business disruption." Do you still feel comfortable just measuring availability as a straight percentage?

So, if you aren't going to rely solely on availability as a straight percentage to tell you your uptime situation, what should you also be measuring? We recommend creating a Business Impact Index (BII) that uses a weighting mechanism that takes into consideration the business impact of downtime. Simply stated, the BII is an equation that calculates who couldn't do what and for how long, and how much it mattered to the business. Measuring availability using a weighted stability index will ensure you're accurately measuring the impact of system outages to the business and that your teams are working on solving the problems that cause the greatest impact. And if you have always aspired to be able to associate a dollar value to your outages but didn't know where to start, this approach will get you one step closer to being able to do just that. We'll discuss this in greater detail in the next chapter on measurements.

> ### Definition
>
> **A Business Impact Index, or BII,** captures the relative negative impact to the business of every system incident.

Response Times

Okay, your availability percentage tells you whether you have unplanned downtime, and if you're using a BII, you know even more about what that downtime is costing the business. That's great; you're measuring a key and basic quality indicator, but you're still exposed to numerous quality issues that don't manifest themselves in the form of outages. Imagine yourself again as a CIO (or a system owner reporting to the CIO) in your boss's staff meeting—sitting there among your peers, the business leaders of your company. You're now measuring system availability using a weighted stability index, so you're very confident your system is meeting the business availability requirements and that your teams are working on the problems that cause the most business pain. You even boast about it to your colleagues—you're very proud. Imagine now the sinking feeling you get when the head of customer service announces that even though the system is up when it's supposed to be, it's so slow that it's impacting the call handle times of customer service representatives in the call centers.

> ### Definition
>
> **Call handle time** is the time it takes a customer service representative to field a phone call from a customer and take action to process their request while on the phone.

Average call handle time is up, service levels are down, and increased customer dissatisfaction is the result. How did you not know this was happening? How do you maintain the trust and respect of the business if they know more about how your systems are doing than you do? You've been so attentive to availability issues that you didn't realize that a highly available system could still have quality issues that could cause such devastating effects on the business. This brings us to the criticality of measuring transaction performance.

Transaction performance in OLTP systems and batch performance in off-line systems is a critical indicator of overall systems health. Just because a system remains up and available doesn't mean it's necessarily responding or processing fast enough to meet the business objectives. It's important to monitor and measure transaction speeds to ensure they remain compliant with the Service Level Agreement, or SLA (whether it be implicit or explicit).

An important side benefit of measuring response times is that dramatic or even gradual changes in performance can be telltale signs of impending system failures or scalability issues. To ignore these signs increases your exposure to future problems—future problems that would be less costly and complex to fix if addressed proactively, rather than waiting until after a major incident has occurred.

One of the reasons transaction response times are often unmeasured or untracked is the sheer number of transactions performed daily in high-volume systems and the number of unique types of transactions. Measuring every single one seems impossible given the enormity of it all. And it's simply not necessary; a technique we've had success with is to identify a subset of certain bellwether business transactions and focus on those. We've often called these the "Top 10 Critical Transactions."

There are three main sources to be used when compiling a top 10 list of key business transactions:

- **Criticality to the business.** It is best to actually ask the business what their most important transactions are.

- **Most frequent transactions.** You should be able to sift through historical data to determine this.

- **Most intense transactions.** Some business transactions work a subsystem very hard, such as a database or a file system. Also, some transactions are unique in regard to which subsystems they hit (e.g., a new service activation may require a call to the credit check service), so you may want to include important yet unique business transactions as well.

Once you have this list nailed down and start carefully measuring these transactions, while you won't have 100% coverage of everything happening in your system, you will have a very good idea of what is going on for a reasonable cost. Then, you can monitor and measure the duration of these transactions at regular intervals, using manual techniques or monitoring software. The data collected allows you to create a baseline and begin a trending analysis. Ultimately, your first attempts at monitoring may be primitive, but the key is to get started and continuously improve. Over time, your data sets will become larger and more valuable.

Utilize the SLA for the transactions (or create one if it doesn't exist by assessing business need) and work the issues causing the transactions to be out of SLA. This can be done in real time if desired by alerting key technical personnel when a significant number of transactions fall out of the norm. For transactions within SLA, use the trending analysis to ensure problems in the system or scalability challenges aren't gradually eroding your performance.

Transaction response times are highly prone to confusion. How many times has your IT staff chased phantom issues because someone declared "the system is slow today"? Establishing a critical transactions list, doing some basic objective monitoring, baselining performance, and tracking trends will allow you to assess system transaction health objectively, based on data instead of rumor and anecdote that may or may not be accurate. In the end, it puts you in a proactive position from which you can confidently track performance, make changes based on real data, report specifics to the business, and avoid the thrash of reactive management.

Transactional Errors

Alright, so you're measuring availability and using a stability index to ensure your teams are addressing the problems that cause the most outage-related business pain. You're also measuring transaction performance on key bellwether transactions to ensure the system response times are meeting the business need. You're now feeling confident that you know the health of your system and that your teams are actively managing it to the quality standards needed to meet the business need. Imagine your surprise when the CEO hands you a stack of complaints sent to him by angry employees who are experiencing system problems.

You take these complaints back to your desk and begin to sort through them. It's perplexing because no two of them seem to be alike. The users complain sometimes of web page timeouts and other nuisance error messages they have to click through but that otherwise don't impact their ability to do their work. Others complain of orders that seem to successfully process but never get fulfilled. When they call the help desk, they're told that the order "erred out" or "got stuck" and needs to be manually manipulated before it can successfully complete. In other cases, they mention error messages that simply prevent them from proceeding forward with the order process, so they gave up trying, or started an entirely new order.

You give these complaints to your team and ask them to try and correlate them back to known system outages or transaction slowness. Your team does some detailed analysis, but has difficulty determining any cause and effect relationship between these issues and known problems that occurred. What you're experiencing here is what we refer to as transaction failures or errors. Even when a system appears to be up and fully available with normal transaction speeds, there can still be issues within the system that cause transactional failures or errors.

For synchronous processing, these manifest themselves to the user in the form of an error message or some other sort of undesirable result, like loss of data synchronization or a session timeout. For asynchronous transactions, these can be failures on the back end (unbeknownst to the user) where the failed transaction requires the intervention of a technician to address the root problem. These can be the most frustrating of all problems to a system user because they seem to occur randomly or occur at the end of a lengthy business process that can't be completed or has to be reentered.

This may seem really bad. But it can be even worse. In this example, you have friendly users, your coworkers, who are able to articulate their problems to you. But what happens if your user base is made up of your paying customers who are out on the web? Not only do they not have a straightforward way to let you know there's a problem, but they also tend to be less computer-savvy, so they find errors to be even more frustrating. If you're not contemplating this as a possible problem, then you are doubly exposed.

Your line of defense against these problems is monitoring, quantifying, and managing these errors. To the extent possible, we recommend identifying all unique errors specific to your system, naming them, and quan-

> ### Definition
>
> **Synchronous transactions** take place while the user waits. The user knows the final state of the transaction before she is free to go on to other functions.
>
> **Asynchronous transactions** finalize after the user moves on. The user assumes the transaction was successful but doesn't really know unless she checks later or she receives a success message after the fact.

tifying the magnitude of the business impact. For those that have business impacts, utilities should be coded to capture and log all occurrences. In many instances, these failures are already captured within the logs of the various platforms running your system. Utilities should be written to parse all of the errors you care about and quantify the number of occurrences. Once a baseline has been determined and priorities established, your team can begin to work the root cause of the errors in targeted fashion.

Scalability

Things are looking better for you now. Your availability data and stability index data tells you you're meeting the business needs via uptime SLAs. Transaction performance is being measured, and various improvement efforts have addressed the problems causing the slowdowns that had been impacting the users. You've also put in place error management metrics and improvement initiatives to address those error issues that had been frustrating your users. You're feeling pretty good about your stewardship of this mission-critical system. Imagine what a shock it is to you and your business partners when at the peak hour of your highest volume business day in the history of your growing company, the system completely seizes up and all processing halts for more than an hour while the operations teams restart the system to get it working again.

This is an outage unlike anything your teams have seen before. Everything was working as designed, nobody made a mistake, and yet everything ground to a halt. A detailed root cause investigation reveals that the system reached a capacity limit that was previously unknown to them. And it gets worse: there are no silver bullets to address the problem. You're told that adding some server-side hardware and changing some operating system configuration values will help improve the situation, but only slightly. The problem begins to happen every weekday at about the same time, when processing volumes are at their highest for the day. Your team tells you a large-scale reconfiguration is required that will involve software changes, the addition of new hardware, and the reconfiguration of a portion of the system design. You're told that in the best-case scenario, the full solution to the problem will take several months. All of your other work begins to pile up while you focus your energies on this.

The missing line of defense here that allowed this problem to happen is a lack of comprehensive system capacity monitoring and planning. Scalability is the hardest of the four vital signs to quantify and manage, but until you do so, you'll always be exposed to the real possibility of major scalability failure. One doesn't have to look far to find prominent examples of this in business. In 2004, Comair Airlines was crippled by a multiple-day outage with a key system that grounded the regional airline at the peak of the critical Thanksgiving Day weekend. The problem? The system that performed crew assignments reached an internal limitation, and all processing ceased. The problem code was easily fixed, but it took several days to do so. By then, the company had been devastated by the impacts to business, and within a few months, the crippled carrier had been taken over by a competitor.

Could this have been prevented? Probably so. Our methodology shows how to head this type of problem off, in the chapters that follow.

Are you exposed the same way Comair was? Do you have a quantifiable scalability plan that correlates business growth or changes in business behavior into known system capacity limits? If you don't, just like Comair, you could be a single mouse click away from a major failure.

The first step toward effective scalability quantification is contemplating the system as a holistic solution wherein all of the software, hardware, and configurations must work harmoniously to achieve the business result the system is designed to accomplish. Too often, IT groups will have a data storage capacity plan, a network capacity plan, and a server capacity plan, and assume that they're on top of system scalability. While it's true that hardware scalability is critical, so is software scalability, and the corresponding configurations are critical to software and hardware working together to achieve the desired quality results. Our experience has taught us that to ensure your system can scale to meet expected or unexpected business changes, you must identify all essential choke points in the system, understand how business behavior impacts those choke points both theoretically and empirically, and then map a plan to proactively address capacity problems.

One way to ensure proper focus on this is to have the following goal for scalability: continue to meet or beat your uptime, performance, and error goals as the business grows (expressed in user transaction volumes). This will drive you to ensure that all the factors that contribute to system quality are evaluated for their ability to scale.

Confidence

Making sure you have each of the four DRES areas covered is certainly a significant amount of work. It can seem daunting at first. But once you do it, you'll be able to relax at your boss's staff meeting, knowing that things are under control.

Summary Checklist

✓ **Complexity**: Large IT systems are, by definition, highly complex and consequently difficult to manage.

✓ **Prevention**: If we don't prevent problems, they can have disastrous consequences for the business.

✓ **DRES**: The four key cornerstones of production quality, collectively known as DRES, are:

   ○ Downtime

   ○ Response times

   ○ Error rates

   ○ Scalability

✓ **Full picture**: No single metric actually captures overall production quality. Ignoring any of these four vital signs creates a situation in which IT is not aware of how a system is actually performing.

   ○ All four must be monitored and measured concurrently in order to fully assess overall systems health.

✓ **Predictable results**: By proactively focusing on the four key quality areas for your mission-critical applications, you are much more likely to provide a predictable quality result and help the business succeed.

✓ **There's more**: While DRES covers the vital signs of production quality, there are other aspects of quality that shouldn't be ignored, such as security and usability.

## CHAPTER 3

IT Orienteering

Key Measurements for DRES

Chapter Overview

We all know you can't manage what you can't measure. In this chapter, we'll go into detail about why you need IT quality metrics and how without them, you're lost.

In addition to the whys of metrics, we'll cover the specifics of what to measure to show you how to track the multidimensional aspects of the four cornerstones of quality. We'll discuss going beyond basic availability by using the Business Impact Index to truly quantify the pain caused to the business by unplanned downtime.

Complementing these innovative new ways to track availability, we'll cover the elusive and often overlooked need to track transaction response times. We'll also take you through errors—the hidden killer—and the all-important yet elusive measure of scalability.

Why Measure?

Measuring at first seems to be obvious—we all measure what we run, right? At companies and other entities with IT shops, we *generally* do this well. We track sales, financials, customer satisfaction, and statistics on our own employees. But how well do we track IT, and in particular IT systems? Do we do it as thoroughly and with as much rigor as we do for key business metrics such as profits and losses? Often, unfortunately, we don't. Typically, we measure IT systems in some ways, but frequently we don't measure the right things, or aren't methodical enough. Measuring CPU alone doesn't cut it. Sending out alerts when we're running low on disk is useful yet insufficient. The larger and more complex the system is, the more systematic we have to be about keeping track of it.

There are many different levels of sophistication when it comes to measuring our IT systems. At a minimum, we typically have some level of business measurement available (e.g., we processed 4,500 orders yesterday), and we trust our technical experts to keep on top of the details (e.g., your lead DBA can tell you that the database server is running at 62% CPU currently). You expect your administrators to head off any problems that they can, and to warn you if there is something out of their control.

Similarly, if we were running a small mom and pop business like a neighborhood café, we might play fast and loose with some of our measuring. How is our supply of eggs looking? Check the cooler. How's business today? Check the till. If, however, we were operating a large and complex nationwide fast food restaurant chain, that informal and often mostly intuitive approach really wouldn't do. In our experience, we have found that too many IT organizations measure as if they were a small business rather than the complicated maze of interdependent technologies they truly are.

Fortunately, there is a much better place to be. By implementing the monitoring, measuring, and trending guidelines set below, you will have data readily available that will allow you to implement repeatable scorecards for all of your most important applications. These scorecards examine various aspects of each application to determine its viability in production, and are sometimes referred to as "health checks." These scorecards serve three main purposes:

- Predict application failures before they actually happen

- Determine areas where improvement is needed

- Measure whether the changes made to improve various areas were effective or not

Making Good Decisions

In many ways, measuring is the foundation of everything else in this book. Why is that, you say? Because one of the most important roles a leader has is to make sure that important decisions are made well. And decisions made with faulty or incomplete information are often made wrong. It's that simple.

If you ran a large fast food chain, and you didn't have historical sales figures for each of your stores, how would you know if same-store sales are increasing or declining? If you didn't have sales data by product, how would you know how to evaluate the success or failure of a new menu item? If you didn't have empirical data on customer satisfaction, how would you know if you were meeting the needs of your clientele? There will be times, of course, when all the right data is not available to decision makers, and it's part of their job to make the best of it. But you should strive to gather the right data when you have the means to get it.

So, as alluded to in the previous chapter, to make things run smoothly, it is important to instrument and monitor all important aspects of your system. Here we'll discuss what to measure (we'll leverage the previously introduced categories of Downtime, Response times, Error rates, and Scalability) and just how to go about doing it. However, we'll save the discussion on how to *use* the data to achieve outstanding results for the following chapters.

Downtime Measurement

Measuring the particulars of when your application isn't working is important. There are many possible ways to do it. The best three are raw number of incidents, availability, and business impact.

Raw Number of Incidents

The raw number of incidents (a.k.a. outages or breaches in service) is the simplest thing to measure in the realm of downtime. Imagine in your national fast food chain not knowing if your thousands of restaurants were open and fully operational when they're supposed to be. Unthinkable, right? Simply counting the number of system outages is the most basic of IT quality metrics. Keep track of how many times your application became unavailable when it was supposed to be available (i.e., during the online window). It doesn't matter if it was down for three minutes or three hours, in this simplest metric, an outage is an outage is an outage.

While this is crude in some ways, it can also be very powerful, because it is easy to comprehend. If your application has averaged three outages per month over the last six months, that's a specific metric that both senior management and your line-level employees can easily understand because it intuitively makes sense. The other two methods below are more precise, but the downside is that they are more challenging to make sense of, sometimes to their detriment.

If you set goals regarding numbers of outages, you can have spectacular results. We have seen a yearly goal of a 50% reduction in the raw number of outages, when shared across an entire department, achieved time and

> ### The Root Cause Hierarchy
>
> When tracking outages, in addition to the details, it helps future efforts to categorize each outage according to
>
> 1. The applications that were the victims of the problem;
>
> 2. The system that caused the problem in the first place;
>
> 3. The subsystem the problem occurred in (UNIX, Oracle DB, network, etc.);
>
> 4. The root cause category (hardware failure, human error, etc.).

time again. It's something everyone can be excited about. When employees see goals that they can personally impact, they make things happen.

When a system incident occurs, investigate it thoroughly to determine what caused the failure, a.k.a. the "root cause." Then the causes can be categorized and trends kept on each. It likewise makes sense to keep track of what subsystem the failure took place in (e.g., client, server, network, DB) in order to know where to place additional focus if needed. And obviously it is necessary to keep track of how many outages happen over time to detect improvement or degradation.

The raw number of outages is especially powerful when your systems are having a lot of outages. If your systems are having few outages, excellent, you'll need to read on.

Availability

If your application or service is doing well from a downtime perspective and having few incidents per month or year, then a more precise metric is called for. One of these metrics is *availability*, expressed as a percent. What percent of the time is your service working properly?

Within availability are several subtly different flavors. There are several ways of calculating the percentage, depending on how your organization defines availability. We will cover three of the most useful methods here: basic availability, absolute availability, and weighted availability.

Basic Availability: Is your application working properly when the business expects it to?

Availability is one of the more popular and useful IT metrics, and is more confusing to calculate than one might initially think. Availability is a measure of how much of the time your users are able to access and use your application or service, and it is generally measured as a percentage.

For instance, there are 10,080 minutes in a week. If your application had only one incident during the week, which lasted 25 minutes, your availability for the week would be (10,080-25)/10,080, or 99.75%. This math would be typical for some applications, particularly web applications or applications with a global user base, that don't have a maintenance window at all.

But for applications that aren't expected to be up 24 hours a day, there is a twist. Typically for an OLTP application, the working timeframe (often during the business day) is called the "online window," and when it is acceptable for the application to not be working (so that maintenance can be performed on it, often at night), it is called the "maintenance window" or sometimes the "batch window." So if there was a four-hour maintenance window, then there are only 8,400 online minutes per week—and assuming the 25-minute incident happened entirely during the online window, this changes the result: $(8,400-25)/8,400 = 99.70\%$.

This can be made much trickier for applications, typically those in less mature shops that don't have a formal agreement with the business on what the online window is. If there is no basic SLA with the business, creating one is a great place to start.

Even more challenging, some businesses require systems to be up 24 hours a day, 365 days a year. For this reason, there is no natural maintenance window when the system can be taken off-line. In this situation, it's common for the system to be designed in a way that allows components to be taken off-line and have maintenance performed on them while other redundant components remain up. Once the maintenance of those components is complete, they are brought back online and the next set is taken down for maintenance and so on until all have been serviced. To the user, the system continues to be up and responsive, yet in the background, pieces of it are off-line and being worked on.

It's also possible to architect high availability systems where so much redundancy is incorporated into the design that a single failure or even multiple failures don't result in downtime. These systems are typically more costly and complex. It's simply a matter of cost versus reward to determine if you want to go this route. In some cases, a single minute of downtime could be so devastating or otherwise unacceptable that the investment in high availability (HA) is a wise one. There's more to come about HA in chapter 6.

Accurate Inputs

Once you've decided what to use for the denominator, you need to determine how you will collect data for the numerator. How long was your application truly down? For some applications, this is relatively easy. If your company has a dedicated service desk, they can handle keeping track of up and down time. However, with this approach, you're possibly missing part of the picture due to the inherent lag between the time an outage occurs and the time it gets reported to the help desk, as well as the lag between the time corrective actions are taken and the users are able to fully use the application again. Assuming you have sufficient monitoring, this can be partially remedied by having technicians verify the timelines in the relevant logs after an incident has been resolved.

Additionally, it is important to represent the end-user experience as much as possible. Measuring availability from the data center has some value but is not appropriate as a stand-alone metric for this purpose. You could show 100% availability on your application servers, but if your users access the application through a wide area network (WAN) and via a web server before reaching your application servers, your metric is missing two important possible failure points. Try to represent the end-user experience as much as possible, because ultimately that is what is important.

Yes, the details should be covered during the root cause investigation, but the availability metric endeavors to display how well your applications are working—not where they failed.

Fortunately, the monitoring industry has recognized this need and offers products that allow you to monitor your application from the end-user perspective, either by purchasing end-to-end monitoring tools, or paying an external service to keep track of this for you. We'll discuss this more later in the chapter.

What % of the time is the app up?

99% availability (a.k.a. "2 nines") = 1% or less unplanned downtime.

Assuming an 18-hour online window, application is down 5.4 hours per month.

Adequate for immature application or non-mission-critical application. Insufficient for customer-facing application. Less than 2 nines is lousy no matter the nature of the application.

99.9% availability (a.k.a. "3 nines") = .1% or less unplanned downtime.

App is down 33 minutes per month.

Adequate for mature, complex app.

99.99% availability (a.k.a. "4 nines") = .01% or less unplanned downtime.

App is down 3 minutes, 14 seconds per month.

Extremely good. You might not want to aim any higher than this in most industries because if you do, you're likely not getting good return on investment (ROI) due to high costs—though ultimately it's up to the business. (In some medical systems, financial systems, and at NASA, however, you want 5–6 nines and doubly-redundant systems!)

Alternate Approach: Absolute Availability

A maintenance window, however, may or may not occur during normal business hours. If the system is needed 24x7x365, any maintenance window will happen during normal business hours. Effectively, the business is saying "yes, we need the application to always be up, but we understand that is not realistic in this case, so are granting you some time to do maintenance." Taking this into consideration, you need to decide whether you will exclude maintenance windows from your calculations or leave them in. Since this metric is meant to represent the extent to which the application is available when the business needs it, you will have a more accurate representation if you use normal business hours as your denominator, and add planned downtime (utilized maintenance windows) in addition to unplanned downtime (outages) to your numerator.

Absolute availability is a metric that helps you best understand the cost-benefit of minimizing or increasing maintenance windows. Can you achieve greater overall uptime by going to a shorter maintenance window that results in slightly more downtime for a net overall gain in availability? Can you achieve greater overall uptime by taking longer maintenance windows, doing more preventive maintenance, and achieving overall greater availability? These are all questions the absolute availability metrics might tell you.

Absolute availability is an advanced practice. It could be used in place of basic availability, or as a complementary metric.

> **Absolute Availability Formula**
>
> Absolute Availability % = 1 - (Unplanned Downtime + Planned Downtime) / 24 x 7 x 365.

Weighted Availability

Further complicating matters are "partial outages." It is possible in a large, complex system to have a partial outage. Perhaps one business office is down while four are still up, or 33% of the functionality doesn't work, but the rest does, or 8% of the documents won't display, but the rest will. In this case, it makes sense to prorate the incident. So in the first example, assuming all of the geographies are equal in size, a 2.5-hour outage would only be counted as 30 minutes of downtime for the system overall. (If three of your restaurants ran out of cheese at noon and were unable to sell cheeseburgers, would you count them as 100% down?)

Deciding whether to track partial outages will partly depend on the likelihood and frequency of such partial outages. In distributed architectures with geographically dispersed data centers, it is more useful than in centralized systems with a concentrated user base.

Beware, though, these gray areas, which are intended to make the availability metric more precise, are tempting areas in which to "fudge" the numbers in order to make your application look better than it really is. Resist this urge! To achieve accurate availability numbers, you have to be harder on yourself than you want to be. Salvation comes from judging yourself more strictly than your customers do. If your customers suspect your numbers aren't real, then you've lost credibility with them. It's not worth the risk. Whichever method of calculation you use, you will always have a better chance of objective and accurate data if you (1) have an automated system to calculate availability and (2) leave the manual intervention to a neutral group, such as the help desk.

> **Pop Quiz**
>
> Is 99.7% almost as good as 99.9%? It sure sounds like it...
>
> But no, it's three times as bad, because .3% downtime (100%–99.7%) is three times as big as .1% (100%–99.9%) downtime! You have to think in the inverse!

Keeping all of that in mind, what's a good availability goal? It depends entirely on the needs of the business. A customer-facing application in the financial products industry may need 99.999% uptime. An internal IT tool may be just fine with 99.9%.

The thing to keep in mind here is that the higher the uptime requirements, the higher the cost to build and run the application. The CIO might ask for five nines across the board, but unless she's willing to pay for fully redundant hardware and well-architected applications across the board, it isn't going to happen. And even if the funding is there, it won't happen overnight. Change takes time.

In lieu of any hard science for setting these targets, it works well to look at recent history, and, if it is less than perfect, to try to make a reasonable improvement. So if one flagship application ran 99.92% last year, you might aim for 99.96% this year, which would be 50% better. Conversely, if you are happy with your numbers today, it's fine to have a goal to simply hold steady so you can focus on other areas.

If you have a large portfolio of applications, you'll also want to consider classifying them by tiers (e.g., gold, silver, and bronze), with various levels of availability requirements. For example, your most mission-critical applications with revenue-generating functions would have higher availability targets than your internal reporting applications. This is a good way to maximize your IT investment. Criteria to use in such a classification approach would include level of criticality to the business, number of users, and interdependency with other applications (more on this in chapter 11, "Where to Start").

Business Impact

The raw number of incidents and availability are great measures. But as we mentioned earlier, they're missing something—they're one dimensional. The problem with availability is that it doesn't necessarily tell the full story. It doesn't tell you how badly the downtime hurt the business.

If you're running an online retail business and you went all year without any downtime on your web site but then went down just after your Super Bowl advertisement aired, you might have hurt the business a great deal. But your numbers won't reflect it! Conversely, if your application happened to go down several times at 10 p.m., but was reliable during the peak hours of the day, you might be doing better than your availability figure indicates. So here is a way to gain clarity on how well you are helping (or hurting) the business: the Business Impact Index (BII).

The Business Impact Index

The BII is not commonly used in IT yet, both because it's new and because it takes more effort to define and calculate. We believe the BII should be a main staple given its power. It provides you a number quantifying the business pain caused by an incident. Ideally, that number is the dollar amount the incident cost the enterprise. If your business relies heavily on web sites to facilitate sales, and you can get sales data by the hour, this may be doable for you. The advantages of assigning dollar amounts to incidents are that (a) it makes the cost-benefit analysis of remediation efforts easy to perform, and (b) it's an extremely objective way of knowing how much the business has been harmed.

If, however, the dollar amount is not easily determinable, a scale can be used to classify outages from small to catastrophic. The scale is somewhat exponential, such that a small outage rates 1 BII point, while a massive outage that takes the business down for a day is worth 250 points (feel free to create your own scale). But these ratings need to be achieved as objectively as possible. So how would you do that?

To calculate to the point rating for a particular outage, you need to know who couldn't do what and for how long. Follow these steps to make that determination:

Discounted EUDT	Class	Points
<10,000	S	1
<50,000	M	3
<250,000	L	10
<1.25m	XL	50
>1.25m	Catastrophe	250

table 3.1. Example BII Point Scale

1. Determine the length of the outage in minutes.

2. Calculate the total end-user downtime, or EUDT. This is the total number of application users impacted multiplied by the duration of the outage.

3. Discount for applications that are lower-priority from a business perspective. That is, your customer-facing sales web site going down is a much bigger deal than your intranet going down, even on a per-user basis…so discount intranet incidents by a percentage to make the relative business impact reflect reality. See appendix for examples.

4. Discount for partial outages (as you would for weighted availability, above). If your application was working in some geographies but not others, or some functions worked while others did not, this is where you take that into account.

5. The result is discounted EUDT. Compare these to the scale your IT department has established and assign the indicated point value.

Let's relate this back to the national fast food chain analogy we introduced earlier in the chapter. Perhaps if one of your largest and most profitable restaurants in Chicago was closed all day, it would be a large or extra-large incident. But if a rural, lower-volume restaurant had to close one hour early at 9:00 p.m., it would be a small incident. All incidents are not created equal, even those having the same duration.

The Business Impact Index is a great complement to the raw number of incidents and availability. In a tactical sense, it motivates your employees to resolve outages quickly. "Hurry up, we don't want this one-pointer to turn into a 3-pointer!" In a more strategic sense, it encourages your deployment managers to make sound decisions about when to take risks. Perhaps by delaying that change to the weekend, the maximum exposure is only a 3-pointer, not a 10-pointer. It also becomes a useful guide in your problem management process, by allowing you to prioritize problems by business impact, ensuring your teams are working on finding root causes and fixes for the things the business cares about the most.

The business will also understand and appreciate this when you are communicating with them about what kind of job you're doing. When you admit that the Super Bowl outage was a 50 or 250 pointer, and what you're doing to resolve it, rather than point to your sparkling availability figure, they will know that you get it.

The BII adds value by means of aligning the non-production-facing parts of IT as well, such as architecture, development, and testing. And from a planning perspective, use of the BII helps drive commonality of investment and expectations among all concerned parties.

Downtime Summary

If your fast food chain has 5,000 restaurants, on any given day some of them are going to open for business later than advertised, have certain products unavailable, or close early…which means they are making less money and will likely be disappointing regular customers. You need to know the trends and the reasons behind the trends in order to make sense of this and take appropriate action.

The above three types of downtime metrics allow you to

- determine an important aspect of your production quality;

- measure actual business impact;

- gauge your progress;

- compare relative quality across a portfolio of applications.

You should leverage all three types.

Response Time Measurement

Another quality metric that gets a lot of publicity is performance. Performance is a word that, over time, has come to mean a great many things, so let us emphasize that in this chapter we will refer to two specific types of performance, both of which are variations of "response times":

- **Response times of user-driven system events:** For human-client interactions, how quickly can a human navigate from screen to screen, or retrieve a record? These are often (but not always) synchronous transactions. For simplicity, we'll call this *client response times*. At your restaurant chain, how long do customers have to wait before they can place an order, and once they are able to, how long does it take to submit their food and drink orders and receive change? In the fast food industry these metrics are taken so seriously that companies calculate them right down to the tenth of a second. Ironically, many IT organizations don't measure transaction performance at all! Is yours one of them?

- **Performance of system-driven events**: Often other events need to transpire that are driven purely by interaction among systems. These are back-end, often asynchronous response times. For example, after a human clicks "OK" and moves on, how long does it take for things to complete in the back end? How long does it take for these same restaurants to prepare the food and drinks and serve them to the customers? How long does it take to refill the shake machine? How long does it take the janitorial staff to clean the restaurants at night? If you have a business process that depends both on client-side user-driven transactions and system-driven transactions, and you're only looking at client-side response times, you're missing half the picture.

Any system that has a human user interface (UI) has client response times. Client performance is the amount of time that a user must wait between certain keystrokes, such as saving information on a panel, switching panels, or logging in. Apart from the frustration a user can feel with a slow UI, this metric becomes very important in large call center environments with thousands of users, because a slow UI costs the company money, as it must hire more representatives than it otherwise would to do the work. In some cases, shaving a few seconds off of a popular transaction can save millions of dollars per year, and conversely a slight degradation can cost millions!

On the web, the impact can be even greater, because if a particular web page takes a long time to load, customers will often search out a different site (your competitor's!) to find the same information or product. Users have no patience for slowness and will only get more judgmental as they become more technically sophisticated.

While in many cases it is possible to ask your users how fast they think a particular application is, or simply if it is fast enough, the data returned will only give you a very rough idea of how things are going. In complex environments where the users are leveraging several applications at once, it can also be misleading, because the bad performance of one application will often bleed over into frustration with their other applications.

Armed with only this subjective data (or worse yet, no data!), production management is wide open to vague accusations that waste time and resources to address. With measurements, you'll be able to defend yourself against the call center VP who didn't make her numbers and is looking for a scapegoat. When you're vulnerable to anecdote, your job security is 100% tied to the whims of others. You also can't drive value in the organization. You need to be a true partner of the business and proactively look for opportunities to improve the systems and business.

A better method is accurate and objective measurement of the response times of the application in production, as your users experience it.

Active vs. Passive

There are two types of performance monitoring available for use in production:

1. **Active Monitoring**: This approach involves the generation of synthetic (test) transactions in a controlled manner and collecting response times of the transactions. In this approach, data is usually collected at regular intervals (e.g., every 10 minutes) by programs (which incidentally are usually referred to as robots) that fire off the transactions. For your fast food chain, you'd be hiring undercover customers to try out the food and service at your various locations and report back to you. The main benefits of active monitoring are

> **TIP**
>
> The best way to know how fast your application performs is to use software tools that capture the actual production response times.

   a. It allows collecting performance and availability data 24x7x365;

   b. It involves executing well-defined, controlled transactions on a regular basis, allowing the detection of trends, including degradation from the norm.

   A few caveats about active monitoring:

   - Be wary of running tests with the same exact transactions over and over again. This repeat data may get cached in several places, yielding artificially fast results.

   - Be careful not to launch too many test transactions at once. If you do, you may end up slowing down (or worse, causing scalability failures in) the production system. A good rule of thumb is to launch less than 1% of the overall production transaction volume. But on the other hand, you need enough samples for each major transaction to be statistically significant.

   - Pay special attention to results achieved during peak hours, and discount results from off-hours and weekends. It is much easier to get good results when there are relatively few users on the system.

   - Be careful to make your tests as production-like as possible. For instance, if you locate your test clients in your data center, but most of the users are in six call centers across the nation, your test robots are cheating by getting superior network performance. Put the robots where your end users are.

2. **Passive Monitoring**: In this approach, real system transactions generated by real users are measured. In your restaurants, this would be akin to hiring someone to look over the shoulder of people taking orders and take notes about their actual experiences, including the time for each step of the ordering process. The main benefits of passive monitoring are:

   a. It gives visibility into performance of transactions not covered by active monitoring. The transactions could not be set up any more realistically because they are in fact real transactions!

   b. It can help with the troubleshooting of specific problems reported by users if their "problem transaction" is covered by the passive monitoring solution.

The Four Approaches

While there are two types of end-user monitoring, there are four main approaches to collecting the data:

1. Stopwatch timings

2. Instrumentation of custom code

3. Software that you install in your environment

4. Monitoring as a service provided by an external company

Stopwatch Timings

The crudest approach for collecting response time data is to perform stopwatch timings of key transactions. This means there are literally humans carrying stopwatches, timing the transactions, and manually entering the results into a spreadsheet. For obvious reasons, this approach is not very accurate and doesn't scale. It can also be expensive in terms of manpower. However, it is still better than responding to anecdotes, and it is extremely fast to implement. When automated end-user monitoring is not an option, stopwatch timings can begin to tell the story about response times. Figure 3.1 shows an example of timings for eight transactions in two locations, and how the numbers differ in both places fairly consistently. While this kind of data should be taken with a grain of salt, it is still more useful than responding to unsubstantiated complaints.

We once were involved in a "crisis" caused by the CEO of a company visiting a call center who, while looking over the shoulder of a customer service representative, witnessed a "very slow" performing transaction. The account of this event quickly traveled by word of mouth, and by the time the IT support team got wind of it, the story had morphed into a rumor that a whole application performed poorly. Unfortunately, no performance monitoring of that application was available, and for several days, the team scrambled to try to find out what the root cause of the "major performance issue" was.

Eventually someone went out to the call center with a stopwatch to collect real data about the problem. As it turned out, performance was generally acceptable, but under a very specific scenario used infrequently, a transaction performed slowly. A simple set of stopwatch timings laid the issue to rest, but not before many hours were spent chasing an elusive problem.

In this example, stopwatches were used for passive monitoring, meaning the real

Average Production Client Response Times (seconds) by Call Center

#	Function	Denver, CO							Jacksonville, FL							% faster	Comments
		Oct 17	Oct 24	Oct 31	Nov 7	Nov 14	Nov 21	avg last 3	Oct 17	Oct 24	Oct 31	Nov 7	Nov 14	Nov 21	avg last 3		
	sample size	6	9	15	15	5	15		4	11	14	13	15	14			
1	Login	17	14	17	18	41	19	26.0	9	12	21	11	38	11	20.0	23%	Incident 34878, dropped index.
2	Search	8	5	7	8	9	8	8.3	6	7	10	5	6	7	6.0	28%	
3	Add new acct	31	29	23	33	30	29	30.7	18	20	44	17	19	21	19.0	38%	
4	Change address	7	6	8	8	7	8	7.7	5	3	8	2	3	3	2.7	65%	
5	Change svc level	49	33	34	31	37	36	34.7	39	22	29	25	21	25	23.7	32%	Code fix #4529 on 10/22.
6	Apply credit	4	4	3	4	4	4	4.0	3	2	5	2	3	2	2.3	42%	
7	Cancel service	12	11	14	13	12	15	13.3	8	6	17	9	6	8	7.7	43%	
8	Post comment	2	2	6	3	4	3	3.3	2	1	8	2	3	1	2.0	40%	
	total	130	104	112	118	144	122	**128**	90	73	142*	73	99	78	**83**	**35%**	

*Network latency in Jacksonville on Oct 31, incident 34720.

figure 3.1. Example stopwatch timings table

production transactions performed by an actual user were timed. It is also possible to use stopwatches for active monitoring, by selecting a set of frequently used or high-importance transactions to time at regular intervals, although doing this for extended periods with large samples would require a small army.

While stopwatch timings are better than rumors, and are by far the fastest to implement, they are still not as good as data collected automatically and continuously as discussed next.

Instrumentation of Custom Code

In applications that are custom-developed, there is an opportunity to build in some facilities that will allow you to track the performance of the application. This approach can be very powerful because you can get very granular in where you put hooks (subroutines) into the code such that you can time the execution of every user-driven or system-driven event. This approach typically involves building a reporting framework, too, so that you can extract and present the relevant data. While instrumenting code allows great flexibility, it is also a significant undertaking and can only be done well if it is designed into the system from the onset. Typically, it is not an option with commercial software.

When instrumentation is done well, it can give you a very comprehensive passive monitoring solution that allows you to know about the performance of all transactions for all users. In such cases, it might make the need for active monitoring obsolete.

If you do decide to forego implementing active monitoring because of the presence of a solid passive monitoring solution, keep in mind that you'll be giving up the ability to monitor the system when no users are on it, which can have the side benefit of identifying possible issues before users log on.

Packaged Performance Monitoring Software

Such software is available from vendors, though it varies greatly in what it does. Both active and passive solutions are available, yet the scope and accuracy of some passive solutions is limited. Success is in part tied to the degree to which the service being monitored contains proprietary code. Simple web applications are easier to monitor than commercial software for which source code is not available.

Monitoring as a Service Provided by an External Company

Some companies have developed a market out of monitoring your application for a fee (e.g., Keynote, Gomez). The most frequent use of this approach is for active monitoring of applications that are accessible via the Internet by a large number of users (e.g., a sales web site available to the general public). In such cases, it's not practical to deploy software to all the locations from which your users might be accessing your application, and it's more cost effective to leverage the infrastructure of these monitoring service providers. This also presents the benefit of not having to worry about installing performance monitoring software.

These services are also able to provide results from computers with various types of bandwidth available in different parts of the world, so you can tell how well your application works for a dial-up user in Brussels compared to a broadband user in Los Angeles.

The main limitation of this approach is that it works only for applications accessible from outside your network (with some exceptions), and generally cannot be used for passive monitoring of non-web applications. It can also be expensive for small applications and companies.

Errors: The Hidden Killer

At our fast food chain, how often is the incorrect change given back to a customer? How often is a food order served inaccurately? How often is something over- or undercooked? These are key things to know if you want to keep your customers happy.

If you interviewed 100 customers at your restaurant, you might find that nine were served late, seven got the wrong order, five received cold food, four were billed incorrectly, and two had burned food. The food critics will all publish different stories. These individual failures could add up to an overall drop in sales, but since they're isolated and difficult to spot, you don't make the connection. Don't kid yourself that you're getting 91% or better in each category. You've got a service delivery problem that you have to get to the bottom of—pronto.

After downtime and response times, the next thing your user community can be hampered by is high error rates in their IT systems and services—so we'll now discuss how to measure them. We need to start by defining what an error is. There are several standard forms:

1. An error (sometimes resulting in a pop-up window or error page) preventing a human user from performing a legitimate business activity. (This is different than the desirable pop-ups [a.k.a. guardrails] that prevent users from entering faulty data).

2. A client application that stops responding while in the middle of a transaction, even if it doesn't return an error message.

3. A line in a batch file that is not processed properly by a batch program.

4. An asynchronous transaction that is not processed properly in the back end. For this error type, the user does not receive a failure message, but whatever they asked to have happen did not happen (e.g., a package does not arrive or there is a billing error on a customer invoice).

The Elusiveness of Errors

If your application has outages, or is universally slow, the business will let you know loud and clear (but hopefully you will already know before they tell you). However, if your application has errors of different types, the customer will be unhappy, but will have a much harder time telling you exactly why. If the errors are of 100 different types, the business will not immediately be able to articulate the pain they are feeling. They might complain that their average call handle times are up, or that customers are dropping off the web more than they used to.

But you probably won't be able to link either of those conditions directly to errors. In fact, over time, the business might adjust by adding more representatives or buying more advertisements to achieve equilibrium. Of course, this is bad for business. This type of condition can persist for a long time, like undetected cancer, until it gets really bad.

These errors can occur for a variety of reasons, including bad input data and bad logic in the code. The main effects of these errors are user frustration, possible lost sales, and the effort to resolve the errors.

If your application processes 1,000,000 business transactions per day, and it has just a .5% error rate, that's 5,000 errors per day, which could take a small army of technicians to resolve each day, and it's also 5,000 unsatisfying user experiences. It's a place you don't want to be.

This is a hidden killer where a business can die a death from a thousand cuts. Many IT managers don't even know about errors. Errors are microorganisms, and these managers are living in the eighteenth century, so they only believe what they can see with the naked eye: large, obvious events, such as a database server crash or a firewall failure.

For an example of how complex error patterns can be, take a look at figure 3.2. With complex provisioning systems, there can be many stages in the process where errors can occur. The table below shows how 43 distinct error types interfered with the ordering and provisioning flow at one company. Categorizing and counting the errors was the first step in getting a full picture of the system's effectiveness at completing orders, and allowed bringing the issues to the attention of management, who didn't realize how many customers were experiencing these issues.

This activity is certainly daunting because there are so many errors, and what's worse, the resolution to each error is unique! This is an excellent example of "facing the brutal facts."

If your restaurant gives too much change back or too much food away for free, you'll never get a customer complaint, but it will hurt your business. If you give too little change back, or give out the wrong order, it makes for an unhappy customer,

43 Error Types for the Provisioning Function of a System

#	System	Error	Mon May 22	Tue May 23	Wed May 24	Thu May 25	Fri May 26	Sat May 27	Sun May 28	Mon May 29	Tue May 30	Wed May 31	Thu Jun 1	Total	Avg Per Day
1	CRM	Could not connect to DB	20	7	8	8	18	8	5	4	902	6	5	991	90
2	CRM	Request timed out	30	53	59	78	89	23	0	67	40	14	16	469	43
3	Billing	Mutually exclusive features	62	55	40	14	44	37	7	44	59	10	64	436	40
4	Middleware	Billing system not responding	4	13	32	220	15	5	1	4	26	12	25	357	32
5	Inventory Check	Unspecified error	29	20	29	41	14	26	11	47	51	27	10	305	28
6	Middleware	Record in queue >8 hours	28	18	24	41	26	7	4	31	30	43	25	277	25
7	CRM	Out of memory	22	20	32	12	46	12	13	25	31	43	5	261	24
8	Address Verif.	Zip code mismatch	13	14	22	30	28	8	1	30	20	30	9	205	19
9	Web CRM	404 File Not Found	12	24	12	32	19	13	6	31	24	17	4	194	18
10	Provisioning	Command failed	20	18	17	22	7	12	4	15	36	27	13	191	17
11	Billing	Ineligible date	17	15	24	10	16	11	2	24	27	13	17	176	16
12	Billing	Invalid state for given command	12	12	25	27	12	13	9	12	14	10	18	164	15
13	Billing	Invalid state for given command													
14	CRM	Arithmetic overflow in module	29	1	4	12	22	6	5	22	18	12	14	145	13
15	Billing	Cannot change after cancel date	6	21	14	4	18	2	4	15	12	21	23	140	13
16	Billing	Account already cancelled	136	0	0	0	0	0	0	0	0	0	0	136	12
17	Credit Card Valid.	Security certificate expired	27	13	10	4	20	6	3	11	27	3	5	129	12
18	CRM	Segmentation Fault	0	14	27	8	24	3	2	13	1	24	12	128	12
19	Web CRM	Unable to Connect to Remote Host	10	14	15	11	16	2	2	23	13	1	19	126	11
20	Billing	Invalid account type	17	1	19	9	2	6	7	17	12	11	17	118	11
21	CRM	627 Error	22	6	13	16	4	10	5	7	11	12	9	115	10
22	CRM	Null pointer	13	8	8	6	10	1	5	14	13	18	12	108	10
23	Middleware	Invalid value length	16	5	17	20	3	1	2	2	9	19	12	106	10
24	Provisioning	Requested service incompatible w/ device	1	0	28	7	6	4	1	15	13	18	4	97	9
25	Middleware	Order number not found	4	21	4	3	4	1	2	18	12	14	13	96	9
26	CRM	Deadlock victim	0	0	0	0	0	0	0	0	0	73	19	92	8
27	Credit Check	Violation of PRIMARY KEY const.	23	2	1	9	16	1	3	7	0	3	17	82	7
28	Provisioning	Insufficient free memory	9	6	9	13	8	2	4	6	8	9	2	76	7
29	Provisioning	Required field missing	4	3	21	2	3	9	4	14	0	2	3	65	6
30	Billing	Record not found	3	12	7	3	1	4	4	2	11	11	7	65	6
31	Middleware	13-123 error	7	5	1	9	8	3	1	3	2	9	2	50	5
32	Inventory Check	Unknown error	6	4	2	6	4	2	1	1	7	0	5	38	3
33	CRM	BUS Error	5	1	4	6	1	0	0	5	5	2	6	35	3
34	Billing	Number invalid	3	2	3	3	4	0	2	5	0	3	5	30	3
35	CRM	Record locked	3	4	2	6	3	1	1	4	0	1	5	30	3
36	Billing	Service name must match acct nm	2	1	2	1	3	1	1	2	0	1	2	16	1
37	Web CRM	Failed DNS lookup	1	1	0	1	5	0	0	0	1	0	0	9	1
38	CRM	Error converting data type varchar to %s	0	1	0	1	1	1	1	0	0	1	1	7	1
39	Credit Check	First name must be at least 2 characters	1	1	0	1	0	1	0	0	1	1	0	6	1
40	Tax Calculation	Network error: Connection refused	0	1	0	1	1	0	0	1	1	1	0	6	1
41	Tax Calculation	Cannot divide by 0	0	1	1	0	0	0	0	0	0	1	0	3	0
42	CRM	Could not write to filesystem	0	0	1	0	1	0	0	0	0	1	0	3	0
43	Middleware	"Last Name" entry too long	1	0	0	0	0	0	0	0	0	0	0	1	0
		totals	618	418	537	697	522	242	123	541	1437	524	425	6084	553

figure 3.2. Example error types list for a complex system

takes time to resolve, and impacts other customers due to delay. While you might get letters occasionally, complaining of these various problems, it can be difficult to assemble them into a unified metric that helps you understand what is really happening in your stores.

On top of the fuzziness surrounding this issue is the cost to resolve. A production error hits the large end of the 1/10/100 rule. Just a single production error can cause turmoil. For example, a customer calls to order a product, and the rep gets an illegitimate client error during the call that they cannot work around:

1. The customer service representative (CSR) calls the help desk to ask for advice. He is put on hold for three minutes.

2. The CSR is told to try to resolve the problem by restarting the client.

3. The CSR puts the customer on hold for an additional four minutes while the client restarts.

4. It works! Seven minutes later, the CSR brings the order back up, but some of the data entered is missing.

5. The customer gets upset due to the wait and having to repeat data.

6. Other calls increasingly wait on hold because the CSR is tied up on this call.

7. After resolving the first call, the CSR hurries to try to keep up with call volume, but makes other mistakes in the process.

8. The CSR's job satisfaction decreases.

9. The same problem happens again in the afternoon…

Worse yet, if a customer calls to order a product, and the CSR enters the necessary information and everything looks okay, and there's an error on the back end, here are the events that will likely follow:

1. The customer won't receive the product and will be upset.

2. The customer will call in to see what happened.

3. The new CSR or even the original CSR who entered the order won't be able to figure it out.

4. The CSR may try to enter a new order, which may or may not work.

5. The CSR will contact technical support for assistance.

6. Technical support will assign a technician to sort it out.

7. The technical support rep will research and fix the problem on the back end.

8. The customer may get one or two products, both of which are late. They decide the company is completely incompetent and calls to send both of them back.

9. An escalation representative gives the customer a $100 credit to stay with their product. Many of these credits are given out, which hurt the company's bottom line.

10. The customer is less angry, but still doesn't respect the ability of the company to service him properly, so leaves six months later when a competitor is having a sale.

Yes, these scenarios are dire, but are also entirely realistic. Imagine these scenarios multiplied hundreds or thousands of times over, per day or per week. Significant costs from numerous touches on the same order, reduced employee satisfaction, and plummeting customer satisfaction. Error correction and prevention must be made a serious priority, because the potential downside is too great to ignore! Better understanding the hidden cost of errors can help you make a strong case for greater testing, better tools, better development processes, longer release cycles, and more.

Do You Need a Dedicated Error Correction Team?

If you don't have a dedicated error correction and prevention team in place for your major applications, and yet you know (or suspect) that you have a significant issue with errors, consider creating one.

The error data should be captured via some form of instrumentation, perhaps as simple as logs (and if it is not possible to do so, great effort should be made to modify the code so it does capture the errors), and categorized by type of error. Then each unique error type can be analyzed to try to identify a fix. Often this work is complex and needs to be performed iteratively. If your software wasn't built and tested with error-handling in mind, don't be surprised to find that you have hundreds of error types in production, many of them unreported. Sadly, if so, your best approach is to prioritize the discovered types based on the amount of pain they are causing, try to find fixes in the software for the most important ones, and iteratively release code to address the problems.

And in the meantime, of course, you need to keep a team in place to manually resolve the errors until relief is found. If you're in a bad spot for a long time, you can develop tools to make ticket resolution less labor-intensive, but an ounce of prevention is truly the way to go here if at all possible.

Needless to say, you need dedicated people looking after this in any sizeable software deployment. This is not a part-time job by any means.

Crashing and Hanging

Also related to errors are the phenomena of crashing and hanging. Crashing is when a process dies due to an error condition that is not caught. Hanging is similar, except instead of disappearing, the process simply becomes nonresponsive.

If either of these happens on the client machine, it will be a scenario similar to the first error scenario above. However, if processes routinely crash or hang on the server side, nobody in operations will notice unless appropriate monitoring is set up. Don't let anyone try to convince you that crashing and hanging are not a big deal. It is entirely possible to create operational jobs that monitor for crashing and hanging processes on the server, and automatically restart these processes if that happens. But that's only a Band-Aid and nothing more, because in all likelihood, the transaction that was in progress while the crashing or hanging occurred is in an invalid state—an error, unless your error handling logic is very good.

You may also be tempted to restart your software every night to prevent crashes (particularly those caused by poor memory management). While sometimes effective over the short term, this is not ideal either. Any software that must be restarted frequently or even occasionally to run properly will put you in a jam in the future. If you have to restart it nightly today, and your business volume doubles next year, what will you do then? Restart it during lunch break too?

Scalability Measurement

If you're running a mom and pop neighborhood café, perhaps you don't think too much about growth and expansion. Your business is just the right size and you like it that way. However, if you're running a national fast food chain, you're probably very focused on new markets to move into to or locations where you could open a new restaurant. If business is good, you might even have issues with existing restaurant locations overwhelmed with customers at peak hours like lunch or dinner time. Perhaps it's time to add another cash register or make room for more tables. Almost certainly you would have extensive metrics focused on understanding your growth challenges to help inform your corporate expansion plans. You probably even have an entire department thinking about this and only this. With IT systems, scalability measuring is one of the trickiest things to get your head wrapped around. Unlike previously mentioned measurements where you are capturing the current state of something, here you are measuring the past and present in order to predict the future. The intent is to head off a scalability crisis or meltdown, where your system ceases to work properly under peak load. Initially, this may manifest itself as a performance problem or in bouts of sporadic errors at peak hours. Eventually, if not corrected, the system will cease to function at all.

What is Scalability?

A system is said to be scalable when it can gracefully handle additional business load (volume) placed upon it.

If your system is not growing or changing (like the small corner café), this is not as big a concern, but if it is growing or changing or both (or if you don't know if it's growing or not!), then you really have to be armed with the best data possible.

Note that for most systems, extending scalability is not a straightforward matter of adding more servers; it simply isn't that easy. Most systems have multiple bottlenecks...some of which are only constrained by processing power, in which case you can buy bigger or faster equipment. But some bottlenecks are a function of the software itself, and they are the most difficult ones to predict and resolve.

Ultimately, your hardware, software, and configurations must all grow in concert in advance of increasing production business volume. Sounds tricky, doesn't it? It is tricky, even when things are going right and you have cushion—cushion meaning having a significant difference between the business volume today and the business volume that would trigger a scalability crisis. What makes it trickier is being right up against the wall with no margin for error and little to no time to analyze the situation and pick the right next step. Then you really can't take any risks, so in many ways your hands are tied. So it certainly pays to get out in front of these problems to buy more time to fix them. For a growing system, if you always know you can support at least 20% more transactions than you are currently processing (or 50% or more if you're concerned about unexpectedly high business demand, low-quality software releases, or other crises), that gives you confidence and the ability to relax a little.

These scalability crises happen when you grow a system beyond what it was designed and tested to do. When you are doing things in production that have never been done in testing, your production instance in essence becomes your performance test or load test bed. Perversely, there are upsides to this approach:

- reduced initial cost from not having to buy a production-like test area

- the test bed is extremely production-like (because it *is* production!)

Conversely, the downside is that if there is a problem, it is a production problem. So this is generally not a good idea, but it happens out there, usually due to resource constraints or poor planning/awareness.

At a high level, to be able to predict system scalability, you have to measure both the supply side and the demand side of the scalability equation.

Supply

There are two parts to the supply side:

- **All the resources available to the system**. This should be formally inventoried in a detailed manner (for instance, down to the patch level) and include the OS version, database management system (DBMS) version, specific server types down to the number of processors and their speeds, available memory, storage capacity, and network bandwidth. These are all fine things to measure and track in the raw: simply how much "oomph" are we throwing at our workload? It's also important to note how the software is configured. For instance, how many threads are there of process X? In fast food, this would be the number of cash registers, drink machines, deep-fat fryers, employees, seats, and parking spaces.

- **Drag or contention on the system**. These are bottlenecks in the system in which conflicts for the same resources are slowing it down.[4] Oftentimes, these are locking and blocking issues, either in the DBMS or file system. For instance, if two processes are trying to modify the same data at the same time, the second process must wait until the first process is finished. Even if the waiting time is under a second, if it happens hundreds or even thousands of times per hour, the drag will be significant. Quantifying the size and frequency of these blocking issues is critical.

The concept of drag can be confusing. Let's say that your particular restaurant should be able to serve 2,000 customers per hour at lunchtime. You have all the staff, equipment, and food there to make it happen. But when it gets really busy, all of those resources are configured in such a way that you don't get the full results you'd expect.

For instance, people get into each other's way at the fry station because it's cramped there. Order-takers queue at the ice machine because, even though there are plenty of ice reserves, the employees are all waiting to use the same ice scoop, and there are too many escalations to the manager for him to respond to them in sufficient time. Therefore only 1,700 customers actually get served in that hour, and a line piles up. That's drag. Conversely, if two employees call in sick, and you just don't have enough people to do the work, that's not drag; there just aren't enough resources available.

In the software world, this phenomenon is typically called contention, but other words like locking, blocking, deadlocking, or even thrashing are often used. Devices and software that aren't configured optimally are prone to have this happen, where

---

4   See excellent technical white paper "Characteristics of Scalability and Their Impact on Performance" by André B. Bondi.

multiple processes fight for the same scarce resources. Or sometimes, when multiple applications share the same resources (for instance, reside on the same physical server), they fight over resources there. Examples are database memory contention, database row-level contention ("blocking" and "deadlocking"), and disk contention. If you measure this contention and subtract it from your supply, you will find your truly available supply:

Supply – Contention = Net Supply

This net supply concept is very important. Most scalability problems are simply situations in which there aren't enough resources available to meet the demand. Maybe there aren't enough memory or disk or CPU cycles to get the job done. So you add resources to resolve the issue. The formula in these cases is inconsequential.

But in a less common case, contention is the key problem. Contention is eating away at your resources. And the solution of adding additional resources may or may not work. In some cases, adding resources will actually make the problem worse, by increasing contention. So the root cause of the contention must be addressed to succeed.

Demand

The *demand* side is simply the volume of business transactions being requested of your system. You need historical volumes, as well as projections of future load; these can usually be obtained from the business, but it makes sense to create your own projections based on your own historical data as well, because the business may use overly optimistic projections for various reasons. If it is a complex system with many different types of transactions, it can be helpful to break it down to the business transaction type level, as those transactions often place varying levels of strain on the system, and also it will help your projections be more accurate. How many orders of fries did I sell last month? Burgers? Shakes? Soft drinks? Business transactions are the ideal unit of work to use as a scalability demand statistic.

Transaction Type	Average # per Hour	Load per Transaction
Open Account	3,000	High
Cancel Account	1,000	Low
Change Address	7,500	Med
Change Device	4,000	Low

table 3.2. Transaction types by frequency and intensity

In addition to the basic transaction volumes, it can be handy to track certain key ratios. Knowing the ratio of soft drinks to burgers sold might be a good way to predict soft drink demand by only knowing the forecast for burgers. Oftentimes, the business will have forecasts for only one major transaction type, such as number of customers. So if you know the typical ratio of orders to customers, you can more accurately predict overall demand, especially if certain transaction types tax the system more than others.

Named Users: Number of users who have access to the system. Useful to know for the purposes of:

- Security – Do the right people have the right access?
- Licensing – How many seats are you/should you be paying for?
- Scalability – What is the maximum theoretical number of users who may be logged in at once?

User Log-in Events: Number of user log-in events over the course of a period. Users who have logged into the system several times in the period will be counted multiple times.

Useful to know for scalability purposes when log-in operations are resource intensive.

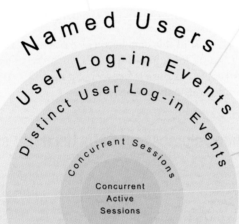

Distinct User Log-in Events: Same as above except each user is only counted once, even if they've logged in multiple times during the period. Useful to know for scalability purposes when considered as a percentage of named users. If that percentage stays fairly constant over time, and the business is able to give you a forecast of named users, then you can forecast actual usage of an application.

Concurrent Sessions: Relevant in systems for which the concept of a user session exists.

Concurrent Sessions equates the number of users who are signed into the system at the time the measurement is taken. They may have signed in several minutes ago and be actively interacting with the system, or several hours ago, and have not performed any activity since then. However these sessions are using system resources (e.g. memory), so being able to track them and forecast them will allow planning for capacity needs of those resources.

Concurrent Active Sessions: Users interacting with the system right now (or at least within the last few minutes), and who are actively consuming system resources (beyond the memory required to maintain the session).

This metric is generally the most useful for scalability planning purposes. It does require being able to make the distinction between an active session and an idle session.

figure 3.3. User count types

Sometimes, in larger systems, demand can be expressed as a number of active users as well. Transaction volumes combined with user counts are meaningful and helpful measures. However a user count by itself is overly simple and often lacks clarity—are the users using your application 100% of the time? Are they idle sometimes or using other applications instead? Figure 3.3 depicts various ways of counting users. Each type of user count has a distinct scalability implication.

The third type of demand metric is the number of customers that the application supports. This can be useful because it is somewhat precise and easy to track, but it only applies in some narrow situations, such as when you are providing a service to a customer that they pay for on a monthly basis. The typical place this works well is customer-supporting applications, and it may not apply otherwise.

TIP

Don't choose the number of users as your only scalability metric, because it is too simple to stand alone.

Most of this data becomes particularly interesting during peak load, because that is when the system is at its most fragile state. If your system is at its busiest between 2 p.m. and 7 p.m. Eastern time, put most of your collection and analysis efforts there.

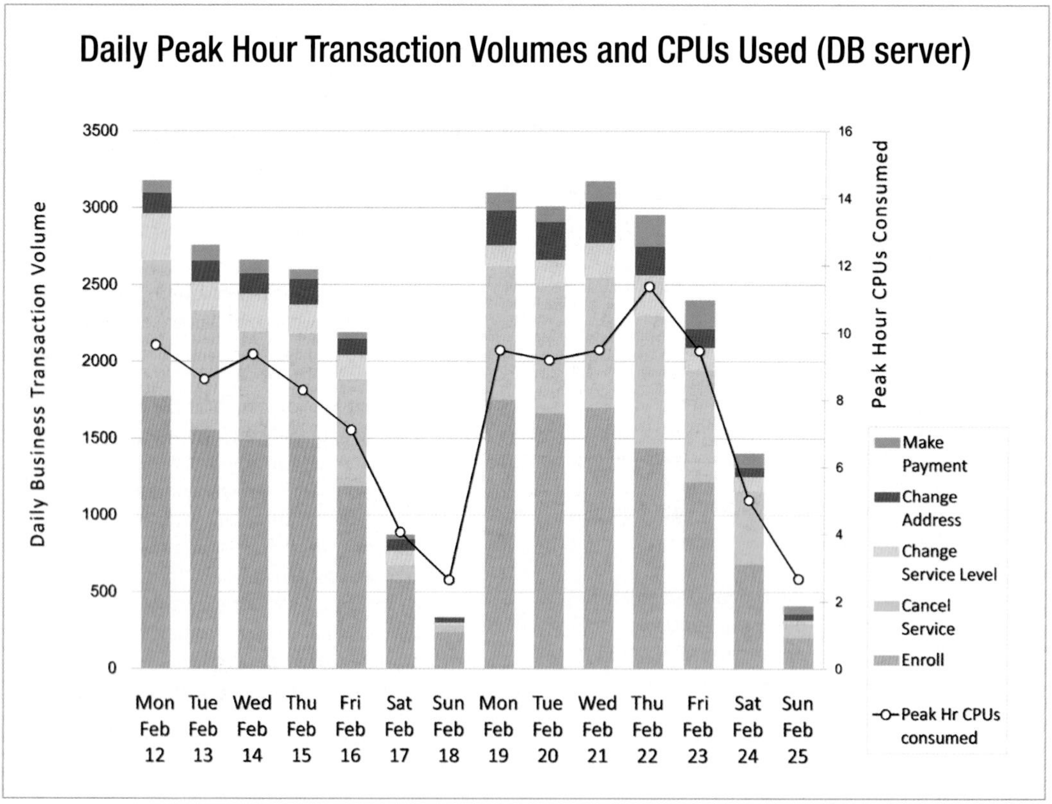

Daily Peak Hour Transaction Volumes and CPUs Used (DB server)

figure 3.4. Example peak hour supply and demand data

Once you have the demand calculated from a business perspective, it's time to translate it into a technical cost. That is, when you have 10,000 business transactions pumping through a system each hour, how many of your available resources are being consumed? You need to keep a specific inventory of how many of your physical resources (CPU, memory, network, etc.) are being consumed by the system at peak load. Depending on the system, this data can be collected every 1 to 15 minutes. The example in figure 3.4 depicts how combining supply and demand data during peak hours shows the relationship between the two. Showing both supply and demand data on the same graph can be a great way to track whether the utilization of your infrastructure evolves linearly with the demand (expressed in business transactions). Also note that here we use number of CPUs used instead of CPU utilization percent. "CPUs used" is determined by multiplying CPU utilization during peak hour by number of CPUs on the system.

Projection

If your database server is at 80% CPU, and your network is at 60% utilized bandwidth, and everything else is less taxed than that, then a very simplistic model suggests that you have 20% spare capacity, or headroom, available (assuming you push your database server to 100% CPU capacity), and, using the previous example, you could ramp up to 12,500 transactions per hour without failing.

Net Supply – Technical Demand = True Spare Capacity

This model is extremely rough, mainly because it ignores unknown software bottlenecks, but it's helpful nonetheless. You at least know that you probably won't be able to do 14,000 transactions per hour without making changes. One caveat to pay attention to is that some subsystems perform more poorly when pushed to the limit; for example, if you take some flavors of a DB server from 60% CPU to 70% CPU, it's not a big deal. But if you take it from 85% CPU to 95% CPU, you might start getting degraded performance, which in turn will yield you less headroom.

The Mystique of Load Averages

Oftentimes, we represent how busy a particular machine is (and conversely, how much headroom it has) in terms of CPU percent utilized. For instance, 90% CPU utilization means that 10% of the time, the CPUs were idle and doing nothing. At a high level, this is useful practice.

In addition, on UNIX systems, we can obtain a broader picture of what is happening by using load averages. Load average takes into account both the processes currently using CPU and those waiting in line to use CPU once one frees up. Rather than being expressed as a percentage, it is a number that changes meaning depending on how many CPUs the machine in question has. On a 4 CPU machine, a Load Average of 2 indicates that the CPUs are 50% busy, and a load average of 4 means that the CPUs are 100% busy. Where it gets interesting is when things heat up: a load average of 6 means that the CPUs are 100% busy, and on average there is one waiting process in the queue for every 2 CPUs. And so on.

So on a busy 4 CPU machine, depending on the OS, application type, and other factors, a load average of 4.1 might not make you worry, while a load average of 10 probably would. There is much more detail and richness to load average (for instance at http://www.linuxjournal.com/article/9001), so please consider this merely a primer!

Also, if you start approaching the ceiling in multiple subsystems at the same time (such as network and database), any negative effects can multiply, and also make diagnosis more difficult. So prevention is the only way to go here as well.

Inefficient Code

When new code is written for a business application, the number one thing that seems to matter is whether the business's official functional requirements are met. So the development teams go through design reviews to make sure they are on the right track, and the testing teams repeatedly test against detailed functional test conditions.

But what about efficiency? It is possible to write code that meets the functional requirements that is terrible from a production standpoint. It could make excessive calls to the database or waste memory. Ultimately, these problems reveal themselves as performance or scalability issues—problems that simple, functional testing would never reveal.

We once encountered a mature system that was having scalability problems where a database call to retrieve information was accidentally placed inside of a loop...so every time the information was needed by the program, it asked the database for the same exact thing *hundreds* of times! How was this allowed to happen?

Ultimately, to have high-performing code, you need four things:

1. Standards for what high-performing code looks like.
2. A development staff that has the expertise to develop with real-world operational aspects of software in mind. This may require training with your own operations personnel or industry experts.
3. Mandatory reviews and testing that checks for compliance with the standards.
4. A culture that values the efficiency of the product being delivered, as much as the functional content.

If you don't have these things, you are leaving your code efficiency to chance. At low volumes, it might not matter much...but at scale, it is a killer.

Note that the desired balance between functionality and efficiency may tip either way depending on the nature of your business. You will get better results by having it be a conscious decision rather than an accident. For instance, for some businesses, it is possible to go overboard, thus expending too much effort by making code too "elegant."

When you have all of this data available on a regular interval, it becomes possible to do true capacity planning (although the less common term "scalability planning" is more clear, as capacity is often confused with simple storage capacity or network capacity). Calculating processing cost per transaction is one technique we've used successfully (see example fig. 3.5).

In order to predict future supply needs, a straightforward method is to determine the amount of "horsepower" each transaction consumes, on average. This can be done by taking the CPU utilization or load average during peak hour, and dividing it by the number of key business transactions executed in that same period (figure 3.5 demonstrates that the CPU needed per transaction has gone down over time due to system improvements).

The ratio can then be applied to the predicted numbers of transactions to approximate needs in CPU capacity. This model assumes that

1. CPU utilization needs progress linearly with business transaction growth, and

2. All transaction types used in the model have fairly equivalent processing needs.

While this model is not perfect, it is simple and has proven to be accurate in forecasting capacity needs for large OLTP databases. See chapter 8 for an example of how this data was used to produce a demand forecast.

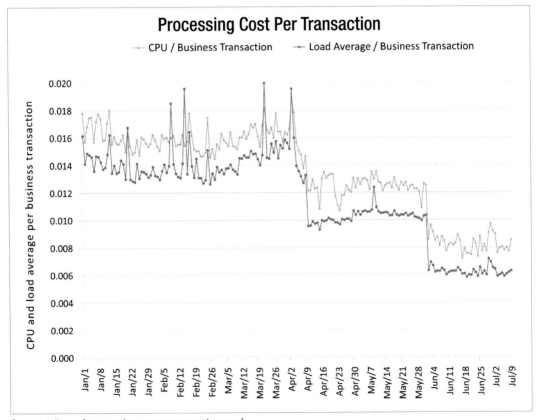

figure 3.5. Example processing cost per transaction graph

Using this technique, you can project whether your system will be okay three months in the future, or six months, or handle the holiday rush, or marketing's latest promotion, or a server failure, and be prepared to take appropriate action. Make a line chart that overlays the projected demand with the supply of resources (see example in the "Scalability status charts" section of chapter 8). See when they overlap. Know that the result won't be 100% accurate, but it is a helpful planning tool. Surprises are an IT manager's worst enemy.

Finally, when you have interlocking applications (applications that share resources or feed each other inputs), you need to measure all of them together and compare results, because trends from one can easily impact another.

Making All This Work for Your System

We have just listed numerous suggestions for aspects of your system that are critical to measure (with examples to come in chapters 7 and 8). Many of these metrics are universally applicable to all systems. But some are not, and all large enterprise systems are somewhat different.

So please treat these suggestions as a flexible framework. Use what works. Discard what doesn't (but have a long, hard look before you do). And most importantly, when your technicians encounter a specific metric of paramount importance, add it in!

You will find that when you begin this rigorous measuring journey, your deliverables will seem somewhat basic. But rest assured they will mature quickly, and as the months pass by, you'll have better and more useful data to rely upon, and you'll have the context of previous months' data to make the current data even more valuable.

Can you trust a measuring package or tool to magically take care of all of this for you?

Several vendors now tout products that you can plug in to your existing production environment that will monitor, measure, alert, predict, and basically claim to solve all of your problems. While some of these tools can be helpful assistants to your staff, rest assured there is no magic pill. There is no substitute for your staff knowing exactly what your applications are doing—being familiar with all aspects of the systems and any changes that are coming their way.

What to Do with the Data

Now that you have all of this data, what are you going to do with it? This data is the foundation of a quality IT shop. You are going to be able to use it many different ways, as you'll see in most of the remaining chapters of this book. But we'll note one very important use here:

Real-Time Monitoring and Alerting

If there is a problem brewing, it is imperative that you know about it first so that you can deploy your forces to take corrective action before the business is harmed. The last thing you want is to be surprised by a call from the business that their systems are impaired or down. As production managers, the most embarrassing thing should be having to hear first from the customer that the system is down. Or slow. Or sprouting errors at a brisk clip. How could they know and not you? We all know that sinking feeling when you think everything's fine and then a customer calls and says, "Are you having a system problem?" Is the system working for you, or are you working for the system?

So, for many of the parameters described in this chapter, it is very important to flag in near-real-time if anything is far outside of healthy parameters. If a server normally runs at 70% but hits 99% or 100%, an automatic notification should be sent out to have someone investigate—i.e., someone should be paged. If response times are over double what is normal, someone should be paged. If there have been five times the normal rate of errors over the last hour, someone should be paged.

Be prepared to monitor every piece of your infrastructure in whatever way you can. It is okay to have some parts monitored by a software package and other parts by some custom scripts. The important thing is to find ways to bring all the relevant data together and find correlations where they exist, which requires strong analytical skills. In our experience, a well thought-out "portal style" system health dashboard can do the trick if you have people who know how to get the most out of it.

In some cases, it makes sense for your main measuring infrastructure to be the one used for paging out problems. In other cases, it may make more sense to have redundant quality-checking systems. But in either case, make sure your department is the first to know.

The Value Proposition

Knowing if you are in trouble, or are going to be in trouble, and exactly where that trouble is located is extremely useful, because you can head off problems before they are felt by your business customers. Knowing if things are trending better or worse helps you manage. You can decide where to focus your efforts and know whether you are being effective or not.

If your restaurant had unplanned closures three days out of the year, would you take action? If orders were taken slowly or served slowly, would you take action? If orders were filled inaccurately, would you take action?

If you simply didn't know…would you be able to take action?

Summary Checklist

✓ **Monitoring, measuring, and trending** are essential activities for managing IT quality.

✓ **Four essential measurements**: You must measure all four of the corner-stones of quality (downtime, transaction response times, error rates, and scalability) to ensure you're delivering and will continue to deliver the level of service your customers expect.

✓ **Downtime**: Measuring availability is a critical but also very basic and some-what limited quality metric.

  ○ **BII**: To truly understand the ramifications of outages, you need a metric that translates downtime into a quantifiable measurement of damage done to the enterprise. We call this the Business Impact Index, or BII.

✓ **Response times**: If you aren't measuring transaction response times, you may be delivering a poor customer or user experience and not even know it.

  ○ Monitoring transaction responses can be done by active monitoring, whereby dummy transactions are created solely for the purpose of timing them, and passive monitoring, whereby actual business transactions are tracked as they happen.

  ○ These are the four main methods of monitoring transaction response times:

    1. Stopwatch timings

    2. Instrumentation of custom code

    3. Installed monitoring software

    4. Third-party monitoring as a service

✓ **Errors** are the manifestation of single transactions or jobs that don't produce the expected result. Even when a system or service has high uptime and good response times, you can have serious quality issues if errors are happening.

  ○ Errors are the hidden killer because they are not obvious like transaction slowness or a full-blown outage. They often go unreported and untracked, resulting in user frustration, increased costs, and customer dissatisfaction.

  ○ Errors must be identified and categorized, and you must implement a sys-tem to track them.

- You need to understand the business impact of errors to rally the focus needed to eliminate them by fixing the broken technology or process that allowed them to be created in the first place.

✓ **Scalability** is the hardest of the four cornerstones to quantify and measure.

- Supply – Contention = Net Supply

- Net Supply – Technical Demand = True Spare Capacity

## CHAPTER 4

Turning Problems into Opportunities

Why Problem Management Is Your Best Friend

Chapter Overview

System trouble manifests itself in the form of incidents. An incident interrupts service. The cause of the incident (and potentially multiple incidents) is a problem. While resolving incidents is an important tactical matter, addressing problems in your environment is a prime way to make your systems more stable over time.

This chapter will be especially relevant to those who are up to their ears in quality issues right now. We will not only discuss some of the basics of a solid problem management philosophy but also some important intangibles that are essential to creating a strong problem-solving culture in your organization—a culture that will generate the most quality improvements over the long term.

We save discussion of the tactical approach for solving specific technical problems for the following chapter, "Hands-On Problem Solving."

Why Is Problem Solving Important?

System problems are like criminals who commit crimes in your neighborhood. Granted, IT system problems don't have intelligence or intent, but they do interrupt normal life, are upsetting, and can be very costly. Furthermore, if they aren't caught and dealt with, they will most certainly reoffend and hurt you more.

Cont. →

If you were a criminal, who would you fear the most: a vigilant, relentless, coordinated, and systematic law enforcement community, or The Keystone Cops, the bumbling policemen from the silent film era that only succeeded in futility (and laughter)? If you were a system problem that didn't want to be found and fixed, who would you want after you: an IT department that was devoted to and effective at problem solving, or one that was too busy, too focused on other things, or too unskilled at the investigative arts to really get after the true source of problems? Sherlock Holmes and TV's Columbo both get their man and are rightly celebrated for their skill and record of results. You need many people just like them in your IT department, and you need them equipped with all the tools they require to get the job done.

Incidents vs. Problems

An incident is a single event that disrupts service to your customers. An incident begins when service is disrupted. Once service is restored, an incident ends. Incidents can be as severe as an outage, but can also be things like transaction performance slowdowns or errors. Essentially, an incident is any breach in service levels.

A problem is the circumstance that caused the incident to happen in the first place. It's the underlying issue that caused the system to go down, run slow, throw errors, or anything else that impacts service. A single problem can cause multiple incidents. Problems are things like bugs, human errors, and incorrect configurations. This chapter is all about getting to the bottom of problems that impact your system quality by causing incidents.

Problems are the things standing between you and the achievement of your quality goals. They are the bugs, incorrect configurations, design mistakes, process errors, maintenance oversights, and other issues that are at the root cause of poor system quality. The more effectively and smartly you solve these problems, the better your quality situation becomes.

Just as effective criminal investigations drive effective law enforcement, effective problem solving is one of the engines that drive your quality goal achievement machine. Later, we're going to cover preventing problems before they happen, but now it's time to discuss something all organizations require: strong problem management.

Just as those for criminology, there are numerous problem-solving methodologies out there, such as Six Sigma[5], Total Quality Management (TQM),[6] and Lean.[7] Problem Management is even an ITIL[8] discipline. All of these are

---

5 Pioneered by Motorola in the 1980s, Six Sigma is a quality improvement program that leverages statistical analysis to help identify and prevent defects. Initially, it was applied to manufacturing but has gained momentum and is now used in various parts of the business.

6 TQM is a predecessor to Six Sigma that was developed in the 1950s.

7 A manufacturing improvement methodology based somewhat on the Toyota Production System and focused on reduction of waste.

8 ITIL stands for Information Technology Infrastructure Library, a popular set of IT standards that originated from Great Britain in the 1980s. While this is not a book about ITIL or how to implement it, we will frequently refer to **incidents** and **problems** in the way they are defined by ITIL, as these definitions are becoming mainstream and do a good job of representing two distinct but important concepts of system quality management.

useful, and it's not our intent to reinvent the wheel but rather to harvest their essential teachings in the IT quality space and marry them to our own practical experiences. We also will focus the discussion on the most relevant and useful aspects of solving operational quality problems on large systems.

The Upside of Outages

We recommend keeping a positive mind-set regarding problems, whether they are inevitable ones or those that were fully preventable. Even though system incidents are what we strive to avoid and prevent, once they've occurred, you should treat them as your best friend and something that's not to be forgotten. Every time a system incident reveals itself in the form of an outage, a transaction slowdown, or an error, it's doing you a favor. How can an outage be a good thing, you ask?

Well, in and of itself it's not, but once it has happened, it becomes something to be exploited. An incident reveals there's a weakness somewhere that needs to be addressed, and it also potentially reveals what was done wrong to create the problem in the first place. It may also indicate that similar problems not related to this particular incident lurk out there somewhere, waiting to cause you trouble later down the line. Incidents are caused by problems, and problems must be resolved to achieve the best system quality.

This leads us to a very important observation we have derived from Murphy's Law.[9] We call it The Ostrich Postulate: A known problem that is not fully addressed will almost certainly reoccur, and next time, it will be of even greater impact. Furthermore, it will be much more uncomfortable and embarrassing to explain to your management than it was the first time it happened!

> ### The Ostrich Postulate
>
> A known problem that is not fully addressed will almost certainly reoccur, and next time it will be of even greater impact.
>
> (In popular mythology, the ostrich would place its head in the sand at the first sign of danger, rather than taking constructive action.)

Would a good police detective be surprised about a series of burglaries, repeated vandalism, or habitual drunk driving? The answer is certainly no. Experienced law enforcement officials know from years of empirical and anecdotal data that crimes are frequently part of trends and that many criminals offend repeatedly until they are stopped. A good detective knows that you have to catch bad guys and put them away to keep them from committing even more crimes. They also know that big-time criminals start out small and become a greater danger over time.

It's the same with IT systems. Until a problem is proven to be fully resolved or cannot reoccur, it must be assumed that not only will there be new incidents stemming from the same problem, but the next time they will be even more severe and come

---

9 Murphy's Law: If something can go wrong, it will.

at an even more inopportune time for your business. To achieve the highest levels of quality, you must have the attitude that known problems are ticking time bombs just waiting to go off and ruin your day. That creates the sense of urgency that a healthy problem management culture has deep down in its guts. The strongest system management organizations see the identification of a problem as an opportunity to improve the system.

Once a problem presents itself, root cause must be vigilantly worked and corrective actions taken wherever possible to generate the maximum possible stability. This is done repeatedly, wherever and whenever possible. Effective law enforcement agencies demonstrate the exact same sense of urgency with brutal and serious criminals, like murderers and arsonists. They simply don't sit around hoping the suspect doesn't do it again. The public demands that they go all out to catch the offender because of what's at stake.

We recognize, too, that in neighborhoods where petty crimes aren't dealt with, a feeling of lawlessness takes over that inevitably leads to more serious crimes. This criminology theory is called Broken Windows,[10] and it states that vigilantly going after lesser crimes like vagrancy, vandalism, and public drunkenness has shown to have been key to the remarkable reduction in crime in New York City in the 1990s. We hold that the same is true for IT. Too many small system problems left unaddressed create an environment where more major problems are likely to happen.

Have a Long, Long Memory

Just as in law enforcement, the foundation for effective problem solving is strong incident management and documentation. After an incident, once service is restored, oftentimes the stakeholders will issue a big sigh of relief that things are back to normal and go about their previous business. This is dangerous behavior! Imagine an FBI agent who arrived at the scene of a bank robbery, found that the robbers had fled the scene, made sure everyone was safe, and then went back to the office and forgot all about it!

---

10 There is some debate about the validity of the Broken Windows theory. For instance, Malcolm Gladwell's *The Tipping Point* (2000) cites it on page 141, while Levitt and Dubner's *Freakonomics* (2005) challenges it on p 121. Regardless of how well Broken Windows applies to crime, we think it's a very useful way of looking at problem creep in IT.

Critical Data to Formally Capture for Each Incident	Example
Start time	6:17 AM Pacific Time
Stop time	6:49 AM Pacific Time
Business applications impacted	Business applications A, B, and C
Primary symptom	Error "unable to connect to DB" for most users
Root cause (or if unknown, what is being done to find it)	Batch job started late due to deployment
Root cause subsystem (what part of the system failed?)	Database
Root cause system (may or may not be the same as the business application impacted)	Business system Z
What was done to restore service	Terminate long-running batch job
Problem owner(s)	Manager DBA
Corrective actions	Carefully schedule batch jobs to end before maintenance window expires and terminate them if they run long.

table 4.1. Example Incident Log Entry

Every production incident must have its impact quantified and documented (in part so that it can be leveraged within the BII!). Data needs to be tracked and stored in a way that best serves the problem-solving analysis to come. An incident undocumented is likely an incident forgotten, or worse, an incident remembered differently than what actually occurred. Poor documentation leads to a poorly organized problem management program. This leads to all kinds of unproductive behaviors, such as chasing red-herring issues and dropping everything to work on escalations or ad hoc problems not critically aligned with the quality goals.

It's become a cliché in the movies and on TV that police officers and law enforcement officials hate paperwork and doing mundane fact gathering at crime scenes, but despite that, the reality is that they do it anyway and in great detail. They know it's essential to solving cases, identifying trends, and reporting accurately on what's happening in the community. Accurately capturing the details of what happened greatly increases the likelihood of an arrest and conviction.

Similarly, a scientific problem-solving approach requires hard data, not anecdote, to generate the best results. Effective documentation of incidents is at the core of any strong problem management program. You should have a team responsible for tracking all problems to resolution across all functions. Doing this effectively requires not only tracking incidents in an incident management system, but also tracking problems as distinct entities, with one-to-many relationships with incidents.

Weekly root cause meetings should be conducted to track progress and ensure consistent focus (see table 4.2 for an example problem management log). Your organization should also look at the same data in a strategic way to identify trends and snuff out the bad ones. Problem solving should be rewarded in your culture (we talk about giving your people the right incentives in chapter 9, "The Invisible Hand of IT").

Problem Management Log

Fields	Example 1	Example 2
Priority	Very High	Medium
Problem ID	3090	5030
Owner	Julie	Jack
Reactive / Proactive?	Reactive	Proactive
Problem Short Description	**Leading wildcard searches cause session to hang indefinitely.**	**Upgrade to ERP vendor patch #66.4.3.03**
Impact or Benefit	Happens 20 times a day on average. Affects 1 user per occurrence.	Improves caching on the client side, increases performance by 20% for some lookup transactions.
Total BII Score	225	n/a
Related Incidents	13453; 13499; 13526; 13546; 13601; 13678	n/a
Date Opened	6/20	7/5
Dev LOE (Range)	40–50 hours	n/a
Test LOE (Range)	20–25 hours	80 hours

Status/Notes	7/12: Business signed off on UI changes. Scheduled for next maintenance release. 6/29: Julie confirmed wildcard searches are causing long running queries in the database. Working with dev on solutions. 6/28: John able to repro in test. Assigning to Julie for DB analysis. 6/27: Leading wildcard searches suspected to be cause. John to repro in test environment. 6/20: Issue first reported. John collecting more information.	7/09: Patch scheduled for testing. 7/05: ERP vendor to release new patch on 8/22. Need to evaluate benefit/need.
Bug#	38-56545587	
Vendor Ticket#		
Patch #		66.4.3.03
Pending Testing?		Yes
Pending Implementation?		
Pending Release?	Yes	
Update Needed?	Yes	
New this week?		Yes

table 4.2. Example problem management log.

Table 4.2 shows some of the key fields to use in a report for your weekly problem management meeting. If you use software to track your incidents and problems, you may have different fields, but here are some of the things to think about if you are creating a tracking tool or are able to modify one. This is by no means a comprehensive list, just some attributes we've found useful:

- **Priority:** Should be based on impact (actual or potential), and problems should be reviewed in decreasing order of priority.

- **Problem ID:** A unique identifier that allows associating incidents to this one problem; also handy for reducing communication issues/misunderstandings about what problem is being discussed.

- **Owner:** It is good practice to have a single owner for each problem. This doesn't mean a single person is responsible for finding the solution; simply that it's his or her responsibility to ensure progress is being made and to give updates at the meeting.

- **Reactive/Proactive:** A good problem management list is one where there are many items that are intended to prevent incidents from happening. Having this field allows tracking a metric about how many / what % of each kind is being tracked.

- **Description and Impact or Benefit:** Impact to business in the case of reactive problems, benefit to the business in the case of proactive items.

- **Total BII score:** Sum of BII points from all related incidents.

- **Related Incidents:** Reference to incidents that were believed to be caused by this problem.

- **Bug #:** It may be useful to cross-reference what bug/defect number has been logged if the problem is also being tracked in a bug tracking system (usually the case for problems that are code related and assigned to development).

- **Vendor Ticket Number:** For problems that need involvement from a hardware or software vendor.

- **Pending Testing:** Indicates if the problem is queued up for some root cause or validation testing.

- **Pending Implementation:** Indicates if problem is awaiting change management approval and/or actual implementation in production.

- **Pending Release:** For bugs that need to be fixed and delivered via a software release (usually has a bug/defect #).

- **Update Needed and New This Week:** Fields for use by the Problem Manager, or other problem management meeting facilitator, to ensure problems are being actively worked.

Keep Asking Why

At the heart of effective problem management is digging as deep as possible to determine root cause and to determine the corrective actions most likely to have the biggest impact when it comes to preventing future outages. It's often possible that a single incident can reveal numerous potential corrective actions that, if addressed proactively, can prevent countless future incidents. Not just the same incident that started the investigation, but other potential incidents caused by other problems that you now know to look for because of what this incident revealed.

The incident has done you the ironic favor of revealing there's at least one problem (and perhaps several) behind it. You need to keep asking why to exhaust every clue of the root cause and to kill that root cause dead. Imagine this dialogue happening after an incident:

Q: Why did the system go down?

A: The application server crashed.

Q: Why did the application server crash?

A: It ran out of memory.

Q: Why did it run out of memory?

A: There's a memory leak in the application.

> ### The Five Whys
>
> Both Lean and Six Sigma leverage the concept of asking deeper and deeper questions to get at the true root cause by advising the use of "The Five Whys."

At this point, we have multiple whys to ask and go down multiple investigative paths.

Path 1—Q: Why did our monitoring not inform us that memory was being leaked before the crash?

Path 2—Q: Why did our code testing processes not identify the memory leak prior to release?

Path 3—Q: Why did our coding processes allow the memory leak bug to be coded in the first place?

Each one of these three investigative paths could require numerous additional whys to be asked before finally getting to the true root cause for each. Along the way, there may be other investigative paths identified that need to be fully analyzed. At the end of the day, this single outage could result in numerous corrective actions that not only prevent future occurrences of outages caused by this memory leak, but proactively identify other existing memory leaks that can be fixed and prevent future new memory leaks from being coded and implemented, even in applications different than the one that had the original issue! As a result of this particular investigation, you could potentially end up making improvements to your monitoring, quality assurance (QA, or testing), and development processes that not only address this problem but countless other problems in a variety of applications that currently exist or would have been created in the future had no action been taken.

Law enforcement engages in the exact same types of behavior. They track small-time drug pushers to get to the kingpins. They use low-level mob informants to go after organized crime bosses. They know that the only way to really corner the true root cause is to keep investigating deep enough until the ring leaders can be taken out of business.

There is enormous power in asking "why," repeatedly, against all known problems. Theoretically, the environment eventually becomes bulletproof through constant improvement, because the same incident is never allowed to happen twice. In a perfect world, every single root cause would be fully analyzed, and every potential corrective action addressed. This, of course, is unrealistic and even unnecessary. The key, however, is zeroing in on the correct actions that will have the greatest overall impact, and that's where prioritization comes in later in the chapter.

Intelligent Extrapolation

There's great power in getting to the bottom of problems and preventing reoccurrence of the same incidents. It's at the heart of achieving system stability. There is, however, even greater power in going beyond this basic problem solving. There are three additional ways we've found to take your problem-solving efforts to a higher level to achieve an even higher level of quality. All three require the existence of a problem management team and robust problem management tools.

1. **Proactively addressing the same problem in other systems—not just the one in which the problem was discovered.**

The classic examples here are problems discovered in platforms like operating systems, networks, database management systems, or any technology that is used in multiple implementations across IT. When a bug is found and patched in the DBMS of system X, it makes sense to assess that same vulnerability on every system in IT running on the same DMBS. It's quite likely they share the same vulnerability. The bigger the size of the IT organization, the harder this can be to do (because of organizational boundaries and communication limitations), yet it's also where the benefits can be the greatest if done consistently and methodically. In our experience, it's all too common for a problem to impact different services on one side of IT when the same problem has already been identified and resolved elsewhere.

The key to doing this well is knowing what you're running across all of IT, who's responsible for the systems and functional components, and having an effective communication channel to alert the owners to known problems. A good way to approach this is to maintain system configuration data for all solutions in a central repository (commonly referred to as a CMDB, or configuration management database). Along with ownership information, send potential problem bulletins to systems sharing the exposure, and then track to the appropriate resolution.

2. Anticipating other problems that may exist and haven't revealed themselves yet.

A good example for this would be a situation where a previously unknown system error is discovered by a production support team. Let's assume the error in question was unknown because it was being logged in a directory the support team wasn't monitoring for error messages. Of course you'd want to address the root cause of the error and put the appropriate monitoring in place for that specific error going forward, but it makes very good sense to then ask the questions, "How did we not know about this error, and what can we do to make sure there aren't other unmonitored directories containing other unknown error messages?" At this point, a full evaluation should be done to ensure all directories housing error messages are being properly monitored and addressed.

3. Preventing meta-problems.

Meta-problems are families of systemic issues in your IT department. They are generally not specific to a particular system, a particular team, or a particular technical platform. They could be due to process, organizational, or cultural gaps in your department, and as such, they are the trickiest trends to identify and address.

Preventing meta-problems is the holy grail of problem solving—using not only the knowledge of an existing problem to change future events, but identifying a series of problems that can be traced to fundamental systemic issues in the IT organization. Doing this effectively requires good data mining capabilities, and can be greatly

> ## Meta-Problems Explained
>
> A meta-problem is a high-level process, organizational, or cultural gap that results in multiple related problems occurring over time. For instance, if your development and testing organization places insufficient emphasis on load testing, and over the years you have had numerous scalability flare-ups in a variety of business applications, that is a meta-problem.

aided by the use of a functionally robust problem management database for all of your systems and services. The problem database must have a common and consistent way of classifying all problems so they can be rolled up and categorized by type. The problem management database must be easily cross-referenced with the database used to track production incidents. Reports can then be run to evaluate trends and the types or categories of problems causing the most business pain (which can be easily determined using the Business Impact Index).

For example, if code bugs are found to be a high-impact problem category, then it may be appropriate to invest in a long-term solution to the overall problem of bad code rather than just fix each individual bug. A strategic investment in improved testing processes (and/or additional segments of the SDLC) may be deemed necessary. If operator error is identified to be a problem category, rather than merely addressing each individual occurrence with the person who made the mistake, it may be strategically smart to focus more broadly on improved change control processes for the production systems. If most of your problems reveal themselves at the beginning of the online window, research needs to be done to determine what is going awry during the batch window (though, in the meantime, performing a pre-online window check of each of your key systems may be a legitimate Band-Aid). The return on investment (ROI) of your strategic investments can be measured based on tracking reduction of the targeted meta-problems over time.

When all is said and done, having the organizational ability, tools, and discipline to take your problem-solving function to these three higher levels can result in extraordinary IT quality.

The Temptation of Band-Aids

The memory leak example is a good one to continue with to discuss something very important: avoiding long-term use of Band-Aids. In order to survive, organizations that are unable, unwilling, or just don't know how to get to true root cause will inevitably resort to Band-Aids as a way of getting by.

We were once brought in to help with a particularly troubled sales application where a memory leak bug caused a server to run out of memory in the middle of a particularly critical production day. When we pushed for root cause, we were told the cause of the failure had been human error. This seemed quite possible to us. We began to wonder where the human error had been made. Was it during the testing process that allowed the bug to make it into production? Was the human error during the coding process that created the bug in the first place? We were eager to hear where the human error had occurred so the root cause could be addressed.

Imagine our surprise when we were told the root cause was an administrator having inadvertently disabled a cron[11] job to automatically reboot the server every night to clear the memory that was being consumed by the memory leak. You see, the memory leak was a known problem for more than a year, and somewhere along the line someone had decided that doing an automated nightly bounce of the server was the right *permanent* solution. In the mind of the manager performing the root cause investigation, the problem had been solved by the nightly auto-restart, and the mistake occurred when the administrator inadvertently turned off the job that kicked off the reboot. Clearly, we had different ideas than the manager about what root cause actually means. He had stopped several whys short instead of looking deeper.

---

11 Cron: a feature in UNIX systems (which stands for "command run on") that allows commands or scripts to be run automatically at a scheduled time.

In this particular case, a Band-Aid had been mistaken for the root cause corrective action. Instead of fixing the code bug causing the memory leak (and fixing the process that allowed the code bug to make it into production), the decision was consciously made to just apply the Band-Aid. This prevented reoccurrence, but also masked the root problem. To be sure, writing a bounce script is a lot easier than diagnosing and fixing a memory bug, and is a valid intermediate step to take in case the leak takes a few weeks to fix, test, and deploy, but the easy way out continues to put you at risk over the long term. The root problem continued to lurk in the environment until, just like The Ostrich Postulate says it will, it reoccurred at an even more inopportune time. Had the root problem been fixed when first identified a year earlier, the repeat outage could have been prevented.

And on top of all of that, it turns out that increases in processing volumes had caused memory use on the server to grow, so the leak effectively became larger. Since running out of memory on the server causes an incident, the nightly bounce would have only worked for a few more weeks before it would not have been enough, memory would be consumed by midday, and daily outages would have begun to occur. This is a classic example of The Ostrich Postulate in action.

Get Focused

In any complex systems environment, there can be literally thousands of problems that exist at any given time (think about how many bugs probably exist in a major commercial piece of software alone). Most problems are relatively minor or even benign, but many of them are causing quality issues or will eventually cause quality issues.

Many of these small problems that seem isolated can often be related to the same root cause. These seemingly unrelated small problems are actually a single big problem disguised as dozens or hundreds of little problems. You cannot fix all of the problems, so how do you distinguish between the ones that need attention and the ones that can wait? The trick is to get focused on the problems that matter the most to your quality objectives and not waste time on the ones that have minimal, if any, impact or can simply wait until more important problems have been dealt with. After you have compiled a fairly comprehensive list of all known problems, the next step to achieving this focus is aligning your problem management activities with your defined quality goals. Your goals are, by definition, the things that matter most to you, so your problem-solving efforts must be focused around resolving the problems that have the greatest impact upon your goals. We'll discuss goals in greater detail in chapter 9.

If you have the analyst bandwidth available, another approach is to perform a light return on investment (ROI) analysis for each of the known combinations of problems and fixes. Perhaps there are several fixes that only address moderate issues, but the fixes themselves are relatively inexpensive (in terms of time, resources, or dollars). In that case, it *might* make sense to do them, even though they don't zero in on your top quality goals, because of the return. That being said, you still must spend most of your focus on your big-hitters in order to meet your quality goals.

The best results happen when your various IT organizations (DBAs, SAs, Production Support, Development, Architecture, etc.), work together to solve big problems just like different law enforcement agencies (local, county, federal, international) do. Sure, if you're just writing a speeding ticket, there is no need for interagency cooperation. But if you're tracking a notorious ring of bank robbers, then it's time to coordinate. Both system problems and criminals benefit from jurisdiction issues and lack of coordination. Get aligned around your quality goals to unite IT overall. Communicate and share information. Put solving the problem ahead of who gets the credit.

The Ten Most Wanted List

Imagine a big city police department where murders are treated exactly the same as petty thefts. It doesn't happen, and for very good reason! It's the same for system problem solving. We strongly recommend the use of a top ten problems list. This is a great time to utilize the Business Impact Index to determine the problems causing the greatest business pain. For scalability, it may be the areas in your key systems that have the least amount of known headroom. For error rates, it may be the errors that occur most frequently or the errors that take the most time to fix. For performance, it could be the slowest transactions or the most popular ones. A good rule of thumb when prioritizing is to try to figure out what is hurting the business the most today or what may hurt it the most tomorrow.

There's nothing magic about the number ten—it's a good round number and "top ten" is a catchy phrase, but it's the concept of narrowing down that counts. You can pick any reasonable number that makes sense. The idea is to not have too few on your list and minimize your ability to develop solutions in parallel or have too many and lose your focus.

Your top ten list contains the problems causing the greatest impact to your quality goals. Rank the problems from one to ten with number one being your primary enemy. The top ten list does several things for you:

1. Helps you get what you need. Whether you need staff, budget, hardware, or time, you'll be in a better position to ask if you always have your top ten

list ready in hand. Opportunities present themselves at unexpected times: a senior executive drops into your office or your boss needs a case ASAP to justify not losing some budget. You should always be ready to show your top ten list at a moment's notice. If you're in a situation where timing is everything, you'll be happy you were prepared, and as a bonus, you'll develop a reputation for being organized and always on top of things.

2. Prevents you from spreading resources too thin by tackling too many problems simultaneously. You can't get traction and momentum trying to solve too many problems at the same time.

3. Keeps your resources aligned and focused on the problems that impact quality the most. There are forces at work out there that will try to pull your resources away to other things. This will help limit that. It also provides an intuitive communication tool for senior management that will help you enforce discipline rather than allowing senior management to refocus resources on flavor-of-the-week issues that have happened to come to their attention. We can't even count how many times we've seen real progress on systems issues halted or slowed down by some well-intentioned executive who became aware of a system issue via an escalation or some sort of customer complaint and unwittingly shifted resource focus off of problem number one to problem number 37, due to lack of knowledge of what the true objective priorities should be.

The organizing glue around your problem management efforts is the focus on knocking problems off the list and adding in new problems as necessary. Rally your resources around these efforts, using the organizational and communication techniques we've outlined in other chapters. Your team will take great pleasure in wiping problems off of the list and watching the subsequent improvement to your quality metrics.

Revealing and Embracing Problems

How can you solve a problem that officially doesn't even exist? The answer is, not very easily. You can't solve problems you don't know about, yet many organizations suffer from problem avoidance or cover-ups. That's when problems are intentionally hidden or not brought to light.

Consider the Ford Explorer Bridgestone/Firestone recall of 6.5 million tires in 2000, due to the rollover risk when used on Ford Explorers as well as thread separation reports. While both companies have denied any cover-ups and pointed fingers at each other, some consumer groups such as Public Citizen claim that both the tire and automakers knew about these problems for years. However, it took pressure from lawsuits for the tires to be recalled, costing the company hundreds of millions of dollars (and possibly into the billions if you take into account the damage caused to the brand). We are not here to add to the debate about who's ultimately responsible for this problem, but it certainly doesn't look like either company actively took corrective action until too much harm had already been done.

In some IT organizations, availability numbers are subtly or blatantly manipulated to hit defined targets, or problems are classified at lower severity levels to avoid embarrassment, additional scrutiny, or the scorn of the customer. This is the worst thing that can happen to your quality efforts. Every person who hides or ignores a problem is conspiring to hurt your quality, because problems are only solved when they are brought to light and understood.

Why do problems get concealed? Because some organizations punish people who cause them or make those who found them wish they never had. This happens in many different ways. An administrator causes an incident because of a fat-fingered mistake and doesn't own up, and even goes so far as to eliminate any log evidence. What would cause someone to act this way? He does this because in the past he's seen others get yelled at, humiliated publicly, or given unimportant assignments as punishment. This is just a typical example. Help desks can also be complicit by downplaying severity levels for friends or to avoid the arguments that come with pushback. Sometimes incidents are even downplayed just because the root cause meetings take too long! Whatever the rationale, it's no good. Per Jim Collins, you've got to confront the brutal facts.[12]

> ### Fat Finger
>
> n. slang for typo, or typographical error. "The operator meant to delete the files in the current directory, but fat-fingered the command and deleted everything on the drive."

Sweeping problems under the rug is like burying parking tickets in your glove compartment without paying. You can only get away with it for so long before all of those individual problems grow into one big monster problem that can potentially wreck your business in the form of catastrophic failure.

Confess to all known problems and actively work them. That's the best way to gain the customer's trust. It's your job to create a work environment where accountability exists, yet people don't fear reprisal for honest mistakes. In organizations where a one-strike-and-you're-out culture exists, behavior regarding problems will naturally be less than candid. What you want is an organization in which your people honestly identify problems (after all, an incident is doing you a favor, right?) and where those who cover them up are dealt with appropriately. In short, finding problems should be rewarded, and burying them should be seen as a terrible offense.

And look on the bright side: if you confess to all 45 problems you had this quarter, but only have 38 next quarter, that's 16% improvement—not bad! But if you don't start confessing to all of your problems now, you'll be aiming at a moving target until you do.

---

12 *Good to Great*, Jim Collins, 2001, p. 13. Confronting the brutal facts is one of the six key concepts of the Good to Great framework.

Accountability vs. Crucifixion

When it comes to getting people to have the right focus on reducing incidents, one problem that organizations find challenging is getting both the message and delivery right. How do you let your people know that business as usual is not okay, while at the same time not coming down so hard as to negatively impact morale?

> **One strike and you're out?**
>
> Don't have a one-strike-and-you're-out policy for making mistakes, but do have such a policy for covering up mistakes.

What we're shooting for is to hold people accountable but not encourage cover-ups or other evasive behavior. The primary answer here is to focus accountability around the quality results in the ways we've previously discussed. If the members of a department know they're being held accountable for how the system performs, they have an incentive to be careful around production and get key problems into the problem management pipeline. Since their performance is being graded based on specific quality outcomes, it's simply in their best interest to do so. Because they're being measured objectively against the quality goals, it will be no surprise to them that they are being held accountable for poor results.

Managers must use good judgment about how harshly to address mistakes that cause quality problems. When people know that they're going to be treated objectively and fairly, they deliver high performance.

The Blame Game: The Tic-Tac-Toe of Problem Solving

Just as in law enforcement, there's a finite amount of energy in your organization you can assign to problem solving. You want to maximize that energy on productive activities that resolve your problems and not waste it on finger-pointing. Every minute of every day spent on these nonconstructive activities is time wasted, so when you hear and see people engaging in blame, you should move to get them back on the problem-solving track as quickly as possible.

> **The Perkins Maneuver**
>
> We have a friend named Dan Perkins who has been known to take blame for things he never even touched in order to refocus discussion on what really matters: fixing things. Sometimes it's comical, and it's almost always effective!

Focusing on solving problems objectively is your best way of putting internal politics aside and avoiding these unproductive negative behaviors. The example set by management is crucial. If leaders don't practice what they preach, their people see this and act accordingly. However, when leadership demonstrates honesty, forthrightness, and a strong focus on solving problems as opposed to pointing fingers, people below them quickly see that the best way to get ahead is to make the maximum contribution to the resolution of the most important problems.

No Silver Bullets

Rarely are there any silver bullets for troubled complex systems. Looking for a silver bullet and repeatedly gambling on long shots is a rookie mistake and will rarely get you the system stability results you need. Imagine you were a quarterback playing American football, and you only threw Hail Mary passes…it might work once in a blue moon, but your team would lose almost every game it played.

Instead, the most successful systems are managed diligently using a relentless approach that chisels away daily at problems. Progress against your goals should mimic the hour hand of a clock. You never actually see it moving, but every once in awhile you glance up and see that progress is being made. The relentless, evenly paced approach will get you farther in the end if you're patient and stay with it. The turtle wins for a reason.

Time for Fieldwork

There are thousands of books about management, most of which have extremely useful information about how to manage, such as interviewing, inspiring, delegating, organizing, and so on. These are all great skills to learn, and you should embrace them. What we are recommending overlays all of those techniques as specific to production-oriented IT management.

In doing so, it's important to remember that effective problem solving is at the center of system stability. And at the center of great problem solving are the organizational alignment and problem-solving philosophies we've described here. However, that's not enough.

Just as in crime fighting, you'll need a full complement of scientific problem-solving disciplines to achieve your quality goals. The equivalent of crime scene preservation, fingerprint identification, DNA testing, forensic medicine, and more are all critical to your problem management efforts. We jump into those in the next chapter. Once you marry your constructive managerial problem-solving focus with specific technical methods, you can start putting your most wanted list in jail and watch the volume of crimes start to plummet.

Summary Checklist

✓ **Incident:** An incident is a single event that disrupts service to your production system or service.

✓ **Problem:** A problem is the issue that allows one or more incidents to happen.

✓ **Resolving problems:** By focusing on resolving all known problems, rather than just quickly closing incidents, you will be practicing a simple yet effective form of prevention that will improve quality over time.

   ◦ If known problems are not worked, more incidents will occur from them.

   ◦ A surplus of known problems that are not being worked can create an environment where quality is not valued, both because people can see that problems are acceptable and also because the "clutter" from having many open problems makes it more difficult to ascertain which problem caused a particular incident.

✓ **Attitude** is important. Every time an incident happens, treat it as an opportunity to make your systems better.

✓ **Tracking:** For trending purposes, carefully track the particulars of each incident in a database.

✓ **Band-Aids** are temporary solutions that mask problems but don't resolve the true root cause.

✓ **Keep asking why:** If you are unsure that you are getting to the true root cause, use the "keep asking why" technique to get to the bottom of things.

✓ **Prioritize:** If there are many open problems to pursue, prioritize them based on the business benefit of solving them. Always have a prioritized list handy, because it can be used for several things.

✓ **Culture:** Ingrain the culture of transparency and openness about problems into your group. Public criticism, blame, and heavy punishments will yield a culture of hiding problems, which doesn't serve your best interests.

✓ **Perseverance:** Problem management takes time and numerous actions to be successful. Work your prioritized list, and over the weeks, see your system quality trend in the right direction.

## CHAPTER 5

Hands-On Problem Solving

Powerful Problem Management Techniques

Chapter Overview

Analogous to crime investigation techniques used by law enforcement, there's a systematic and scientific approach to technical IT problem solving that can help you identify the true root cause of problems more reliably and quickly.

At a very high level, the typical process flow of the problem-solving process is to

- collect all possible relevant facts;

- analyze the facts to generate a list of hypotheses;

- if needed, test the hypotheses to determine which of them are valid.

By sorting through the forensic and circumstantial evidence and consistently performing relevant detective work, a disciplined IT organization uses vigilant problem solving to eliminate the root cause of system problems in order to increase stability.

This chapter gives you a solid overview of the steps that need to be taken and also how to create an effective discipline of troubleshooting in your IT organization.

Groundhog Day

It's 10 a.m.; your cell phone buzzes. You have a nasty feeling it's a notification about the same old problem that happens on most days around this

Cont. →

time. Sure enough, you check your messages, and the help desk has opened yet another ticket about some reported slowness with the system.

You know that the problem eventually disappears without any specific action being taken by your team. But you also know you're probably going to get another page tomorrow. The trouble is, nobody seems to be able to find anything wrong with the system. The monitoring tools your team uses merely confirm that things do slow down for the users around midmorning. You know there's got to be a better way to approach this situation and get to the bottom of it. The business is getting increasingly irate, and they need some answers.

You think to yourself, what if lives were at stake here? How would we go about solving this problem? What if we were confronted with a serial killer who would keep striking until we caught him? You know he's getting bolder with every crime, and the citizens of your community are pressuring you to catch him.

So you decide to get serious about finding the culprit, and you implement rigorous criminal investigation techniques. You put your detective hat on and decide to treat every occurrence of the problem as a crime.

Scope Clarification

This chapter doesn't attempt to solve every kind of technical problem out there; there are simply too many! But we aim to provide a line of reasoning that can be used to solve most problems, along with some common examples. To solve tough technical problems for your given applications and associated platforms, you will certainly need to supplement this recommended technical problem-solving approach with platform-specific technical insight appropriate to your situation.

We all know that many famous criminal cases were solved thanks to the leadership and tenacity of a single detective. What we often overlook, however, is that behind the scenes a small army of individuals is providing him with critical information without which the case can't be broken. Forensic science, which relates to the use of science or technology in the investigation and establishment of facts or evidence in a court of law, is often used in the process.

While in IT our burden of proof isn't tested by a court of law, we can improve our chances of making our systems fundamentally better by applying the same amount of rigor to our problem-solving approach as detectives apply to crime solving. Following the steps below is a great way to accomplish this.

1. Preserve the crime scene

2. Search for evidence

3. Analyze the evidence

4. Formulate hypotheses

5. Reconstruct the series of events

6. Reenact the most likely scenario

7. Solve the case

Preserving the Crime Scene

The first thing investigators do at a new crime scene is protect it from destruction and contamination. They need all the evidence they can glean from it. So they limit access to the scene to only those who strictly need it. There are two main reasons for this: (1) they don't want evidence to be lost (e.g., someone stepping over some footprints), and (2) they don't want someone's actions to generate false evidence (e.g., their own footprints are thought to be those of the culprit).

When your staff is investigating an outage situation, make sure their approach to troubleshooting doesn't allow key information to be lost. For example, if they are going to suggest that users reboot their desktops, they should think about whether information needs to be collected about the state of the machine and software (such as available physical memory, CPU utilization, processes that are running, and any applicable log files). The same is true when troubleshooting servers.

One word of caution, though: while it's a good idea to take a few moments to gather evidence, you can't dillydally. If the scene of the crime is a busy intersection, keeping it closed for several hours while searching for clues can place an unfairly large burden on the users. Get in, collect your evidence, and restore service as soon as possible. In some cases, it may even be possible to automate evidence gathering in advance of a system problem to expedite service restoration. The ability to gather diagnostics quickly requires advanced planning. You must ensure that log files are small enough to be manageable, you have sufficient disk space to store them, and the scripts needed to run traces are ready and accessible. Trying to figure these things out reactively in the heat of an outage will result in mistakes and the loss of valuable diagnostics.

If several technicians are going to be troubleshooting the servers, ensure there is clear communication among them on who's doing what during the incident. This way, they can get in and get out faster. They will then have a better chance of understanding the data they'll be analyzing later regarding the evidence and series of events. This also reduces the chance of someone's corrective action being confused with a symptom of the problem.

Searching for Evidence

This is probably the most critical piece of the investigation. Collecting evidence is the only way to prove you have found the culprit.

Collect the Facts

Here you want to collect as many facts as possible. Focus on just the facts, though. At this stage, resist making assumptions until you have collected sufficient evidence. If this were a criminal case, you'd want to make sure your assertions couldn't be challenged in court. So collect hard facts about the locations of the users affected, specifics about their machines, their network connections, the level of access to the application they have, if applicable—anything that will help you identify trends and commonalities.

As with any investigation, witness accounts can be useful, but they should be treated with caution. People's perceptions can be subjective, so if you're going to ask for input from users, corroborate that information with other facts.

When searching for evidence, look for

- what can be seen with the naked eye (e.g., an investigator's visual inspection of the scene, or your own observation of a slow application);

- what can be seen with the help of some tools (e.g., the inspection of a crime scene with flashlights and luminol,[13] or the collection of data via system monitoring tools);

- what needs to be sent to the lab for analysis (e.g., fingerprint analysis, or analysis of a core dump by your system's vendor).

Gaining Vendor Support

An additional reason for obtaining thorough root cause data is to get relevant vendors to help you. Vendors are more likely to partner with you effectively if you make good use of facts and data instead of innuendo and anecdote. Chasing down red herrings is costly for vendors, and most have lines of defense in their support process to avoid this. If you suspect a problem in a piece of vendor code, you will get the best support if you provide hard evidence!

We were once involved in a scenario very similar to the hypothetical one described in the introduction. Sporadically at first, then regularly, a number of users from various call centers complained about extreme slowness and even the inability to log in to their credit card payment system. Only when we had collected enough facts did we realize that while the problem was happening in several call centers, what all these call centers had in common was that they were outsourced call centers (not company-owned). So why these call centers?

The List of Suspects

When searching for evidence, you might start identifying potential culprits, and those are good leads to follow. But if you run dry on potential culprits, proceed by elimination.

---

13 http://en.wikipedia.org/wiki/Luminol: Luminol is a versatile chemical which, when mixed with an oxidizing agent, glows blue—that is, it exhibits chemiluminescence. It is used by forensic investigators to detect scant amounts of blood left at crime scenes.

Look for evidence that rules out components of the system from your suspect list. In complex technical problems, it can be effective to treat all layers of your architecture as suspects. Collect evidence at the application, database, operating system, hardware, software, file system, and network layers. Leave no stone unturned.

In our investigation of the third-party call center issue, we checked all the usual suspects: PC configurations, authentication mechanism, and network bandwidth and latency. Everything checked out as "normal." We knew this was going to be a tough nut to crack, but we had to figure it out. At this stage, the only viable lead to follow was to learn more about why this was happening only to these third-party call centers. We knew there was something different about them, but what?

Zero in on the Top Suspects

A broad search for evidence may be necessary if no obvious suspects emerge, but a deeper search should be performed on highly likely culprits. Once you do have some suspects, you want to get very granular with the information you collect. While a crime investigator might want to know about all the people who were in contact with a victim in the past month, he might only request extensive information about a handful of them to start with.

If you suspect the application server is causing slowness for the users, then probe for more detailed data. We've seen load balancing problems manifest themselves not at the server or even process level, but at the thread level. Finding this type of problem requires staff who know the inner workings of computer processing and who can get creative about how to collect the right data at the right level of granularity.

Search Warrants

Low-level information may not always be readily available. Sometimes you need permission to get it (e.g., you don't own some piece of the system). So, as a good investigator, you want to first ask the suspect if he will allow you to "look around." If the suspect doesn't agree to let you have access to private space or information, you may need a warrant.

When we asked the third-party call centers for additional information about how their computers connected to our Wide Area Network, most saw the value in it because they knew we were trying to help them, so they volunteered all the information we requested. Others felt that it was our problem to figure out what the cause of the slowness was, and didn't provide any of the extra information we requested. So we had to resort to escalations with the management teams, which eventually provided us the warrant we needed to perform the search. In the end, good technical problem solving works best if all the players put their agendas aside and focus their energies on solving the problem.

Circumstantial Evidence

There are times when the evidence doesn't point to an obvious culprit, or will take time to find and investigate. Although we believe most, if not all, root causes of computing problems can be identified and proven with the right tools and data, the use of circumstantial evidence will often help zero in on a suspect. For example, you might see an e-mail communication about seemingly unrelated activities being performed in the environment around the same time (e.g., security scans or reports being generated). While this is not evidence that proves a cause-effect relationship, collect it carefully and bring it all to the table for analysis.

One effective approach to searching for such evidence is to look for things that have changed, because degradations in D, R, E, or S are often caused by change. There are five main families of change to consider:

1. Something in the software or hardware configuration changed to your detriment: code, variable settings, etc.

2. Routine maintenance didn't get completed, and as a result, one or more of your subsystems are performing poorly. Typically, this would be database maintenance (such as index rebuilds or data archival) or purging of log files.

3. Your load grew (more users or transactions), but the system stayed static, and you hit a scalability ceiling.

4. Another system that shares some resources with your system is behaving differently (could be shared disks, shared network, or shared server resources).

5. Usage patterns changed. For example, users started performing new actions for which the system is not tuned; this is often the case when an OLTP system starts being used for reporting activity.

Single-Threaded Processes: Bottleneck Bait

Asynchronous, back-end processes are often prone to scalability problems. If you're processing 1,000 transactions per hour, and they complete on average in 5 minutes, it's possible that at 1,500 orders per hour, it would take an average of 30 minutes as the queue grows.

Be on the lookout for areas where serial processing (e.g., single-threaded processes) may become a bottleneck, backlog, and cause transactions to take a significant amount of time to perform. If your design allows for parallel processing, (e.g., multi-threaded processes), you can usually just add more instances of the same process to, say, set up a billing account. However, if you are stuck with a single-threaded process for a technical reason, and, for instance, each billing account creation takes 5 seconds to complete, then your peak transactions per hour will not exceed 720, no matter what you do.

This may not align with what we typically think of as changes. Changes are not only things that your technicians do to your systems—change can come from the user community, other systems, and the Internet as well!

Unless your measuring software is extremely sophisticated, you will usually have to answer the following two questions the hard way, by doing research:

- Did my configuration change in any meaningful way just before the problem started?

- Do any of my subsystems behave abnormally just before or during episodes of the problem?

During our investigation of the call center performance issues, we looked at the application servers for some clues. When we considered CPU and memory utilization for the entire environment, we saw we had plenty of headroom. But when one analyst performed a server-by-server review, he noticed that a handful of servers were seeing abnormally high utilization. The most intriguing aspect of this was that it happened to different servers every day! On the surface, this seemed like a separate issue from the call center one. That is because traffic coming from all locations nationwide was load balanced evenly and randomly across the whole server farm. None of our servers were dedicated to any specific group, such as geography or location type (call center vs. retail store). Such a problem was expected to affect users completely randomly. Nevertheless, this was interesting information for the evidence room.

Extend the Search Area

The obvious focus on any crime investigation is the crime scene itself. But good crime scene investigators extend the search to a larger perimeter. If a crime was committed in a given room, is there evidence in other rooms to indicate where the criminal may have entered or exited the building? If your system interfaces with other systems, is there evidence you can collect in these other systems?

As it turned out, when we extended our search to include the third-party call centers' network configurations, we collected a crucial new piece of evidence. They were the only ones making use of NAT IPs.[14] The analyst who brought this piece of information back didn't know it at the time, but he had found the crime scene equivalent of a tire track in the mud from a very rare tire.

Simultaneously, we had someone investigate the "circumstantial evidence" (the few servers that were seeing spikes in utilization). He extended his search area by learning more about the way we balanced traffic between servers. He learned that we were using a network device that uses the client's (workstation) source IP address as the discriminator to assign a session to the appropriate server. By that time, we had quite a bit of new information that needed to be put together and analyzed.

---

14 (NAT, or network address translation): A technique in which a router or firewall rewrites the source and/or destination Internet addresses in a packet as it passes through, typically to allow multiple hosts to connect to the Internet via a single external IP address. (*The Free On-line Dictionary of Computing.* Denis Howe. http://dictionary.reference.com/browse/network address translation [accessed: November 23, 2008].)

Analyzing the Evidence and Solving the Case

So now you still might not know what the true root cause of your incident is. But you have mountains of evidence! So where do you go from here?

Reconstructing the Series of Events

Once all evidence is collected, investigators piece it all together to make it tell a story. What happened when? Do any of the findings contradict themselves? This process starts with such simple things as what time the crime took place. In the case of homicides, a number of techniques can be used to determine time of death, such as victim's lividity, body temperature, or chemical changes in the body. Fortunately, in IT, we don't have to deal with corpses, and we shouldn't have to estimate the time a problem occurred. With appropriate monitoring and log surfing, we can get precise to the millisecond.

Where it gets tricky is in understanding the whole series of events that lead to a failure in service quality. Sometimes this requires a tedious piecing together of the known facts and timelines. You'll have to rely on your various departments (client, network, server, DB) to compare the statistics in their systems to the times that the problems were happening in order to deduce a correlation. Examining the logs for clues (such as retry errors) can also be helpful. Don't try to keep it all in your head. Use a diagram to help all involved in the troubleshooting to understand what's known and to fill in the blanks. A situational diagram like the one in figure 5.1 can be handy when a complex problem arises that everyone needs to understand before action can be taken.

And that is exactly how we solved the third-party call center case. When we put all the data together (the time of the slowness reports, the times at which some servers were spiking, the fact that some call centers used NAT IPs, the fact that our load balancing system used source IP addresses to assign sessions), we were able to determine that since the load balancer saw all clients from the NAT call centers as originating from a single IP, it loaded them onto a single server. This was causing the server to run at unacceptable CPU loads, resulting in poor performance for all clients connected to that server. That IPs were randomly assigned to a server explained how the spikes in utilization were happening on different servers every day. When the first user from one of those call centers logged in, a session was assigned randomly to a server, and then all other users logging in later in the day from that same call center would end up having sessions assigned to that same server. In essence, hundreds of users sharing the same IP appeared to be a single user, creating disproportionate load on a single server. The result was poor response times, in some cases so severe that the third-party call center representatives could not log in at all.

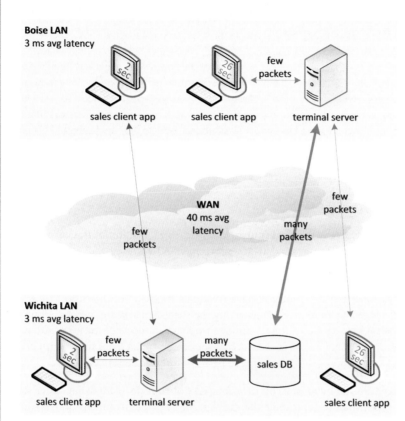

Boise LAN
3 ms avg latency

sales client app   sales client app   terminal server

few packets

WAN
40 ms avg latency

few packets

few packets

many packets

Wichita LAN
3 ms avg latency

sales client app   terminal server

few packets

many packets

sales DB

sales client app

This diagram shows how the current physical architecture of this sales system yields poor client response times to users who connect via terminal servers in the Boise data center.

The reason is that the sales client application is extremely chatty with the database, sending in excess of 100 different calls to the database for some business transactions, each DB call needing an average of 6.5 packets.

For users of a terminal server in Wichita, this is acceptable because the network is relatively fast:

100 DB calls * 6.5 packets * .003 seconds = 1.95 seconds

The terminal server sends far fewer packets to and from the client, so even the Boise users who are using a Wichita terminal server fare just fine. However, users of a Boise terminal server are sending the chatty DB traffic over the WAN, and pay a hefty penalty:

100 DB calls * 6.5 packets *.04 seconds = 26 seconds

This impacts users in Wichita who are leveraging Boise terminal servers as well. The solution? Either co-locate all the terminal servers with the sales DB, or reduce the number of database calls the application makes to the DB for each business transaction.

figure 5.1. Example situational problem-solving diagram

One thing we've found that you should avoid is relying too much on application error messages that blame the network. More than once we've seen the application teams find those messages in the logs, and then call the network team and wait for them to report back. All too often, the network folks correctly report back that the network is just fine—and meanwhile, the application team has wasted several hours of valuable troubleshooting time. In our experience, the network often gets an undeserved bad rap, as many programs have error messages that indicate they are having a network problem when they don't get an expected response from another subsystem—talk about shooting the messenger!

Reenacting the Crime

Even seemingly open-and-shut murder cases deserve a minimum standard of proof. One technique commonly used in law enforcement is to put together all the known elements of the crime and ensure that the hypothesis about who did what, when, and why is plausible. This process can involve creating a mock-up of the entire crime scene and reenacting the suspected series of events. Along with this, specific reproducible aspects of the crime are reproduced, such as shooting a bullet from the firearm used in the crime to perform forensic ballistics analysis.

TIP

Just because an application complains of a network problem, don't assume the culprit is the network; often, it's a different nonresponsive subsystem instead.

If you have a solid hypothesis on the root cause of your problem, what better way to obtain proof than to reproduce the problem in a test environment? Once you can reproduce it, you'll have a way to verify that a proposed fix actually works.

Get Inside the Mind of the Serial Killer

Law enforcement agencies have gotten very effective at profiling repeat offenders. Over the years, they have identified characteristics of crimes that correspond to attributes of individuals. In the same fashion, you want to leverage the collective experience of your teams to identify characteristics of service quality problems that can be traced to typical root causes. You also want to analyze all the evidence you've collected and look for trends and commonalities. Is the same piece of evidence found in more than one crime scene?

FBI profilers are not your everyday cops. They are very experienced and, over the years, have developed a knack for guessing what a suspect's characteristics are. Make sure your problem management process involves such high-caliber individuals. We've too often seen problem management being a process involving just a few nontechnical people who look at problem tickets and look for excuses to close them without resolution. The only way to get to the bottom of your toughest recurring problems is to get your top talent thinking creatively about ways to find root cause. The goals and targets of your problem management function must be on solving problems and preventing repeat occurrences of incidents—not on just closing out tickets or checking things off a list.

Prosecute!

Now comes the fun part. You have a hypothesis about how the problem occurred, and you have your smartest

> **Clarification**
>
> We're recommending prosecution of the problem, not the people involved!

minds on the problem to figure out a fix. Now you need to prove that the fix works, and put that problem away forever. While it is sometimes tempting to try a new fix ASAP in production, the prudent approach is to test it and confirm that it solves the problem before deploying on a large scale.

Case Closed

Good job—one less problem roaming in cyberspace. Enjoy some peace and quiet from your pager (and your customers!). But beware, the next serial killer is out there, and he could be smarter than the previous one. So make sure your team stays on top of the latest tools and techniques. If they're at the fingerprint analysis stage, get them to start using DNA analysis. Who knows, they might solve some of those cold cases you've given up on!

Summary Checklist

✓ **Evidence and expertise**: Like a detective investigating a crime, an effective IT problem troubleshooter leverages evidence and expertise to get to the bottom of the problem.

✓ **Facts and data**: Systematically gather data and collect the facts of an incident.

✓ **Forensics**: When resolving an incident, while it is important to restore service as quickly as possible, it is essential to ensure forensic data, such as logs and dumps, are not lost.

✓ **Enlist** the help of all relevant technical experts.

✓ **No limits**: Obtain the appropriate permissions to cross organizational boundaries as part of your troubleshooting efforts to enable capture of all technical data you may need, no matter which organization the system or subsystem in question may lie in.

✓ **Circumstantial evidence**: Although factual evidence is most effective, circumstantial evidence can often be helpful in driving to root cause.

✓ **Proof**: Recreating an incident in a safe and controlled manner can be an effective way of achieving a high level of proof.

✓ **Use testing and validation** to ensure your hypothesis was correct and that the fix adequately addressed the problem.

Prevention

In production IT, there are two main modes you can be in: experiencing quality issues, or smooth sailing. The way to maximize your time smooth sailing is to resolve quality issues ASAP, and to prevent issues from occurring in the first place. This section covers the latter.

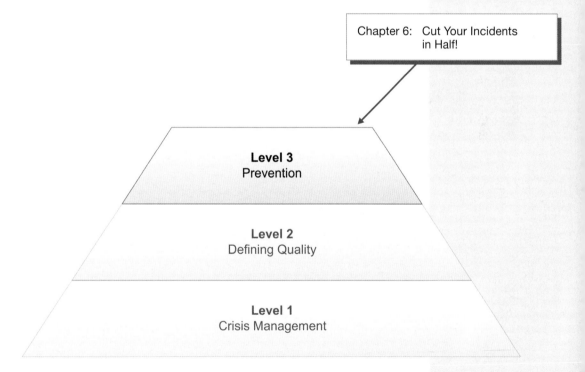

Chapter 6: Cut Your Incidents in Half!

Level 3
Prevention

Level 2
Defining Quality

Level 1
Crisis Management

CHAPTER **6**

Cut Your Incidents in Half!

Prevention, Prevention, Prevention

Chapter Overview

On television, all the highly rated medical dramas place emphasis on trauma and emergency—lifesaving procedures that rescue a person from the brink of death in the nick of time. To be sure, these are exciting events that merit the limelight. The same tends to hold true in IT—firefighters who successfully lead us out of immediate trouble receive the lion's share of the glory.

However, a substantial portion of the factors that determine our health (or lack of it) are within our control. If we want to enjoy a life with minimal health issues, we can stack the deck in our favor by making it a high priority to care of ourselves. On the other end of the spectrum, if we are content to simply be reactive, to seek professional help (at significant cost and risk) only when we have a serious health issue, that avenue is open to us as well. It's a choice we make.

Without getting caught up too much in the specifics of the analogy, at a high level, the early chapters in this book emphasize procedures that are more reactive in nature. In this chapter and the ones that follow, the focus becomes much more preventive. These are complementary sets of techniques that should both reside in your arsenal.

Systems failures and issues are costly and have all kinds of negative impacts to the productivity and reputation of your business. This chapter is all about the lifestyle that best positions an IT organization to prevent systems problems from happening in the first place.

Table of Contents

Cont. →

An Ounce of Prevention

Being an operations manager can be a very satisfying job. There are many important decisions to be made, and the work you do has an impact on a large number of people. But often, when you ask people about work in operations, they groan that you are tied to your pager and are constantly working crises, often at odd hours, without the time or tools to get into a proactive mode. It's not being on call and responding to incidents that's frustrating; it's the constant firefighting with little hope that things will get better. In that paradigm, it takes quite a strange fellow to find it a fun job. Being in constant crisis is not just bad for the customer; it's also bad for your employees.

However, there is another way. Although you'll always need firefighters to deal with unexpected incidents, to get off the constant firefighting treadmill, you have to put more of your efforts into fire prevention instead of just fire extinguishing. This can be difficult when you're responding to a two-alarm fire downtown every day. But it doesn't take sirens, asbestos suits, or water hoses; it just takes time for organized people being diligent to rein in the chaos.

Taking Good Care of the Patient

IT systems are complex organisms, as are humans. If IT systems were patients, being in constant firefighting mode would be like having to make frequent trips to the doctor's office or even to the emergency room. While that is sometimes unavoidable, those who grossly neglect their health are more likely to require doctor visits because of problems. It is no surprise, then, that people are encouraged (by health care professionals as well as insurance companies) to do *preventive* care.

Preventive care aims at taking preemptive actions that will have a positive impact on your health, or at least minimize the risk of negative things happening to your well-being. It includes everything from having regular checkups, during which vital statistics are collected, to taking proactive measures against known risks (e.g., immunizations).

Beyond preventive care, there are many things people can do toward increasing their chance of getting or staying in good health. This includes simple things, such as diet and exercise, and less simple things, like having a plan for dealing with all the surprises life will throw at you.

It's no different with your IT systems: there are no substitutes for preventive monitoring, regular maintenance, and healthy living.

Preventive Health Monitoring and Trending

Heart disease is the leading cause of death in the United States. Yet simple monitoring of certain key vital signs can indicate whether one is at high risk of heart disease. High blood pressure, for example, increases your chance of heart failure. While high blood pressure is not easily identified via any kind of visible symptom, it can effortlessly be measured and tracked with the right instrument. Why wait until the symptoms move to the heart (when it may be too late to avoid a crisis) if they can be identified earlier?

Similarly, with IT systems, there is basic monitoring that can be put in place to identify symptoms invisible to the naked eye before it is too late and users or the business are negatively affected. In a previous chapter, we discussed the various means of measuring systems so we won't cover them here, but we do want to stress the importance of collecting data about the health of your systems, not only when service quality is degraded, but also when the systems are still healthy. It will allow you to compare your data with what a "normal" system looks like and observe any trends that might indicate that a problem could happen in the future. The more aspects of the system you monitor, the more likely you are to detect such problems early enough that you can do something about them before service quality is noticeably degraded. And if you're doing that, you're moving up the Production Maturity Model pyramid.

There are obviously some limits to how far you can go in monitoring the patient before the act of monitoring itself has more negative consequences than positive ones. Some kinds of monitoring can be too intrusive, whether it is in IT or in preventive health care. For example, while most pregnancies are monitored using ultrasounds (among other means), a smaller number warrant an amniocentesis (a test in which a sample of amniotic fluid is removed and examined). Even though the test detects defects that other methods cannot, there are also some drawbacks to performing it: it can be painful and risky. Consequently, the procedure is performed only if the potential reward is considered to be greater than the risk.

With an IT system, certain kinds of monitoring can also be intrusive (by using too many resources or injecting synthetic transactions that need to be discernable from real transactions) and should only be performed if they will help avoid a bigger problem.

Preventive Health Monitoring for DRES

When determining what kind of *preventive* monitoring to implement, keep all areas of DRES in mind.

- For Downtime, think of all the possible failures that could cause an outage and how these failures can be detected before causing the outage (such as setting an alarm to notify an administrator when disk space usage reaches certain levels).

- For Response times, you'll want to have regular monitoring of network latency and response times measured at various levels of the architecture.

- For Errors, you'll want to capture your error rate on a regular basis and react to any growth patterns or spikes. Preventive monitoring for errors requires good knowledge of all the potential root causes of errors (e.g., poor data quality, data discrepancies between systems), and therefore tailored monitoring (e.g., scripts that regularly run through databases and look for the presence of "bad data" and discrepancies).

- For Scalability, it's more a question of trending than just monitoring. Preventing a scalability problem requires collecting data about both sides of the supply-demand equation, which we covered in chapter 3. The prevention aspect is in being able to predict what future supply needs are going to be, based on expected future demand, and ensuring there is always sufficient supply.

The Discipline of Routine Maintenance

We all know about the virtues of taking good care of our bodies and minds. We've seen what happens when one neglects basic hygiene practices, doesn't sleep enough, constantly eats unhealthy foods, never gets out, and never exercises. It leads to degraded health and ultimately can lead to serious medical problems, perhaps resulting in a shortened life.

The same is true with our production instance of enterprise software and hardware. There are certain things that must be done to keep everything running well. The following are a few examples.

- A restart schedule for various components that must be cycled. For instance, most of your physical servers should be cycled quarterly so that any hardware failure that would occur during a system startup will happen during a scheduled downtime window, not during an unplanned reboot. Your database (DB) instances might need to be cycled monthly. And your custom software might need to be cycled weekly. However, beware of recycles done to mask deeper problems. For example, a daily or weekly reboot is never a satisfactory long-term resolution for a memory leak.

- DB index rebuilds. For DB tables that typically have many rows added or deleted, the indexes must be rebuilt on a regular basis. In some cases, rebuilding tables might be necessary, too. Performance can really degrade if this is not done.

- Log file archival. Sometimes when a log file gets too big, it decreases the performance of your application. Or the log files themselves get too unwieldy to be used for troubleshooting efforts. So they need to be pulled and archived on a regular basis.

- Data archival. Sometimes data stores that are very large can impede both transaction performance and the ability to complete maintenance. If data is no longer in use by the system, and it is of a scale to cause such problems, it should be moved elsewhere. If it is old enough (no doubt your legal department will want some say here) or of transient nature, perhaps it can be simply deleted. Hopefully, your architects have designed the system in such a way that it is possible. But that being said, don't expect miracles here. Archival will not speed up a properly tuned OLTP system all that much. This is particularly true in the database, because well-designed indexes are fairly efficient whether the data size is small or very large.

The source of required maintenance procedures can come from vendors for vendor products, such as physical equipment and third-party software. Maintenance required by your own company's custom software ideally comes with the documentation provided with the release, though in reality your operations department will probably discover some things that need to be done in addition that you should manually add to your list (and feed back into the formal documentation).

If there are issues with not having enough time in the maintenance window to get all of the maintenance done, you have a few options:

- Try to tune the maintenance jobs to complete faster.

- Determine if some of the jobs can safely be performed during the online window. Safe is a relative term, so perhaps starting at 7 p.m. is an improvement over starting at 11 p.m., but still safer than starting at noon. To a large extent, it depends on the normal pattern of business transactions.

- Determine if more nonconflicting jobs can be run in parallel.

- Work with the business to see if the maintenance window can be expanded. Sometimes they are willing to do this to deal with special circumstances, but not permanently!

If there are activities necessary to make your systems run well, they should not be performed on an ad hoc basis. They should be formally documented, scheduled, and executed. This serves five purposes:

1. You will prevent problems by making sure all maintenance is performed in a timely manner.

2. When problems do arise, you can rule out lack of maintenance as the culprit (if true).

3. The CR board will be in a better position to identify change collisions if it has a formal maintenance schedule to compare other changes to.

4. Training for new employees is made easier and more thorough.

5. Platform vendors can be held more accountable, since they can't point to the lack of routine maintenance as the reason their product isn't performing as it should.

Your technical employees initially may not enjoy the extra effort to adhere to a schedule when it comes to maintenance, but after the lists and schedules are created, the extra work to track task completion isn't really all that much. If you have employees who are totally opposed to this process, you potentially have the wrong type of employees performing the maintenance. This is definitely one of those roles in which you want anal-retentive employees: people who like to keep their houses in order.

If you don't have a program to formalize your execution of routine maintenance, you are operating by luck or blind trust, rather than truly managing. It is in your best interest to create a culture in which maintenance is a priority and is never allowed to be forgotten or unacceptably delayed because "more important things" needed to be done, or because of fear that something will go wrong during the maintenance. Maintenance should be seen as a fundamental activity. In a healthy organization, you shouldn't be able to order your people to not do maintenance without instigating a mutiny.

Tuning

In addition to routine maintenance, there is tuning. Large applications utilize various platforms to accomplish their business functions. They typically run on some flavor of Windows, UNIX, or mainframe operating system, and if they use a database, it's probably Oracle, SQL Server, DB2, Sybase, MySQL, or Informix. These platforms are generic and, as such, are designed to support an enormous diversity of processing tasks.

The good thing is, most of these products are extremely configurable. If you have a batch application running on a Solaris (UNIX) server, there are certain parameters you can set to make your jobs process faster. If you have an intense OLTP application that uses an Oracle database, there are also certain parameters that can be set to make your application run faster and scale further. If you install and run these platforms just as they come on the CDs, it is likely you are running in a suboptimal state.

While this problem is solvable, there are, unfortunately, five main pitfalls here that stand between you and the successful use of these hidden capabilities.

1. The first problem is that setting these parameters correctly can be tricky. It is typically an advanced SA/DBA skill. You can help here by sending your technicians to relevant tuning classes and occasionally by bringing in outside experts to help your staff properly utilize the latest and greatest capabilities. Your staff can also benefit from participating in online message boards.

2. Some of these parameters are dangerous. If set improperly, they can grind your system to a halt. So you have to proceed very carefully. Blindly following some advice off some blog without understanding the internals is not the way to go.

3. If you have multiple diverse applications sharing the same instance of some vendor software, and the applications are equally important, sometimes you cannot take full advantage of tuning. Some parameters that might help OLTP will harm batch and vice versa. If your OLTP application is more important than your batch application, you may still be able to make some wise choices, however.

4. Some of these parameters take a full system restart to take effect. If your application is in use 24x7, finding the room to make system changes can be a challenge.

5. It's a moving target! The proper parameter settings change as your application behavior evolves, and settings also change as new versions of the vendor product come out. So once you think everything is great, you have to pop the hood and start tuning again!

All that being said, fully utilizing the tunable parameters of your vendor software can really kick your production implementation into high gear. Tuning is an important activity, and you should recognize that your senior people need time and other resources to perform. So make the investment and then proceed carefully.

Inventory Control

Similar to routine maintenance, it is vital to track and be absolutely certain of what you are running in the production environment. Most IT shops do a good job of tracking the hardware specifics...and if the documents are incorrect, you can always pop the panel on your server to see what's actually there. But software is a different story. Is it asking too much for a production manager to actually know what's running in the environment? As a production manager, isn't it more than a little embarrassing if you don't know exactly what's running?

To be proactive in avoiding problems, you should audit your production setup on a regular basis to ensure that everything is as it should be. Why would systems get changed unexpectedly? There are two main reasons things can get out of alignment here. The first is that you have dozens of hands in the kitchen performing work. Occasionally they will accidentally make a change that is harmful to production. The second is that during deployments or severe outages, it is common to have numerous changes take place all at once in a rush. During the confusion, it is difficult to be sure that only intended changes took place. You need a way to be sure! Trust but verify.

So what do you need to track? Here's a starter list:

- The configuration for every physical server, including the following:

  ◦ what hardware components are in the box

  ◦ the specific OS version, including patch versions

  ◦ the complete OS configuration, including all tuning parameters

  ◦ all security settings and logins

- The configuration for every instance of DBMS, including the following:

  ◦ the specific version

  ◦ all configurable settings, from global parameters down to table-specific settings

  ◦ all security settings and logins

  ◦ the amount of data in each table

- The configuration for every instance of the application software, including the following:

  ◦ the specific version, including patch versions

  ◦ all configurable settings

- Network essentials:

- inventory of all nodes and their locations

- network cards with their MAC addresses

- IP addresses and NetMasks

- gateways and DNS Server addresses

Ideally, you can have scripts (there are also commercial products) that automatically fire up every morning to check that everything is as it should be before the start of business, or that run on a regular basis. They can also be manually initiated when there is a problem or immediately following a deployment. Here is a sample of things that should be checked:

- Are all of the application processes running?

- Is the middleware up?

- Are all of the databases online?

- Are all of the critical network segments running properly?

This is a good way to catch things before they get out of hand.

Control Change Before It Controls You

A primary source of production incidents is changes gone awry. When you have an outage, one of the first questions always asked is "what was changed?" Sometimes the change itself is flawed. At other times, the change itself may be fine, but the implementation process is flawed, so it breaks something or takes too long and spills over into the production window. And at yet other times, two changes are introduced at the same time that conflict with each other. There is a significant amount of risk when it comes to making changes to your production system. However, there are two main benefits to having a rigorous change control program in place:

1. Increased service quality through reduced chance of changes breaking production.

2. Shorter mean time to restore service by reducing time to diagnose production incidents caused by changes.

If you have a lackluster change control process (or none at all), in which each change gets rubber-stamped by a body that doesn't understand the changes being implemented, do you think that real value is being added? Not much. If your change success rate (defined as the percentage of changes that don't have unintended negative consequences) is less than 90% (or if you don't know what it is!), then that reinforces the answer to that question.

At minimum, your change control process should include:

- Change tracking

- Change review and approval

- Risk assessment and mitigation

Change Tracking

One of the key foundations of controlling change is to be able to track it. Many vendors offer solutions to help with this, but regardless of the tool used, you need the ability to document changes, their attributes, their status, and their history.

Understanding the causes of some ailments requires very good change tracking. Anyone who has consulted a doctor to treat migraines knows that many of the questions asked by the doctor are aimed at understanding what the triggers of migraines are. If the patient is able to remember when they consumed caffeine or stopped consuming it, when they ate certain foods, performed certain activities, how much sleep they got, and so on, they have a better chance of identifying what triggers the migraines. For someone with a keen sense of observation and a great memory, this might be possible without keeping track of all these changes that happen to the body. But for most, it is necessary to track this down on paper. Dealing with IT systems is no different. You can't count on collective memory to know what happened when and to which part of the system.

Since all changes will need to be approved (see next section), make sure the details of each proposed change are clearly documented and the reason why it is being proposed is articulated. At minimum, the following points should be addressed:

- Core attributes of the change: Is it a change in software, hardware, configuration, or data? What specific components of the infrastructure will be changed?

- The value that the proposed change provides: Why is it worth taking the risk of making the change?

- How routine the proposed change is (or conversely, how unique/risky it is).

- Documentation supporting that the proposed change is high in quality (that is, it achieves the intended result and doesn't break anything in the process). Usually this means discussing the testing procedures, how production-like the test environment was, and the results.

- The time that the proposed change will take place and its duration, as well as why that is the proper time, and that the time doesn't conflict with other changes or routine maintenance activities.

- The person responsible for implementing the proposed change and their emergency contact information.

- How the success of the change will be verified.

- The back-out plan in case things go wrong: How will the system be reverted to the previous state, if necessary? Is the plan good enough? If critical, was it practiced to make sure it works?

Change Review and Approval

Change review and approval can sound like a bureaucratic function. And it can easily become that way if the true intent and value of change control is lost or forgotten. How would you feel if drugmakers were allowed to sell prescription medicine without going through some sort of review process to ensure certain quality standards are met? Whatever you think of the Food and Drug Administration (we are by no means in a position to evaluate it), we take comfort in knowing that if our doctor prescribes us a migraine treatment, a third-party organization has scrutinized the drugmaker's research on the treatment's safety and effectiveness, the design of the clinical trials, the severity of any side effects, and the drug's interaction with other drugs.

As most people can easily understand the value provided by the FDA's process, people involved in the change process should understand that the reason it is in place is to

- detect change collision (will a change be incompatible with some other change?);

- encourage cost-benefit analysis by preventing the introduction of change that is too risky for the reward it is expected to provide;

- allow potentially impacted stakeholders to raise an objection to the change: for instance, the representative of a downstream system, or a representative from the business who might object to the timing of the change.

Therefore, the change review process should involve representatives from all the systems and business units that may be impacted. It is also advisable to have a senior management person accountable for the change involved.

Routine Changes

Not 100% of production changes truly belong in a change review meeting. Production administrators need to have the flexibility to perform minor and routine changes in order to keep the system running optimally. Not all SAs and DBAs need a "license to kill," but they should have some clearly defined leeway as to what they can do without a Change Request (CR). Otherwise, your capability to react quickly to problems is handcuffed, and your technicians spend too much time doing paperwork.

Also, the change review meeting becomes an administrative nightmare when you literally evaluate every single change to production. You want your staff thinking about the big, risky changes, not whether or not your SA should be allowed to add a new login.

For the significant changes that merit it, at the meeting, you have to be prepared to leverage the information documented in the change request to approve, partially approve, delay, or deny changes as makes sense.

There is great value in having control over your production environment. Employees don't always appreciate what they sometimes perceive as low-value-added bureaucracy, but they certainly understand that having fewer outages is better for the business and better for their personal lives. It may even make sense at the beginning of every change meeting to explicitly state the reason you are having the meeting in the first place!

The Reward of Risk

Some drugs have drastic side effects. Chemotherapy and radiation therapy can destroy cancer cells but also have an impact on healthy cells. As a result, these treatments can cause hair loss, reduction of appetite, fatigue, nausea, soreness, and lower resistance to infections, to name just a few. Nevertheless, they are widely used because the potential rewards are greater than the costs and risks. Not undergoing the treatments leads to a fairly certain grim outcome.

With computer systems, all changes involve different degrees of risk, and not making changes has inherent risk as well in a dynamic system environment. Good change control is simply risk management.

As far as risk goes, sometimes you do have to take risks. You want to intelligently manage your risks as much as possible, but it is not always feasible to wait for complete decision-making data to become available, due to costs, resources, or timeframes. It's all a matter of understanding risk and reward. If you have a solid understanding of both, you're positioned to make the most intelligent decisions.

The data is the key. A risky change incorrectly thought to be low risk is dangerous. A low-risk change mistakenly thought to be dangerous can result in an enormous lost opportunity. For instance, if you believe a particular tuning change could save you $50,000 per day, but the full testing process would take three weeks, and the back-out process is dead simple, you probably make the change, depending on the other circumstances. Ultimately, the tough calls deserve a formal or informal cost-benefit analysis, which should make the choice clearer. It also probably makes sense to involve a higher level of management on the hard calls for high-profile systems. In short, change control allows us the flexibility to make high-risk changes when warranted, as well as low to moderate ones.

In addition, there are multiple levels of risk mitigation that should be considered. Obviously, there is testing. But there are also *piloting* and *scheduling* as valid risk mitigation techniques.

Piloting

Piloting is akin to trying a new drug on a small sample of the population before fully launching it to the public. In IT, piloting works when you have a production system with multiple instances. Make the change on only one or two of the instances (preferably the smaller ones in most cases), leave the other instances alone, and watch what happens.

Similarly, if your system's workload is balanced across multiple servers, and you can control the load distribution, an effective risk mitigation strategy is to size your environment such that a server could be taken "out of rotation" without causing any scalability issues. That way, you can apply the change to that server first and put it into service with a controlled set of users (which may or may not be real users). Then, when you are confident that the change is successful, you allow gradually more users on the server. If it turns out you need to back out of the change, the impact on the business is minimal.

Scheduling

Scheduling works on the same principle of managing risk by implementing changes at the most appropriate time. If you must undergo knee surgery that will require you to take a week off from work, when's the best time to do it? Probably not in the final phase of a big project you're involved in, but also not during golf season! When making a change to the system, can you do it in the middle of the night and validate it then? Or can you do it on a day (perhaps Sunday, if that's a light business day) when the load is minimal? Or at the beginning of the month when sales and accounting volume is relatively low? If there is a problem, you should be able to escape with greatly reduced impact. It's very important to understand the business situation to make smart choices about when change risk is lowest for the business.

One other rule of thumb is to try not to stack large and/or risky changes on top of each other. Would you want to take care of that knee surgery at the same time you come in for a hip replacement? Spread them out. You do not want to run big changes four days in a row, for a few reasons. First, you want all of your alpha geeks on high alert when you have a big change in the works, and they can't be on high alert that long. Second, you don't want to expose the business to repeated risks like that. In fact, if you have a significant outage, it is prudent to temporarily curtail all changes that aren't related to fixing the outage, to give the business a breather. Lastly, sometimes the negative impact of a change isn't noticed for over a day, a week, or in some cases even months! So if change A introduced a subtle yet important problem, and you've already laid changes B and C on top of A, then the back-out process has greatly increased complexity.

Ultimately, you have to find a happy medium, where important changes are getting done (you need to get the knee surgery done someday), yet there is enough rigor to keep your exposure acceptably low. Rubber-stamping changes is not the answer. Denying all changes and making changes administratively prohibitive is not the answer (not getting the surgery could cost you the use of your leg). Using a sound process to carefully evaluate changes prior to scheduling them is the answer.

Outlaws

Imagine the FDA's reaction if a drugmaker suddenly decided to bypass the review process and market a new product without approval. The administration would take swift action.

If you discover that your own personnel are going outside the change process for items that they don't have a license to do without a CR, they should be given a clear, stern warning that it is not acceptable. If they persist, take more severe action. Rogue operators, even when skilled and well intended, can easily cause more harm than good. Hear them out the first time on why they aren't using the CR process, but do not let this behavior persist or it will undermine everything. This can often be overcome by creating a change management program that your people understand to be a value-adding process and not just an administrative speed bump.

Health History

There's a reason our doctors keep files with our information and health histories. They even seek historical data about our families to help determine our predispositions to certain problems. This historical data can be very useful down the road.

As we've mentioned already, production incidents are often caused by changes gone bad. If the production troubleshooters don't know what changes have happened recently, they waste valuable time trying to figure out what happened. The problem is compounded when problems don't manifest immediately after a change. The further back in time the faulty change, the less likely it will be remembered.

So in addition to having the system owners contributing to the change call, you should have your outage specialists in the loop. That way if you do have a problem, they are armed with your latest change data. If you have a large IT department, the approved changes can be posted to the intranet for easy retrieval.

Separation of Powers: Basic Internal Security

By no means is this book a reference work on security, and you certainly should have dedicated security experts looking after the security of your key systems—especially to prevent harm from outside the company. However, there are a few easily correctable mistakes that can help a great deal with availability and data integrity issues driven from *inside* the company.

While we might lose sleep about the unstable or revenge-minded employee, the vast majority of our employees are honest and hardworking folks. Even so, they occasionally make mistakes that can negatively affect production. A common mistake is that employees working in the testing or development departments will take an action on a system, thinking they are in a test area, when in reality they are in production! They certainly didn't mean to issue a shutdown in production, or to delete mass quantities of data in production; it was just a mental slip.

The best way to prevent this type of scenario is to both make it extremely clear what is production and what isn't, and to separate access to the environments as much as possible. Here are some tips to get you there, some of them obvious and some of them more subtle:

- In the same way non-licensed doctors are prevented from operating on you, non-production folks should be prevented from harming production. Only grant production access to operations personnel and a very select list of senior troubleshooters outside of production.
    - For the troubleshooters, make their production ID very clear, such as "johnw_production" (provided your systems don't use Single Sign On).

- Limit the powers that these IDs have to the minimum necessary to do their jobs. Many roles such as troubleshooting only require read-only access, so it should be used in those cases. As much as possible, avoid giving any root or admin privileges on production outside of production staff.

- Along the same lines, sometimes when we have one piece of software that logs into another piece (such as seven production programs that all share the same production DB), we assign these programs a common DB login and password. This makes figuring out which process is doing what extremely difficult, especially during the time crunch of a crisis. Fix it by doing the following:

  - Ensuring that each application has a clear and unique user login and password in the DB. When you're looking through logs and at diagnostic output to try and find out what is causing a problem, it's far easier if the specific IDs are being used.

  - Ensuring that the passwords for these apps are protected—only known to a small subset of production personnel.

  - Providing for easily changeable passwords by the production staff as needed. A hard-coded password will be learned by many and abused.

A note of caution, though: it is possible to lock production down too much. If you decide to make your production system into such a fortress that even your own subject matter experts (SMEs) can't get to the files they need to optimize your system, you've gone too far. On a scale of 1 to 10, 1 being Central Park and 10 being Fort Knox, you should, generally speaking, shoot for an 8 (depending on the sensitivity of your business and the particular system in question).

Collectively, these basic security guidelines have two main benefits: they keep non-production personnel from accidentally causing issues in production, and they also make production troubleshooting easier.

Healthy Habits from the Start

Imagine a society in which all the operational aspects of the health care system are top notch: the fire departments are consistently good at responding to incidents quickly and efficiently, the emergency rooms are world class at triaging and treating injuries and poisonings, the doctors are effective at administering preventive care and monitoring their patients, the way new drugs are accepted into the system is safe, and so on. Would that be enough to ensure that society will maximize its quality of health and life expectancy? No. Some critical pieces would be missing: the constant search for a better understanding of the human body's inner workings, and research into new drugs and treatments. Doing this not only requires the presence of researchers but also some good communication between the health practitioners and the researchers.

As good system health care practitioners, many production managers do a good job of handling the day-to-day production-oriented changes that need to happen during the course of business in IT. But what about major software upgrades created by your counterparts in development? When it comes to major software releases, most production managers seem to feel disempowered. Powerful organizational leaders often champion major releases in both the business and development. The CIO is aware of them and wants them to go well. The business is hungry for the functionality they requested many months (or years!) ago.

In such a scenario, production managers feel that if they intervene in the name of production quality, they will be perceived as troublemakers—people who get in the way of progress. Or they feel that their concerns will not be heard anyway, so what is the point? They just have to take their lumps and make the most of it, right?

Wrong. If you are the production leader, it is your duty to scrutinize the quality of anything you put into production. Ultimately, it's your say whether or not to deploy. If you know of bad software coming down the pike, and you implement it anyway, you are not doing your job.

That said, there is a wrong way and a right way to steer the quality of major releases. The wrong way is to come out at the last minute against something that development has been working on for 10 months. You can't show up three days before deployment and say that their testing hasn't been thorough enough. It's just unfair, and they have too many moving pieces in place already—the pain from stopping would be enormous. In addition to being unfair to your development counterparts, you're not likely to be successful or keep your job very long in some cases.

The right way to ensure the quality of a major release takes months of careful oversight well in advance of its production deployment. Here are some concepts you can leverage:

- Clearly establish written guidelines about what production quality looks like (many of the criteria should revolve around DRES, but some can be about operability and hardware usage as well). See the "Production Release Guidelines" section in the appendix for some examples. Mandate that any new software has to prove that it meets those criteria before implementation. Make it publicly available on the intranet, and when you hear of a major release that has been kicked off, meet with the leadership of that release to make sure they are aware of these guidelines, and that you will be checking in on the release to make sure it adheres before you give your permission for it to be released into production. Also let them know if you can be of any help along the way—either in interpreting the guidelines or assessing the release and giving them feedback early.

- Draft a small team of your own experienced folks and give them a new part-time job: monitoring the quality of the release. They should go to design review meetings to make sure the designs are not flawed from a production standpoint, test planning meetings to make sure the scope of the testing is suitable to confirm that the entrance criteria are met, and test result meetings to make sure the quality is actually there. They can even participate in the testing. If development and testing are nervous about you looking over their shoulders, a lot of that mistrust can be taken away if you volunteer to help execute certain kinds of tests with them. People rarely turn away good help. Note that in a large IT shop, this part of your team should be continuous and you should staff accordingly.

- In addition to your folks on the ground checking in on the releases, you should have a regular meeting with development management to keep them abreast of your findings. You need to do everything possible to give them time to react to meet your needs. These meetings will not usually be fun—as development management's number one concern is often to release on time—but you have to be persistent. They have to know you're not going anywhere until you get what you need to be successful.

- Ensure the development organization is equipped to deliver on operational quality requirements. It is not sufficient to give them guidelines or requirements for production quality. Some development teams will need help in being able to meet those requirements. One avenue is to lobby for getting the developers trained in such things as designing and developing for high quality in DRES. Another effective approach (but more taxing for the production organization) is to have production personnel share best practices with the developers. For instance, if you have a DBA or analyst who's very strong at tuning SQL and understands how to write efficient SQL in the application, have that person give a training session to the development team. This will often be very effective because the trainer will be able to use relevant examples that the development team will relate to.

Production Coding Guidelines

In a large IT shop, it is best practice to have formal coding standards, and most do. If you are in operations, how well these guidelines cover what you care about, and how fully they are embraced, is another story. If you have concerns about the quality of the code being delivered into production, make it part of your mission to get a copy of the coding standards and also find out how they are being leveraged. In the event you find significant gaps, you can partner with the appropriate leaders in engineering to improve things over time.

If, however, your friends in engineering do not follow formal standards, you may need to improvise. You likely have experts on your operations staff who know certain technologies inside and out. Perhaps you have a guru-level Oracle DBA, or an amazing batch operator who really knows her stuff. If your team has advice on how to write good code that is specific to your environment or platform, or how to correct specific mistakes you have seen in custom code written by your development group, it is entirely appropriate to write a short document or host a few training sessions in an attempt to improve code quality.

Yes, it takes a bit of effort to create such a guide (the details will likely vary significantly from platform to platform and implementation to implementation), but the upside can be significant. There are books available that provide a solid starting point in the area of coding best practices as well.

Lastly, when delivering this document or advice to development, do you have to come off as superior and arrogant? Of course not. The tack to take here is that you have specific insight from seeing your applications in a heavily loaded production environment, and that you'd like to share things you have learned in hopes that the application will perform better in future releases.

Volume of Change

In addition to proactively ensuring the quality of major releases, you may have an issue wherein development is intent on pushing more change into production than you can handle with quality. Even if every release has high quality, perhaps you can only deal with so much change at a time. Perhaps there needs to be a limit of one large release every two months, or perhaps you should not allow large releases in November or December because your heavy retail cycle requires your resources to be tasked elsewhere. Of course, different industries will have different risk circumstances and different periods in which it makes sense to minimize change.

If the business needs a lot of change in order to be successful, then you may have to make do as best you can. Some business models, particularly for new, rapidly growing businesses, may in fact require the development of new functionality (to attract new customers) to be prioritized higher than quality. This decision should be made carefully, while keeping the long-term view in mind, but sometimes it makes sense. We would argue, however, that if you have hundreds of thousands of customers already, then it probably doesn't make sense, due to the risk of losing the customers you already have.[15]

And you should have a look at your own operation to see if there is any way you can handle more release throughput with quality (by reorganizing, adding staff, or using a new technique). Sometimes you can encourage development to create smaller, more iterative releases instead of huge big-bang ones, in part by leveraging newer development methodologies such as Agile or Extreme Programming, rather than the traditional waterfall.

---

15 Another technique to successfully release with suboptimal quality while protecting against dissatisfied customers is to set low expectations with your user base. Typically for brand-new software this is done by labeling the software as "beta," à la Google's Gmail, which has been in beta since April 2004. It also doesn't hurt that their software is free.

But after you've had that look, if there is a limit to how much change you can accept, and development is asking for more, you should call a meeting or series of meetings to figure out how to do what's best for the company. The CIO should probably be involved here, as this is an IT-wide decision that needs to be figured out.

More on Preventing Scalability Crises

While scalability crises can happen as a result of slow and steady growth over time, that scenario is somewhat rare. Also, in that scenario, because the growth is slow, there will usually be warning signs that will flare up well in advance of a serious system crisis.

We already discussed how to measure scalability at length in chapter 3. This section will help you understand the five situations where you are most at risk and what to do about it.

1. **A new software release.** The bigger and more custom your software changes are, the more you have to worry about. Assuming it's a big release, you'll definitely want to investigate whether the new release will scale in production before going live. There are essentially two choices when it comes to load testing:

   a. **A load test with full production volumes.** This test is helpful because the results are meaningful and give you peace of mind that your system will work properly in the real world. Unfortunately, full load tests on large production systems can be prohibitively expensive due to the amount of hardware required, the effort involved in setting up and maintaining the environment, and the cost of high-volume testing tools.

   b. **A limited load test in which you extrapolate the results.** This can be handled a couple of different ways. In both limited load test scenarios, you pump a moderate transaction volume through the system and collect data telling how hard the various components were working.

      i. If you have results from an identical test performed against the release that is currently in

---

Common Test Phases

Typically software is not just tested once before it is deployed but in multiple overlapping phases. Here are some of the common ones:

Unit Test

This is where your developers test their individual work before checking it in to the shared code repository. If they don't do a good enough job at this, your subsequent testing efforts will take much longer than they otherwise would.

System Test/Functional Test

This is where the system is checked to make sure it fulfills all of the functional requirements. This phase may or may not include an Integration Test, during which the interaction of various components or systems is verified.

Regression Test

This is for upgrades and new releases, where the existing functionality is given a once-over to make sure the changes introduced didn't break the existing functionality.

production, you can tell if the new application fares better or worse from a scalability perspective. If it is no worse, then perhaps that is all you need to know to feel comfortable. If it is X% worse, then try to make sure you have more than that much headroom available in production before releasing.

ii. You can also gain insight from determining the amount of resources used *per business transaction*. For instance, if you ran 500 transactions per minute through the system and needed 3 web servers, perhaps 5,000 transactions per minute would require 30 web servers.

Limited load tests are helpful, but not as reassuring as full load tests, so we encourage you to utilize full load tests wherever practical or economical. If the investment required is very big, do a return on investment analysis.

2. **A new hardware configuration.** These cause scalability problems less commonly, but if you are using a new component (e.g., a new brand of load balancer for your Internet-facing application), be prepared to roll it back if trouble hits.

3. **An immature system.** A brand new system's growth, when looked at in percentage terms, can be astonishing. If your system sold 2,000 widgets in March, and 8,000 in May, you just quadrupled your growth in two months, for an annual growth rate of 4,000 times, or 400,000%. Such steep growth curves can play havoc on your system. To help remedy this, examine the production data weekly for changes in the growth curve, and perform your load testing at a very high level of transactions. In this case, 20% or 50% headroom is completely insufficient.

4. **Seasonal peaks in growth.** Oftentimes, businesses will have steep seasonal growth curves. For instance, because a product being sold is only appropriate during certain weather, or because a product makes a great holiday gift, or because the books close at the end of the year. In these cases, since you know it's coming, it often makes sense to "batten down the hatches" and apply extra rigor a month or two in advance of the peak.

Common Test Phases (continued)

Performance Test
This checks to see what the response times of the application will be, ideally under a variety of load scenarios.

Load Test / Stress Test / Scalability Test
These tests ensure that the application can successfully perform X transactions per minute or per hour. In some cases, it is interesting to keep adding load to a system until it breaks (stress testing), no matter what the requirement is, so that you know where the ceiling is and what is likely to fail.

Exception Test
As the name implies, this test phase handles exceptions. What happens when your network connection momentarily disappears? What happens when the database goes off-line unexpectedly? Exception tests help you understand how robust or resilient your system is when specific components of the architecture fail.

Operational Acceptance Test (OAT)
This test certifies that the operations department can effectively run the system in production. This typically includes things like start-up and shutdown processes, etc.

5. **Atypical peaks in growth.** If your marketing department is planning a huge campaign and is keeping you in the dark (sometimes on purpose for fear of competitive information leaking out), you are at risk. Work with them to make sure you get the inside scoop on any major initiatives that are designed to increase volume quickly.

When you take a step back to see how at risk you are from the five factors above, then you can make enlightened decisions about how prepared you need to be, how often you need to take measurements (weekly? monthly? quarterly?), and how much headroom you need to keep on tap.

Sometimes, rather than just expressing headroom as a percentage, it makes sense to say "I want our systems to be ready today for the anticipated level of load X months from now." Then the percentage can change as conditions do, but you're still giving consistent direction.

Basic Disaster Recovery and Fault Tolerance: IT Insurance

The last category of prevention is *disaster recovery (DR)*. As with security, this book does not pretend to be a comprehensive guide to DR (and there are certainly numerous dedicated references available on the topic), but there are some basic principles that it pays to adhere to, which we will briefly cover here.

Unless you absolutely can't afford it, common sense says you should have health insurance. And the most basic kind is the one that protects you in case of an event that would cause some very big expenses, risking bankrupting you.

If your system is truly mission-critical, there must be a plan to deal with any type of disaster, from the unlikely yet commonly used examples of natural disaster and terrorism (look no further than Hurricane Katrina or 9/11 for powerful examples), to the more mundane (and common) power/server/network/disk failure. Any large enterprise should have a dedicated team to coordinate this, but the specific technical aspects of your system's DR plan belong to you, the production manager.

Prioritization

If you have several applications in your portfolio, start by envisioning some worst-case scenarios. If you lost application A, would you be able to make new sales? If you lost application B, would you be able to bill your customers? If you lost application C, would your employees get paid? There are probably differing amounts of time your business would be able to withstand this disruption, so you must plan accordingly. If you do not, you stand a legitimate risk of running your company out of business. Customers will be sensitive to a natural disaster…for a time. But they have businesses to run as well and will eventually take action to ensure their own viability.

So it becomes necessary to take inventory and prioritize. If you lost every single system, which ones would you rebuild first? Take stock of all of your applications, and work with the business to calculate how necessary they are. Once you have worked out a priority and a needed recovery timeframe for each key app, it is time to assess your recovery capabilities.

Typical DR Setups

For critical enterprise applications, it is standard to have two data centers in different parts of the continent, to reduce the risk from natural disaster, though there are mild advantages to having your data centers somewhat closer together (such as higher data transfer rates and the ability to share personnel between the data centers). Then, to be able to leverage these data centers, you have full or partial duplicate systems on standby in the other center, and the data from the primary system is transferred to the backup center on a regular basis, preferably in near real time. Then, if the first center (or an instance of your system within the data center) becomes inoperable, you flip over to the backup data center. Depending on how sophisticated your switchover mechanism is, you either have a relatively minor interruption in service or none at all.

> ### Definitions
>
> **Disaster recovery (DR)** deals with restoring operations that have been interrupted as a result of a natural or human-caused disaster. Disaster recovery effectiveness and efficiency increase dramatically when DR is planned in advance.
>
> **Fault tolerance** is concerned with reducing or eliminating the impact of component failures in a system, and is often achieved through duplication of components and/or data (e.g., RAID—"redundant array of independent disks").
>
> **High availability (HA)** is achieved via design and implementation approaches that aim for a certain level of availability regardless of disasters or hardware failures. Disaster recovery plans and fault tolerant designs help achieve high availability.

An alternative design is to split traffic between your two data centers continuously, but overbuild them such that one data center can handle the entire load if needed. This technique works great for web sites that are publishing data, but is much trickier for complex applications that modify data in a back-end database, because it requires bidirectional replication.

Duplicate data centers also become handy when you are making upgrades to the primary system. In the case of a primary and secondary data center, if the upgrade in the primary goes very poorly, you can fail over to the backup system, which has not been altered, so presumably it still works. In the case of two primary data centers, you can design your deployment strategy to take advantage of that topology by moving all the traffic to one center while you upgrade the other, allowing uninterrupted service if the system needs to stay up 24x7 (e.g., an Interactive Voice Response System or IVR).

However, this redundant setup, which is essentially an insurance policy, comes at high cost. There are the physical costs of the gear and data center, additional personnel, potential travel costs, and the costs to keep the systems in sync when changes are made. These costs can be marginally reduced by offering a lower level of service in the period after a disaster. With less gear, perhaps your system can support 1,000 critical users instead of the full 3,000, or perhaps it is acceptable for the performance to degrade for several weeks after a disaster.

Another Use for DR Gear

You might also consider finding alternative uses for when all of this extra infrastructure is sitting idle. For example, the hardware in your backup data center can be used for hosting certain testing environments. A perfect candidate for this scenario is if you need a place to run high-volume tests on a production-sized environment. It is typically hard to get funding for such hardware, so why not kill two birds with one stone by utilizing your redundant infrastructure? You'll maximize your investment by having DR capabilities and being able to run tests that can help you ensure you systems will scale.

Of course, there is one caveat with this approach: you have to be extra careful not to jeopardize your ability to cut over to your DR environment at a moment's notice. Since your testing will likely involve changing the configuration of the environment, you need a way to restore it to a fully functional production environment reliably and quickly.

Other DR solution possibilities include taking nightly tapes of your second-tier systems and overnighting them to an off-site location. When a disaster is over, you can bring the systems back up using data retrieved from the tapes. While this is not an appropriate selection for a Fortune 500 enterprise sales system, it may be entirely appropriate for the payroll system of a small company where you can take a few days to bring things back online. And it comes at much lower cost.

System Type	DR Setup Description	Cost
Mission-Critical, Tier-1 System	Fully redundant systems in separate data centers in different states with less than one-minute data replication from primary to standby.	Very High
Important Secondary System	Partially redundant system (can support fewer users but is fully functional) in separate data center. Stand-by data center may be as few as 20 miles from primary data center. Data replication can take as much as one hour.	High
Low-Priority Production System or Important Test System	No redundant hardware or applications online. Detailed contingency plan to quickly obtain new hardware and data center space in place and practiced. Data sent to tape nightly and overnighted to off-site storage service.	Medium-Low
Low Priority Test System	No redundant hardware or applications online. Data sent to tape weekly and overnighted to off-site storage service.	Low

table 6.1. Example DR setups by system criticality

The Bottom Line

There are really three bottom lines here.

- First, you have to choose optimal DR solutions for each of your important systems. Not making enough of an investment here puts your enterprise at risk. Conversely, spending too much money on DR for your needs just saps company resources that might be better spent elsewhere. This is effectively insurance, and only you and the business can decide how much to buy.

- Second, your DR solution isn't just how to recover your systems; there is a human angle as well. You need to know how your employees are going to get in contact with each other. You need to have backup plans in case selected employees are unavailable. You need to know how the recovery process will start. Ultimately, your IT DR plan needs to dovetail with that of the overall DR plan for the business.

- Third, practice makes perfect. If you have all this fancy gear and written procedures, but you don't ever dust them off and try out, they are bound to fail when needed. So by all means, schedule some regular time, perhaps quarterly, to walk all your key personnel through what needs to be done.

Again, your dedicated DR team should be organizing all of IT around this, and they should be reading the detailed texts on the science of DR. But you as a production manager need to start with the above and go from there as makes sense for the systems you are responsible for.

Summary Checklist

✓ **Preventive Care:** As in health care, preventive care of your IT systems creates a more stable environment and better longevity.

  ◦ There's no substitute for leading a healthy IT lifestyle.

✓ **Monitoring:** Effective systems monitoring makes you aware of problems before serious business impact occurs, allowing preventive actions to be taken.

✓ **Maintenance:** Routine systems maintenance is essential to good systems health and must always remain a priority. It may feel like you can get away with not doing it in the short run, but ultimately neglecting it leads to costly problems.

✓ **Tuning:** In order to perform well over time, system tuning is necessary, particularly for highly dynamic environments.

✓ **Audits:** It is vital to track in detail what you are running in production and do regular audits to ensure everything is still configured as it should be.

✓ **Change Control:** Rigorous change control is important and allows you to improve service quality by reducing incidents related to system changes; it also improves your time to restore when incidents happen.

  ◦ At a minimum, a good change control process should include change tracking, change review and approval, and risk assessment and mitigation.

  ◦ All changes involve different degrees of risk. Sometimes it makes sense to take risks, and sometimes it doesn't. Good change control allows you to make change decisions in an informed manner.

✓ **Access:** Be particularly judicious in allowing production access to non-operations personnel. Also ensure software programs all have unique database logins.

✓ **Upstream Influence:** IT operations must have influence in the software development process to ensure the needed quality in releases.

  ◦ Establish clear quality guidelines for development groups.

  ◦ Have operations participate in architectural decisions and design reviews.

✓ **Disaster Recovery:** A solid disaster recovery plan is needed in case unforeseen events cause your primary systems to become unavailable for a long period of time.

Information Promotion

Sure, you can make your own organization run smoothly. But wouldn't it be nice if all similar and adjacent organizations ran smoothly as well? Perhaps, surprisingly, your efforts can make a big difference in the performance of your peer teams.

Chapter 7: The Power of Pictures

Chapter 8: Expand Your Influence

Level 4
Information Promotion

Level 3
Prevention

Level 2
Defining Quality

Level 1
Crisis Management

The Power of Pictures

How to Take Advantage of the Data You Already Have

Chapter Overview

As an information technology professional, you deal with information all the time. This chapter shows how you can more effectively manage and act upon that information by using visualization techniques. Visualizing information is about more than just looking at information differently; it's a crucial way to increase your productivity, improve the efficiency and effectiveness of teams, and move away from a hero and tribal-knowledge culture.

In the following pages, you'll find practical tips on what to diagram and how to do it, with real examples that have done wonders for us and for the health of the systems we've looked after.

The Leg Bone's Connected to the…

If you own one or more large enterprise systems, you probably have a rough idea of how complex they are. Otherwise we wouldn't need dozens (or even hundreds) of personnel to run them, right? To a layperson, it can be every bit as intimidating as comprehending the complexity of the human body. After all, how many of us fully understand how all of our bodies work at a detailed level? The skeletal system, the circulatory system, the nervous system, the digestive system, and the reproductive system are all significant interactive pieces that have their own functions. For the most part, we know the basics, but we don't need to know the details, so we don't bother. To be completely honest, I wasn't sure what my pancreas actually did until I looked it up.[16]

Similarly, there is a very real problem in IT today wherein, in response to this complexity, we bury our heads in the sand (this is a corollary to the Ostrich Postulate, discussed in chapter 4). The difference in this case is that we are the experts, and we need to know! Instead, we convince ourselves that the technical details are an unknowable "black box," and so we trust our technicians and consultants to just "handle it." This can be a grave mistake, for a number of reasons. If there is not a widely shared fundamental understanding about how your core systems work, the following problems can arise:

- Productivity suffers because a lot of time is spent educating (or reeducating) everyone about relevant parts of the systems at meetings. This goes double for new hires, who have no way to quickly assimilate system information. Imagine how tough it would be for medical students to receive 100% of their education from lectures with few handouts and fewer textbooks. Unimaginable. But in IT, it happens.

- Teams perform activities that have unintended negative impacts on other teams, because they didn't understand the connection between their actions and their peer teams' actions. A neurosurgeon would never ignore a patient's blood pressure during a procedure just because it wasn't her specialty. But in IT, these things happen.

- It causes leaders to add less value, because they tend to make poorer decisions (or just delegate the decisions to technicians, who may not understand the big picture). They also don't anticipate actions that need to be taken for lack of perspective.

- Consultants and vendors gain power, because they may understand your systems better than you do. When they want to sell you something or make key decisions regarding the system, you may not be able to find legitimate flaws in their arguments for doing what they want to do. In effect, you can be at their mercy.

- Key SMEs leave your company and take the knowledge in their heads with them.

  ◦ As a corollary, key SMEs can hold you hostage. You don't dare lose them!

Ultimately, lack of consistent system knowledge can be a drag on your entire organization. Even if you have competent teams that know each of their areas of specialty

---

16 The pancreas is a gland, situated near the stomach, that secretes a digestive fluid into the intestine through one or more ducts and also secretes the hormone insulin [Dictionary.com Unabridged (v 1.1). Based on the Random House Unabridged Dictionary, © Random House, Inc. 2006].

and perform well in a narrow field, you won't be achieving as much as you could be if everyone readily understood the medium-level details of your system. Don't you want all of your bright people pondering possible improvements to the system while they're in the shower or driving home? Do you think a cure for cancer will be found by one narrow group of scientists working in isolation, or from a variety of disciplines working together?

Fortunately, building this consistent foundation of system information for your whole department is a modest investment—we don't need to drive down to the molecular level! Just making sure the basics are well covered can make a great difference.

What's Worth Diagramming?

The key activity recommended in this chapter is to create simple, accurate, and powerful diagrams of everything in your organization that is *both important and complex*. Ideally, these diagrams will fit on one page (even if the page has to be larger than standard size—an amazing amount of information can be conveyed on an 11x17" color printout) and be readily available to everyone. They should be posted on the intranet, tacked to walls, brought to relevant meetings, and embedded in training for new hires.

Diagrams are powerful, because people tend to understand them quickly, and they are semi-permanent. You can get the gist of what they mean during a meeting, and study them in detail later.

Conversely, we often rely on verbal communication. When a big decision has to be made, we ask an architect to explain the underlying system to us. He tells us as best he can. If we're lucky, we might get a crude whiteboard diagram (which incidentally goes up in smoke at the end of the meeting), and we pull the trigger. A week later when the same topic is brought up again, we've forgotten half of what we were told. Certainly verbal communication is superior for a great variety of tasks, but in the case of accurately depicting a factual landscape, pictures are key. Furthermore, pictures are often more memorable for many people.

Examples of things that would benefit from being diagrammed:

System Interaction Diagram (fig. 7.1)

When you have a complex set of systems that provide critical business functionality, it is vital for all of your employees to have a common understanding of how it all works. Not everyone needs to know all the details, but a mid-level understanding is key. People need to know how a complex application functions, including how the process flows and what systems are dependent on each other to make it all work. For example, for respiration, blood is pumped from the heart to the extremities via arteries and returns to the lungs via the veins, where it is re-oxygenated and the cycle begins anew.

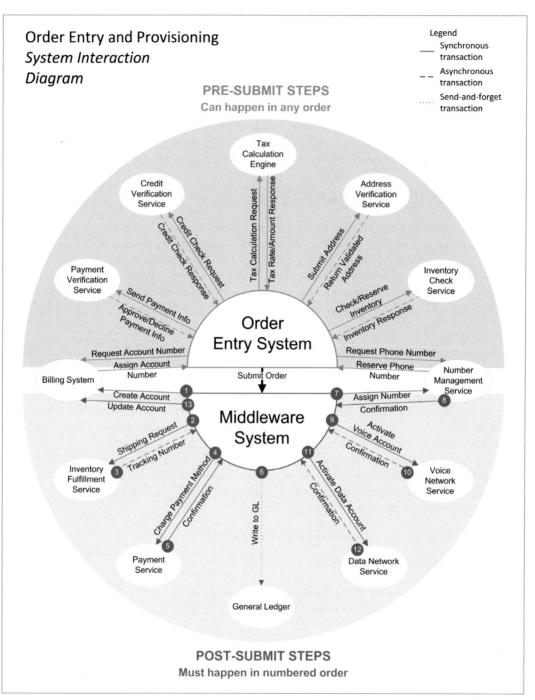

Order Entry and Provisioning
System Interaction
Diagram

Legend

— Synchronous transaction

-- Asynchronous transaction

..... Send-and-forget transaction

PRE-SUBMIT STEPS
Can happen in any order

Tax Calculation Engine

Credit Verification Service

Address Verification Service

Tax Calculation Request

Tax Rate/Amount Response

Credit Check Request

Credit Check Response

Submit Address

Return Validated Address

Payment Verification Service

Inventory Check Service

Send Payment Info

Approve/Decline Payment Info

Check/Reserve Inventory

Inventory Response

Order Entry System

Request Account Number

Assign Account Number

Request Phone Number

Reserve Phone Number

Billing System

Submit Order

Number Management Service

Create Account (1)

Update Account (13)

(7) Assign Number Confirmation (8)

Middleware System

(2)

Shipping Request

Tracking Number (3)

(9) Activate Voice Account Confirmation

(4)

(11)

(10) Voice Network Service

Inventory Fulfillment Service

Charge Payment Method

Confirmation

(6)

Write to GL

Activate Data Account

Confirmation

(5)

(12)

Payment Service

Data Network Service

General Ledger

POST-SUBMIT STEPS
Must happen in numbered order

figure 7.1. Example system interaction diagram

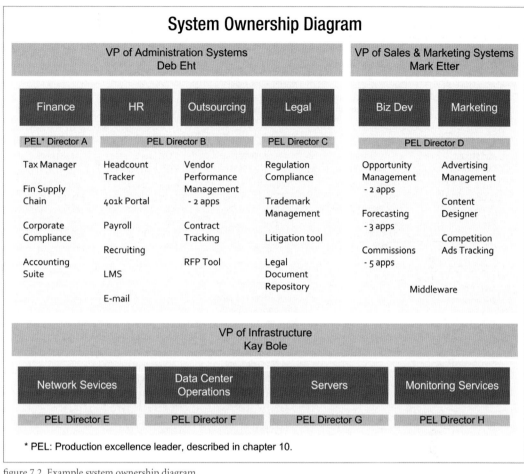

figure 7.2. Example system ownership diagram

System Ownership Diagram (fig. 7.2)

This diagram describes the alignment of your services, applications, and systems with their respective teams and organizations. What teams are responsible for servicing which applications, or what team supports which tiers of your infrastructure (e.g., Who is the head of cardiac surgery? Who is in charge of the ER?).

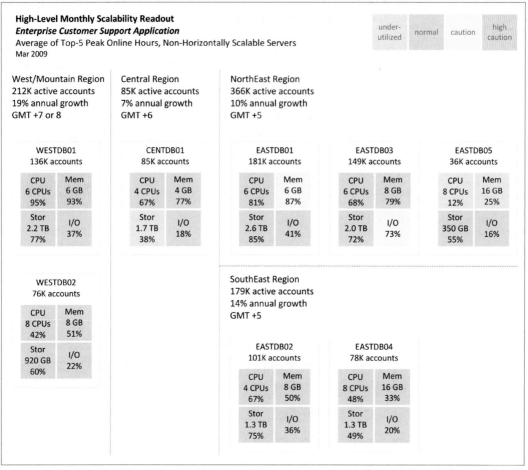

High-Level Monthly Scalability Readout
Enterprise Customer Support Application
Average of Top-5 Peak Online Hours, Non-Horizontally Scalable Servers
Mar 2009

under-utilized	normal	caution	high caution

West/Mountain Region
212K active accounts
19% annual growth
GMT +7 or 8

Central Region
85K active accounts
7% annual growth
GMT +6

NorthEast Region
366K active accounts
10% annual growth
GMT +5

WESTDB01
136K accounts

CPU 6 CPUs 95%	Mem 6 GB 93%
Stor 2.2 TB 77%	I/O 37%

CENTDB01
85K accounts

CPU 4 CPUs 67%	Mem 4 GB 77%
Stor 1.7 TB 38%	I/O 18%

EASTDB01
181K accounts

CPU 6 CPUs 81%	Mem 6 GB 87%
Stor 2.6 TB 85%	I/O 41%

EASTDB03
149K accounts

CPU 6 CPUs 68%	Mem 8 GB 79%
Stor 2.0 TB 72%	I/O 73%

EASTDB05
36K accounts

CPU 8 CPUs 12%	Mem 16 GB 25%
Stor 350 GB 55%	I/O 16%

WESTDB02
76K accounts

CPU 8 CPUs 42%	Mem 8 GB 51%
Stor 920 GB 60%	I/O 22%

SouthEast Region
179K active accounts
14% annual growth
GMT +5

EASTDB02
101K accounts

CPU 4 CPUs 67%	Mem 8 GB 50%
Stor 1.3 TB 75%	I/O 36%

EASTDB04
78K accounts

CPU 8 CPUs 48%	Mem 16 GB 33%
Stor 1.3 TB 49%	I/O 20%

figure 7.3. Example data store diagram

Data Store Diagram (fig. 7.3)

For a system having many databases containing similar information, a diagram of what data is where, including how much data is in each store and possibly even how each data store is doing from a scalability perspective, can be extremely useful (e.g., How many patients are in each wing of your hospital? Do you have enough spare beds to accommodate new patients?). The data stores can be organized a variety of ways, such as by DB platform, by hardware platform, by customer time zone, by customer tier, by size, etc.

A diagram such as this one can show you at a glance where you need to focus your attention the most from a scalability perspective, and also the differing online windows based on the customers contained within the various time zones.

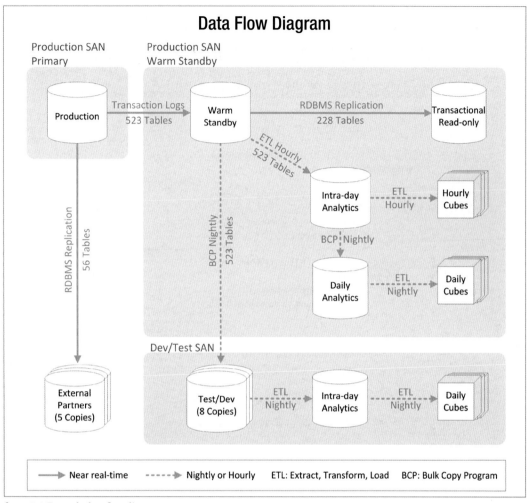

Data Flow Diagram

Production SAN
Primary

Production SAN
Warm Standby

| Production | Transaction Logs 523 Tables | Warm Standby | RDBMS Replication 228 Tables | Transactional Read-only |

ETL Hourly 523 Tables

RDBMS Replication 56 Tables

BCP Nightly 523 Tables

Intra-day Analytics — ETL Hourly — Hourly Cubes

BCP Nightly

Daily Analytics — ETL Nightly — Daily Cubes

Dev/Test SAN

External Partners (5 Copies)

Test/Dev (8 Copies) — ETL Nightly — Intra-day Analytics — ETL Nightly — Daily Cubes

— Near real-time   ----▶ Nightly or Hourly   ETL: Extract, Transform, Load   BCP: Bulk Copy Program

figure 7.4. Example data flow diagram

Data Flow Diagram (fig. 7.4)

If you have data automatically being transported from data store to data store, it is important to have a very clear understanding of exactly what data is going where, how data is routed to your other data stores, including DR instances, your data warehouse, and your reporting systems (e.g., What do you do with a patient's chart after you discharge them?).

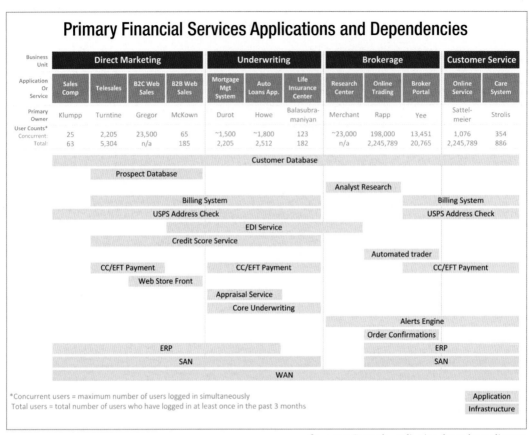

figure 7.5. Example application dependency diagram

Application Dependency Diagram (fig. 7.5)

This type of diagram is helpful to determine at a glance which subsystems must be working properly in order for a particular business application to be functioning. Conversely, it also shows the impacted systems if a particular subsystem goes down. It helps answer questions about which of your applications interface with each other or with external applications and how. (Can a problem in your respiratory system cause other problems in your nervous system? It sure can.)

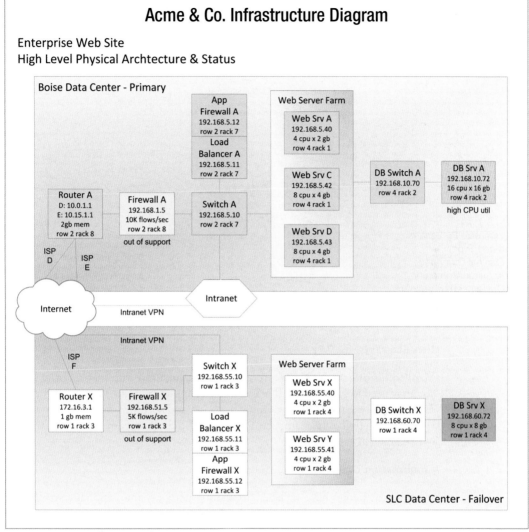

figure 7.6. Example infrastructure diagram

Infrastructure Diagrams (fig. 7.6)

These are logical and physical layouts of your servers and network components with server names, IP addresses, subnet, location, and perhaps scalability information such as bandwidth and latency as well. (What is the physical layout of your hospital? What are the communication systems for emergency response units?)

figure 7.7. Example geo-diagram

Geo-diagrams (fig. 7.7)

Many kinds of data are best represented in combination with maps. For example, you may need to know where the users of your applications are located. This type of diagram can be handy both for tuning purposes and keeping track of the time zones where your activities have impact. The size of the circle corresponds to the amount of personnel in each location.

Combination Diagrams

Inasmuch as bodies have skeletal, circulatory, nervous, and lymphatic systems, IT systems also have multiple layers of depth. Sometimes the layers can be combined into a single diagram, while at other times it makes sense to separate them out.

In two of the previous examples (figs. 7.3 and 7.5), we actually show multiple separate layers of information within the same diagram. The data store diagram overlays database information onto hardware information and then places all of that into a time-zone aware context. Similarly, the application dependency diagram not only shows dependencies, but also gives a rough idea of the scale of each application and also lists the primary application owner. As you begin diagramming the various types of information that are most relevant to your business, definitely explore matching up useful data sets. Your work will be in demand if you do.

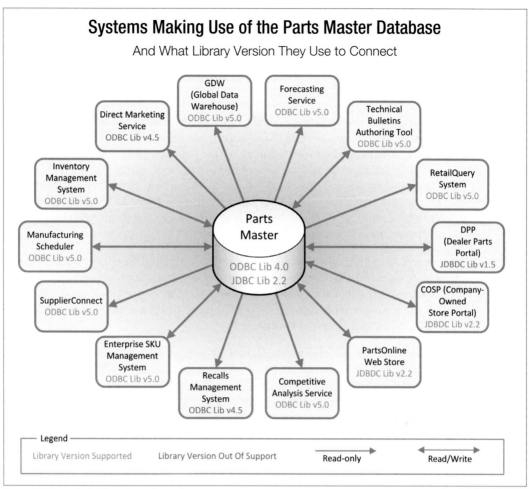

figure 7.8. Example database dependency diagram

Going forward, every time you are asked to make or confirm a technical decision about a system you aren't familiar enough with, ask your folks to provide a relevant diagram in advance of the meeting. If they don't already have one, they'll probably learn things about the system in question along the way that they didn't even know!

How to Paint a Useful Picture

The key challenge in creating a useful diagram is finding the appropriate level of detail. Too little detail and you have concealed significant aspects of how something works. Make sure to capture each key process. Too much detail and the picture can be overwhelming, thus not drawing attention to the important elements. Diagrams with missing legends, hundreds of little boxes and lines, and abbreviations in 4-point all fall into that category. These may be useful to a small handful of technicians, but an "everyman's diagram" should be restrained to mid-level detail and a clear indication of what is being captured.

How do you know if you've hit the right level? Apart from just noticing that it's easy to understand, generally if it fits on one page, is legible, and doesn't leave out any mandatory processing steps (in the case of a process flow) or important physical entities (in the case of a system inventory), you're golden. This can be tricky—sometimes it is necessary to abstract numerous virtually identical components into a single box that says "12 components of type X." A proven approach to address the level of detail problem is to start simple and then add on useful layers of information over time.

If you have an unquenchable thirst for detail, and you have the resources to get fancy, then you can have your cake and eat it too, through use of "drill downs." This means that your primary high-level view of the data is not too detailed, but if you desire, you have more detailed views available (perhaps available via a single mouse click) of various aspects of the system.

Lastly, you can incorporate the real system names (DB names, server names, etc.) into the document to increase their usefulness. Sometimes with large systems it is hard to remember all of the names, even if they follow a logical convention. The same goes for sizes and main configurations. If you have a diagram of physical servers used by a particular system, knowing the number of processors, processor speed, amount of memory, etc., at a glance is also helpful. In figure 7.8, we show a diagram of a very complex environment, boiled down to a view of which systems share a given database. The boxes also contain versions of libraries used by the systems to interface with the database.

Who Should Create the Diagrams?

There are really two valid approaches when it comes to figuring out who does the diagramming. Generally, we like to have the system SMEs be the owners of the documents, because as the systems change, so should the diagrams, and nobody knows the systems like the SMEs. If you have a centralized production excellence leadership team (which we'll describe in a later chapter), the SMEs who live there are a good choice as well.

The other option is to have your technical writers handle this. The upsides are that they have the time, are skilled at diagramming, and can apply standards to all of their work. But the downside is that they don't really know the systems well, so they will be counting on interviews to get the right information. It is also an unfortunate fact that if the technical writers are doing the writing, then it is more likely that no one will pay attention to the deliverables.

In either case, documenting systems can be challenging to do well. Expect early deliverables to be crude. Providing solid examples, as well as appropriate training, can help.

Lastly, don't be afraid that you don't know enough to make a useful diagram. This is yet another case in which you can start small, and as you learn more, you can build more into the diagrams. Early anatomical diagrams were simple (and sometimes incorrect), but they were still useful in their time. Yours will follow the same path but achieve greatness much faster.

One training class that is excellent is Edward Tufte's one-day session; he tours the country giving seminars on effectively graphing and diagramming. He has four excellent and interesting books about visual design from Graphics Press.

Dynamic Diagrams (Dashboards)

Now comes the extra credit section. Let's say you have a large, complex system that is rapidly growing and changing. Let's also say you are producing a regular report that tells how each component of the system is performing (see next chapter for details). A useful document would combine your system diagram with your performance report into a single diagram.

What you get at a glance, then, is the structure of your system and how healthy it is. Truly great diagrams display several key facets of data at the same time, to tell the whole story. Take the baseball box score for instance (fig. 7.9). While not a diagram per se, it only takes up a few inches, and you pretty much know how the whole game went at a glance.

August 27, 2006 at Seattle		
1 2 3 4 5 6 7 8 9	R	H E
Boston 0 0 0 0 1 2 0	3	2 3
Seattle 0 1 0 0 5 0	6	9 1

Figure 7.9

There is a wide spectrum of how timely the information can be. It can be

- **Static.** This is the basic structure of a system with no information about how it's doing (like a generic diagram of a human circulatory system).

- **Partially Dynamic.** This diagram contains system health information at an interval. It could be the server scalability on a monthly basis (or the results of 17 CAT scans taken every 3 weeks for the past year).

- **Fully Dynamic, or Near Real Time.** This would essentially be a display, in which the representation you were viewing held actual data gathered from the system in the last few minutes, such as how many transactions per minute are being processed. (The medical equivalent would be the hospital bedside monitor that captures and displays your vital signs in real time.)

Depending on what you are trying to accomplish, and how many resources you have available, it may make sense to have representations available at all of these levels. But if you don't already have them, it is best to start with static diagrams and go from there.

Third-Party Dashboards

There are several third-party products available to help you construct a useful system dashboard. None of them are completely automatic, but they can give you a big head start if you have the funds to acquire them.

For dynamic diagrams, it is particularly useful to compare the state of something to history, or better yet, to a predefined quality threshold. If you have specific technical thresholds defined for DRES, and you can measure them, then you can get clever. For instance, you can color each component of your system green, yellow, or red, depending on how well it is behaving. Has your blood pressure fallen below established norms? Let's take a closer look.

Two notes of caution, though: Resist the temptation to make a cool-looking automated dashboard before figuring out what data to represent and how. It is far better to create a diagram manually with great data than to automate the publishing of such a diagram but have poor or little data behind it.

The second bit is that the cost for fully dynamic monitoring is much higher than for monthly or weekly monitoring, yet there is a ton of value in doing a monthly deep dive. So don't dismiss the monthly process!

How Is Your Patient Today, Doctor?

While this chapter is mostly about diagrams, it's worth discussing charts as well. Diagrams organize data, often showing how various entities interact. Charts, however, show how one variable changes against another one.

The number one use of charts in this space is keeping track of how things change over time. How many transactions does your system perform every month? How quickly is your database growing? How many incidents do you have compared to this time last year? Is your application faster after 5 p.m. than it is in the middle of the day? What are your top five root causes of incidents?

Charts are more straightforward than diagrams to create (your average spreadsheet package is actually very powerful at charting these days), but they serve a complementary purpose and carry equal power. They are particularly strong in helping you track progress against goals. Use them in your reports and meetings to bring your key data to life!

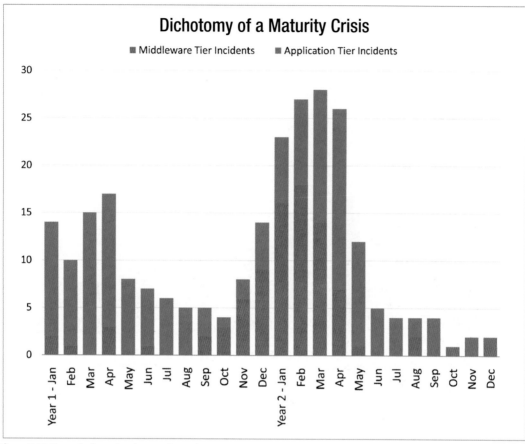

figure 7.10. Example downtime by month graph

Key charts to consider:

1. Quantity and Impact of Downtime

a. ***By month***

Figure 7.10 is a simple graph that shows the number of incidents per month over several months. This particular system started having such significant problems at the middleware level that information about middleware incidents was included, without necessitating the introduction of a drastically different graph. This example tells the story of how an organization had set out to reduce the number of incidents it was experiencing to less than five per month, and was making progress towards that goal, when middleware problems started reversing the positive trend. By representing the number of middleware incidents as a sub-series, it becomes obvious

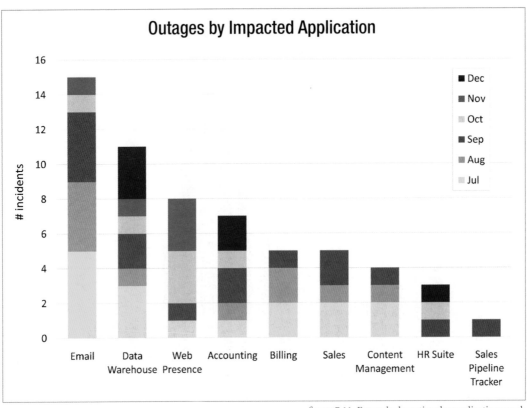

Outages by Impacted Application

(chart legend: Dec, Nov, Oct, Sep, Aug, Jul)

y-axis: # incidents

x-axis: Email, Data Warehouse, Web Presence, Accounting, Billing, Sales, Content Management, HR Suite, Sales Pipeline Tracker

figure 7.11. Example downtime by application graph

that these became a growing proportion of the overall incidents starting in October of year one. This may indicate that while focusing on addressing root cause of the application tier outages, the middleware had been neglected and became a big problem. Further analysis may show that while all resources were shifted towards addressing the middleware crisis, the application tier was once again neglected, causing total incidents to spike sharply. Only in July of the second year did middleware and application outages both get under control.

b. By impacted application

In figure 7.11, the graph still shows number of incidents, grouped by impacted application instead of by month. This kind of graph is also useful to represent how a common architecture component's outages are affecting dependent applications. This will typically be the case in Service-Oriented Architectures (SOA).

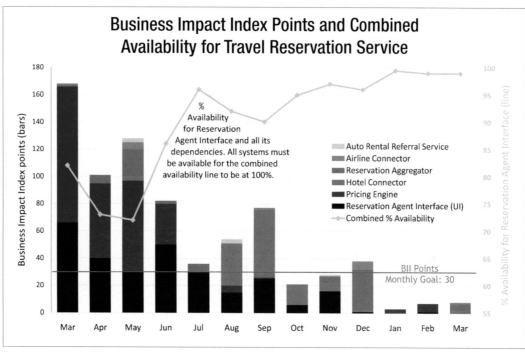

figure 7.12. Example downtime by causing application graph

c. By causing application or by subsystem

While the previous example was a representation of how a single component may affect multiple applications, in figure 7.12 we take the opposite view, where we look at how various components contribute to the downtime of a single service. Additionally, in this example, more than the number of incidents is shown. The graph displays the incidents' translation into BII points (see chapter 3 for a discussion of how to calculate the BII), along with the percent uptime. In one graph, you get visibility to overall availability for an end-user service (the % Combined Availability line), as well as Business Impact points classified by offending system (the UI application, as well as all the subsystems that are required for the service to be fully functional). Lastly, the height of each bar above the red line shows just how dramatic the impact to the business was in some months.

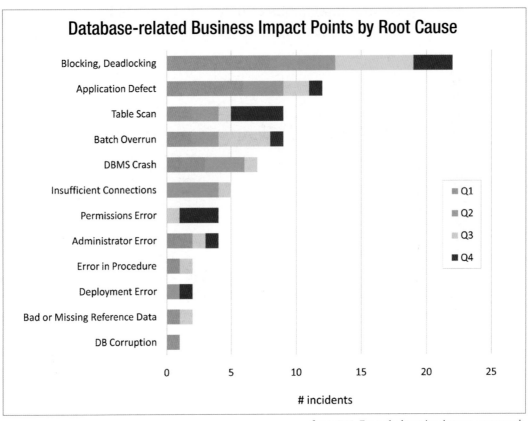

figure 7.13. Example downtime by root cause graph

d. By root cause

In figure 7.13, the graph shows a breakdown of the various causes of database incidents. Such a graph, while simple and not concerned with effect on % availability or BII, can be useful in communicating to the organization about areas of concern that need attention.

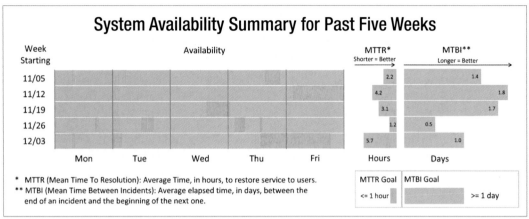

figure 7.14. Example downtime by duration graph

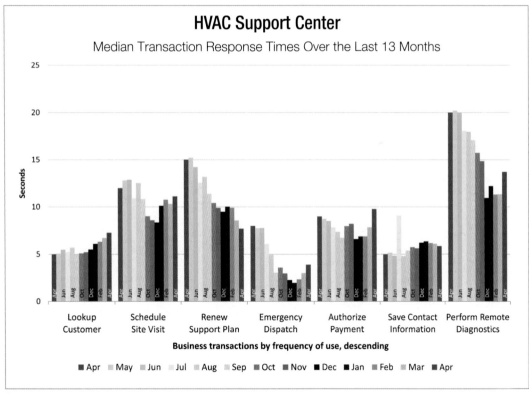

figure 7.15. Example response times by transaction type graph

e. By duration of incidents, and time elapsed between incidents

Figure 7.14 shows two important incident metrics: mean time to restore, and mean time between incidents for an application month over month.

2. Response Times

a. By transaction type

Knowing which transactions are slowest is obviously important. It is also useful to track these over extended periods of time to see if performance is trending in the right direction, as well as to look for possible emerging problems (fig. 7.15).

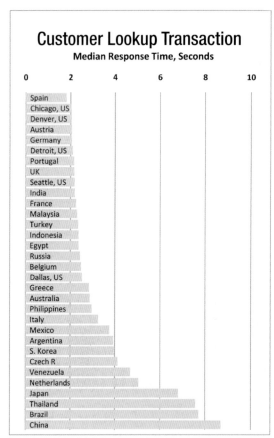

figure 7.16. Example of transaction response time by location and transaction type

b. By location and transaction type

If your users or customers are in many locations, you'll want to get a picture of response times across multiple locations for at least the key transaction or transactions, and perhaps for the "Top X" transactions in terms of volume (e.g., 10 or 20) to show the cumulative effect of performance issues when all frequently executed transactions in the users' workflows are considered.

If most of your transactions perform fairly well, it may not be obvious what differences there may be in response times across locations (a 10% difference on 2 seconds is only 0.2 seconds.). An interesting way of comparing performance across locations is to stack a certain number of transactions together as shown in figures 7.16 and 7.17.

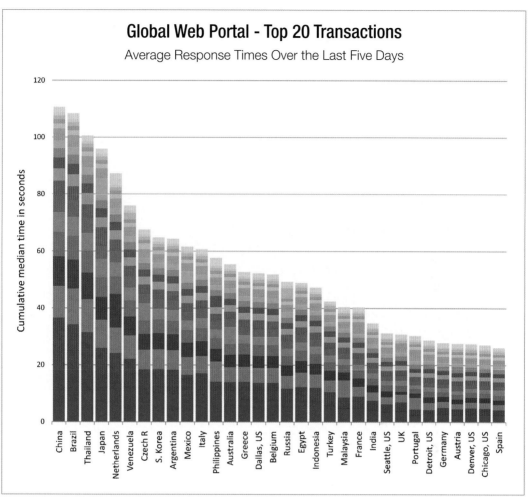

figure 7.17. Example of transaction response time by location and transaction type

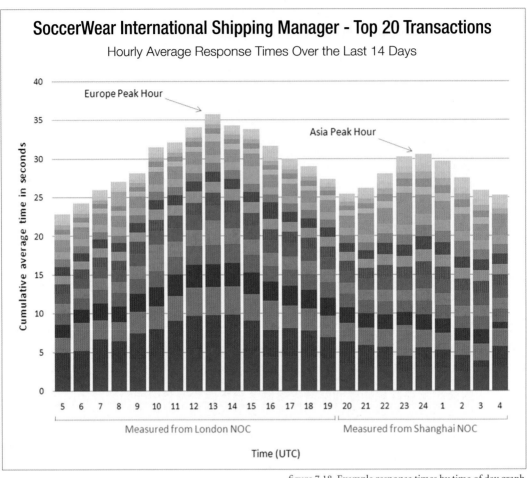

figure 7.18. Example response times by time of day graph

c. By time of day

The same method can be applied with hours of the day instead of locations to determine if response times fluctuate during the course of the day (fig. 7.18).

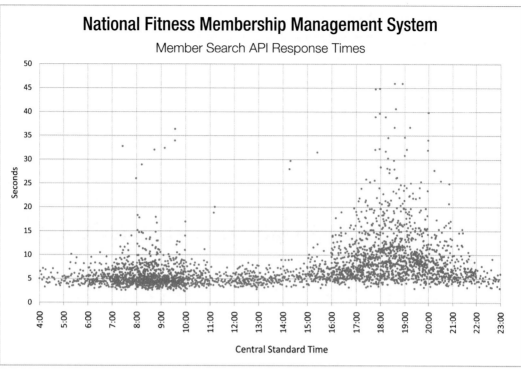

figure 7.19. Example API scatter plot

d. API scatter plot

Monitoring the response times of an Application Programming Interface (API) is a great way to determine if performance problems seen in a client UI or a batch job can be explained by issues in an underlying system. Figure 7.19 is a scatter plot of every single call made through an API. A scatter plot has the benefit of showing the distribution of response times over time. In figure 7.19 it becomes very clear that under high volumes, performance degrades.

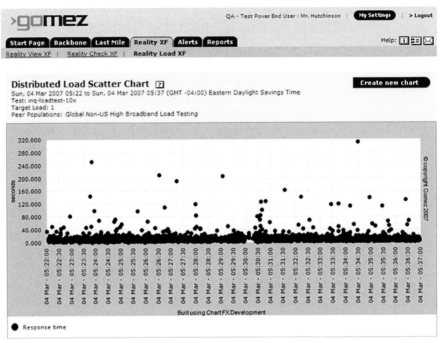

figure 7.20. Client response times scatter plot[17]

In figure 7.20 it is obvious that there are outliers but that their occurrence doesn't seem related to transaction volumes. In such a case it's handy to know what is common among the outlying points. The electronic version of figure 7.20 dynamically displays relevant information specific to each dot when hovered over. In a client response time context it can be useful to depict the differences by geography, browser type, call center, etc.

The scatter plot has use in other situations as well, such as display of web UI response times. Outliers are exposed rather than being folded into averages, and trends are made clear on a micro level.

---

17 Image courtesy of Gomez, Inc., http://www.gomez.com/products/demo-center.php (accessed July 3, 2007).

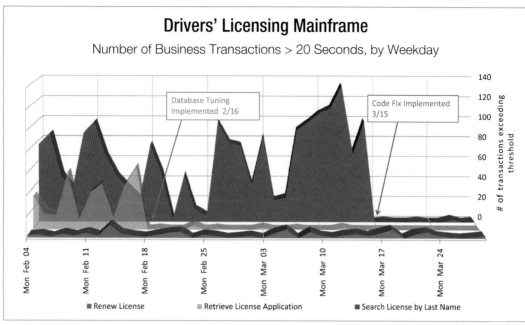

figure 7.21. Example API outlier tracking graph

e. Outlier tracking

If you find yourself in the unenviable position in which things are so bad (or there is so much data) that it's difficult to make sense of the data by simply using averages, sometimes it can be helpful to isolate and trend the exceptions by themselves. Figures 7.21 and 7.22 show two examples for doing so.

When many transactions perform outside of an acceptable range, it can be useful to reduce the noise by only displaying data about the out-of-range transactions. Figure 7.21 shows only the volume of API calls that exceed 30 seconds in duration. In this example, the focus on outliers resulted in a fix implemented in the system, as can be seen in the sharp reduction of transactions exceeding the 30-second threshold.

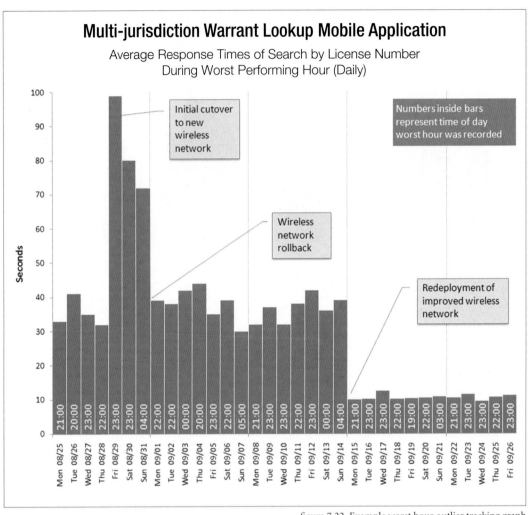

figure 7.22. Example worst hour outlier tracking graph

In figure 7.22, an alternative way of selecting relevant data is used: only the average for the worst hour of each day is displayed. Sometimes when issues only crop up in a small segment of the day, the data can be obscured when averaged in with the rest of the day.

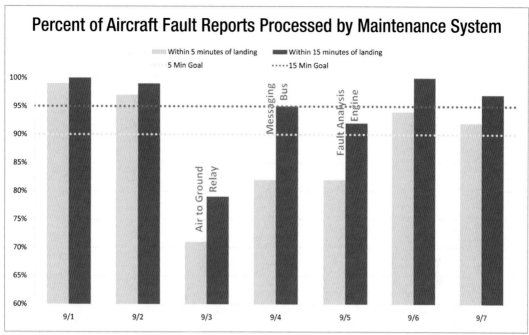

figure 7.23. Example SLA compliance graph

f. Percent within goal

Oftentimes an OLA or SLA will express a target in terms of the percent of transactions that meet some standard.

Column charts such as the one in figure 7.23 give a historical perspective and a quick assessment of not only how frequently the goal wasn't met, but also what systems were at fault those days.

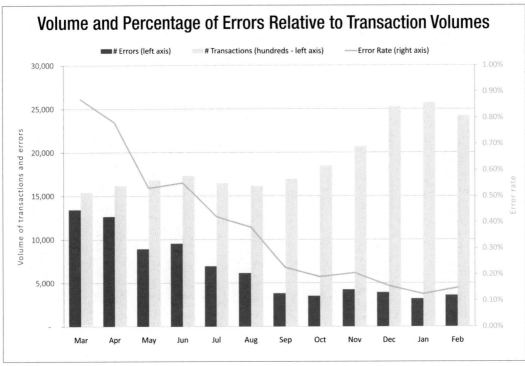

Volume and Percentage of Errors Relative to Transaction Volumes

■ # Errors (left axis) # Transactions (hundreds - left axis) — Error Rate (right axis)

figure 7.24. Example error rate graph

3. Error Rates and Error Volumes Over Time

a. Error rate over time

It's useful to know the error rate of your key systems over time, so that you can tell if the situation is improving or degrading, and also see if your fixes have the desired effects (example in fig. 7.24). At the same time, it is worth knowing how many total errors have occurred. This can be used to estimate impact to the user community, and also the effort required to address any individual errors that cannot be cleared by the users themselves.

figure 7.25. Example error resolution SLA compliance graph

b. Transaction completion error resolution SLA compliance

As opposed to UI errors, transaction completion errors need to be resolved in a timely manner to limit impact to your business. For example, if a percentage of your credit card transactions are failing, you need to track how quickly you are resolving the errors, or you can't recognize the revenue (financial impact), and in some cases can't ship the product to the customer (satisfaction impact).

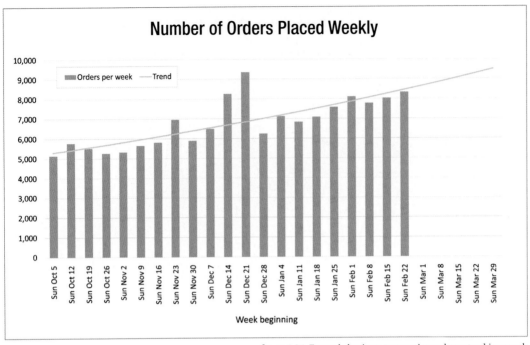

figure 7.26. Example business transaction volume tracking graph

4. Scalability Metrics

a. *Volume of business transactions over time*

Generally it is helpful to look at this type of data on a weekly or monthly basis, as shown in fig. 7.26.

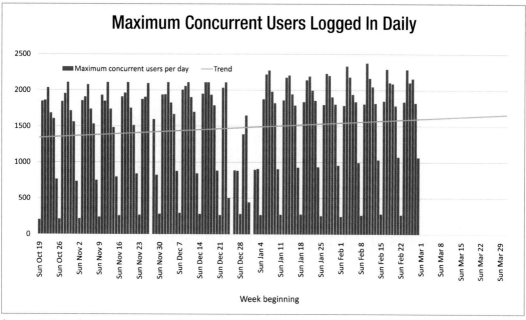

figure 7.27. Example concurrent users graph

b. Maximum number of concurrent users over time

An important usage metric to track for an application is the maximum number of concurrent users each day (fig. 7.27). This provides enough granularity to identify which days of the week are busiest, while giving enough perspective to see if / how much the user base is growing.

For tracking volumes over a long period of time, weekly or monthly aggregates may work better.

> **Stock vs. Flow**
>
> In economics, a stock refers to items you have in inventory, while a flow refers to the movement of items through your inventory over a given period of time.
>
> Applying this terminology to IT systems, a stock could be an inventory of servers, tables, rows, customers, or suppliers. A flow would be the number of orders you process in a day, or the number of customers you add in a month, the number of web pages you serve in an hour or the number of records your batch job processes during the batch window. Both sets of data are useful.

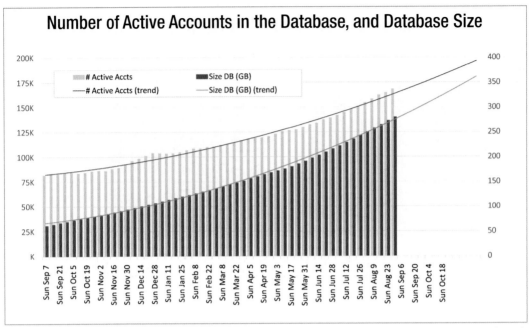

Number of Active Accounts in the Database, and Database Size

Legend:
- # Active Accts
- Size DB (GB)
- # Active Accts (trend)
- Size DB (GB) (trend)

figure 7.28. Example business entities stock graph

c. Number of business entities and/or size of data in the system

The previous two examples are measures of the flow of transactions through a system (granted the number of active users is an indirect measure of flow). Figure 7.28 is different; it shows the stock, the number of active entities in a database (e.g., customers or items for sale in a catalog).

For some systems, it is important to track this information because it can be a good indicator of load (if there is a correlation between system activity and such an entity as number of customers—this is usually true with businesses that operate on a subscription model).

Secondarily, understanding the relationship between the number of entities in the system and the amount of storage used will allow you to more accurately predict future storage needs.

Now you know not only the particulars of your patient, but you know how they are progressing since that operation you performed on them last year. Or since they gave birth. Or since they were born.

Conclusion: The Bargain

To some readers, this chapter may seem like common sense and not worth pursuing on a large scale. In response, our question would be, if you could make everyone in IT 10% more knowledgeable about your key systems at a low cost, would you? Do you think this increased knowledge would pay significant dividends to your organization's performance as a whole? Contemplate the following scenarios, considering their likelihood both with and without high-quality diagrams being available:

1. There are two testers working on testing a new release of a product. The first tester only has minimal knowledge about how the system works, and so follows the test conditions literally, even if they are wrong. He doesn't consider if there are any missing test conditions because he doesn't really know how the system works. The second tester, armed with the diagram, compares the test conditions to both the diagram and her own knowledge of the system. She finds a couple of the conditions to be wrong and identifies a whole subsystem that is missing some conditions. Which one would you rather have on your staff?

2. A consultant wants to bring in a team to write code to optimize a particular subsystem. He says that the subsystem will work twice as fast once they are complete. You agree to the work, and in the end, the subsystem is three times as fast! But that particular subsystem is not the slowest one (i.e., not the bottleneck), so the overall system performance is not improved. If you'd had a diagram, would you have agreed to have them work on that particular subsystem, or the bottleneck instead?

3. A production DBA needs to do maintenance on a particular production database that requires the database to be down. After the applications that use the DB are off-line, he takes down the database. But he didn't know that a particular web service also uses the same database, so he accidentally causes an outage in the web app. If he'd had a diagram showing all the apps that used that DB, would he have chosen that time or picked one that worked for all of the applications? (To be fair, an even better solution to this problem is to have a configuration management database and a change management process that utilizes it. Both solutions together are ideal.)

4. You need to perform an audit of all of your servers to comply with Sarbanes-Oxley requirements. There is no diagram listing them all. Where do you begin?

5. You have just hired a new SA into your organization. You want to make sure she knows what applications and hardware she is responsible for. The previous SA has already left the company. How do you get her started?

6. You're hosting a meeting with all of the managers and architects that work on your flagship application, to decide how to scale the system to support double the volume next year. You only have 2 hours to meet because it's the busiest time of year from a sales perspective. It takes 1.25 hours just to explain to everyone the nature of the problem. Would you like to have more than 45 minutes to come up with solutions and discuss the alternatives?

7. The CIO is paying you a personal visit to discuss the incident you had last Friday. You want to be well prepared and not waste her time. Where should you start?

8. If you were going to a medical facility to have tests run, or to have a procedure performed, would you like the people helping you to be part of an environment in which all key information is clearly documented and shared?

Every day, managers and technicians in your organization are making hundreds of decisions about how to feed and care for your system. Would you rather have them making informed decisions or just winging it? It takes a little effort, but it's well worth it.

Summary Checklist

✓ **Diagram:** Most IT systems are complex. Not diagramming and visualizing them can cost you in several ways:

  ◦ Time wasted speaking a thousand words instead of looking at a single picture

  ◦ Time to train new hires

  ◦ Bad decisions based on insufficient understanding of how systems work or are interrelated

  ◦ Dependency on key staff or consultants who have all the information in their heads

  ◦ Lower service quality due to poor understanding of the health of the systems

✓ **Share:** Big organizations are more effective if all their members have access to the same, easily comprehended information about complex things. Then they can focus on higher-value tasks rather than simply trying to re-collect and re-comprehend vast amounts of information.

✓ **Value:** Envisioning information effectively does come at a cost, but it's a small investment when compared to the benefits.

✓ **Invest** in diagramming in situations that are *important* and/or *complex*.

✓ **Must-haves:** Typically, IT organizations benefit from the following diagrams (at minimum):

- System interaction diagrams

- System ownership diagrams

- Data store diagrams

- Data flow diagrams

- Application dependency diagrams

- Infrastructure diagrams

- Geo-diagrams

- Combination diagrams

✓ **Be creative:** Invent your own diagram that combines the various things that will make it useful.

✓ **Balance:** A good diagram is not too complex, yet not overly simple.

✓ **Expertise:** System subject matter experts need to be involved in creating or reviewing any system diagram, or the diagram is not likely to be used.

✓ **Combine:** Make diagrams come to life by combining static information (e.g., how a system works) with status information (e.g., health status of the system).

✓ **Quality** of data presented is more important than how fancy the representation of the data is.

✓ **Start simple:** It's perfectly fine to start with simple diagrams and enhance them as you go.

✓ **Pace:** Having high-quality information less frequently is better than having poor quality data in real time.

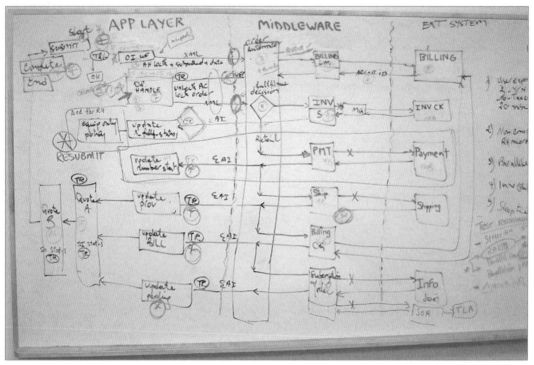

figure 7.29. Dry erase board

This is what happens when you don't have any formal system diagrams to leverage for meetings (fig. 7.29). People put it up on a whiteboard, then—poof!—it disappears forever.

Expand Your Influence

Get All of IT to Understand DRES

Chapter Overview

In the previous chapter, we discussed how to effectively transform information to make it more useful. Here, we'll discuss how to make that information further your organization's success in even greater ways.

At the core of this chapter's message is the notion that using facts, data, and analysis in a completely transparent way across the whole IT organization can make the entire organization work toward your quality goals. In addition to giving specific examples of scorecards and health reports, we discuss how using this information in various forums builds alignment and business success.

Money Makes Data Interesting

At the beginning of the 1980s, the mutual fund industry experienced dramatic growth as more and more people sought to invest in the stock markets. This created a great need for comprehensive and objective information about mutual fund performance, so investors could make informed decisions.

Seeing a demand for this information, Joe Mansueto created a company in 1984 to do just that. By providing useful, informative, and objective data and analysis to the individual investor, his company emerged as a leading source of investment information. They did it by effectively, consistently, and reliably presenting facts, data, and analysis. Simply put, people were willing to pay for useful information—regardless of whether the news was good or bad.

When Joe's company published positive information, like a fund outperforming a benchmark, their business grew. When they published negative information, such as an entire sector of funds underperforming the market, their business grew. They told the good, the bad, and the ugly so that their customers would have the best information available.

But wait, it gets better! When investors began to make informed decisions using this data, mutual fund managers took note and focused their efforts on driving improved results and greater investment. Investor confidence grew, and the entire mutual fund industry and, indeed, the entire investment industry grew at record rates.

The company Joe Mansueto founded is Morningstar, which is now a publicly traded company with a market capitalization of more than 1.5 billion dollars. They are one of the most recognized names in the investment industry and serve more than 4.9 million investors, 185,000 professional financial advisors, and 750 institutional clients around the world.

We're here to tell you that in order to reach the top of the pyramid, you need a Morningstar within your IT organization. When you publish, actively market, and communicate the useful, informative, and objective data and analysis about your systems, regardless of whether the news is good or bad, everyone will benefit in the long run from improved system quality and customer confidence.

The DRES Publishing Imperative

The Downtime, Response times, Error rates, and Scalability (DRES) data you've harvested and started to use is extremely powerful and has the same potential as the financial information published by Morningstar. It is certainly possible to use your newfound data in a vacuum, making things better internally, and building a fence around your department to the outside world. The main reasons for doing so would be to keep outside troublemakers from meddling in your affairs, and keep you from having to explain your mistakes. In short, it's less work.

However, if you do practice isolationism, you'll only be getting half the possible benefit from all of your data-harvesting efforts. Instead of just leveraging your direct reports, you can leverage all of IT to make your systems better the same way good data and analysis drives the growth of the investment industry. It's time to get the word out and let everyone benefit from what you're doing. So where do you start?

Scorecards

The best way for your department to track mission-critical DRES data is to create monthly or twice-monthly detailed scorecards (or one big scorecard with several sections). Typically for each of your key applications you'll want to create the following reports (the categories will be no surprise at this point):

- A downtime scorecard

  - Including the following summary data:

    - Number of incidents per month for each month over the past year, in a chart

    - Availability per month (or better yet, Business Impact Index points) over the past year, in a chart or graph

    - Any large trends that significantly impacted the month

  - With detail in a spreadsheet on every incident that happened over the last month.

- A response times scorecard

  - Including the following summary data:

    - Median client response times compared to previous months (oftentimes it is valuable to have the 90th percentile as well, to see what the slowest times are like)

      - Broken down by transaction type

      - Broken down by geography (if applicable)

      - Broken down by time of day/day of week

      - An error rates scorecard

  - Including the following summary data:

    - Overall error rate

    - Rate compared to previous months

    - Rate by transaction type

    - Rate by error type

> **TIP**
>
> It's probably okay to pilot your monthly scorecard on an internal basis only, but as you gain confidence, you really need to expand your sphere of influence to all of IT.

- Including the following detailed data:
  - Rate by day
  - Correlation to any known system events
- Including the following error correction-related data:
  - Queue depth—how many unfixed errors exist right now?
  - Queue age—how old is the oldest unfixed error right now?
  - Effort to fix—how long does it take your people to fix the various types of errors?
- A scalability scorecard
  - Including the following summary data:
    - Business transaction volume (demand data)
      - Actual historical
      - Projected based on IT's data
      - Projection provided by business
    - Load on system
      - Broken down by subsystem
    - Load projections
    - Areas of concern
- An overall summary scorecard

Many of the possible elements of such a scorecard listed above were covered in chapter 7. Here we will highlight a few more that are specific to reporting the current health of a system, often in context of the goals or SLAs held by the organization.

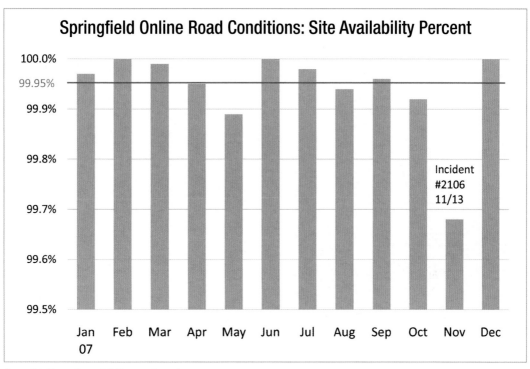

figure 8.1. Example availability trend graph

Downtime Status Charts

Here are two charts (figures 8.1 and 8.2) that clearly show the downtime experienced by two different web sites over the past 12 calendar months. In figure 8.1, it is expressed as percent availability…

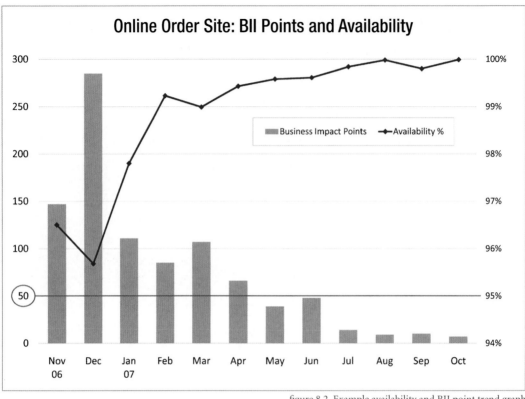

figure 8.2. Example availability and BII point trend graph

…and in figure 8.2 as Business Impact Index points (and availability).

The presentation in both of these charts is quite simple, making both the trend and the adherence to the quality goal easy to discern at a glance.

Response Time Status Charts

In some respects, displaying response time data is the same as for downtime. For instance, knowing the monthly trend is still important. Yet for response times, it pays to break the data out in several ways, such as geography or business function being executed. And lastly, because individual responses can have a wide distribution, you need a way to express that as well. Will a simple average or median do the trick, or do you require something more sophisticated?

The power in a simple tabular format as in figure 8.3 is that it can be sent out multiple times per day to any interested parties to communicate simple operational status. It is also easily displayable on most mobile devices.

```
                    Pager Activation Performance
               for Pager Activation in BC AB SK NT YT

Jan 8 2009

total    median    [  < 3 min  ]    [ < 10 min  ]    [ < 30 min  ]
  #       secs     #       %        #       %        #       %

Billing Account - time to set up a customer acct in the billing system
3187     7         3184    99.9%    3185    99.9%    3185    99.9%

Provisioning - time to activate in the switch (pager can receive pages)
13840    29        12975   93.8%    13790   99.6%    13811   99.8%

Order Completion - time to complete an order in all necessary systems
13840    42        12202   88.2%    12511   90.4%    13101   94.7%
```

figure 8.3. Example completion time status in tabular format

Even though the data is compact, it shows the volume of transactions over a given timeframe for several different key transaction types, along with the median execution time, and the number and percent complete within various thresholds. That's a lot of data!

Note that fig. 8.3 only shows a point in time with no historical data present.

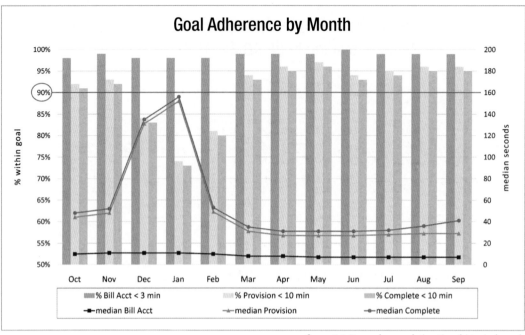

figure 8.4. Example completion time historical graph

For less frequent communication, the diagram in figure 8.4 gives a graphical representation of the data in the previous table, allowing the display of extensive historical data and trends. Of course, this also shows if the goal is being met or not.

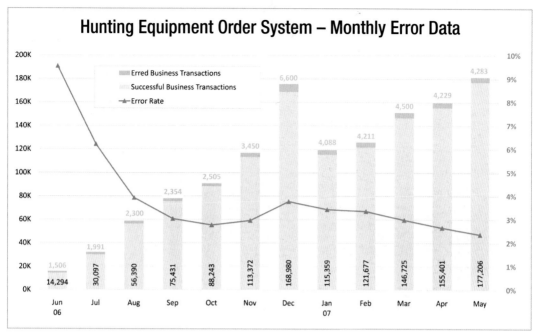

figure 8.5. Example error trending chart

Error Rate Status Charts

In figure 8.5 we have another trending chart, in this case for error rates over time.

If your transactions require some sort of provisioning function (credit card check, billing, shipping, etc.), it is important to keep track of the volume of errors compared to your total transaction volumes. These types of errors not only endanger the customer experience but also take manpower to fix, costing you money.

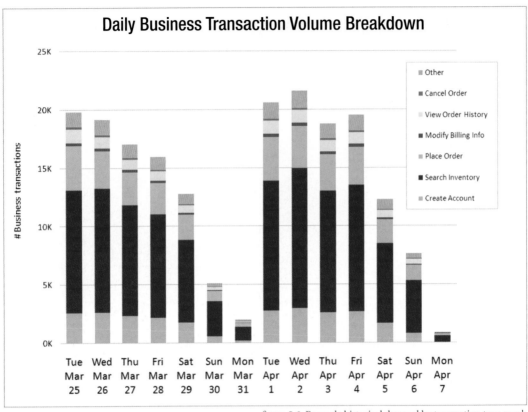

figure 8.6. Example historical demand by transaction type graph

Scalability Status Charts

The main point of scalability charts is to help the reader understand the system's capability to scale into the future. Generally, the first place to start is demand data. If projected demand is flat, there is not too much of a scalability concern, while if demand is projected to increase, there is reason for concern.

The example in figure 8.6 shows the short-term historical view day by day. It also breaks down the business transactions by type. A stacked column graph for your key transaction types gives visibility into overall transaction volumes as well as highest volume transactions. It's worth noting that volume affects all areas of DRES, but it's most significant in the scalability arena.

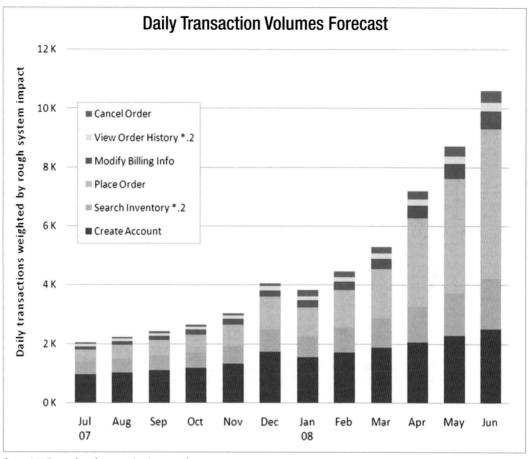

Daily Transaction Volumes Forecast

figure 8.7. Example volume projections graph

The chart in figure 8.7 shows a volume projection into the future, month by month. Still leveraging the stacked bar, it does two clever things. First, it explicitly adds in an increase in transactions that is expected due to an external event (in this case, the winter holidays). Second, it takes note that not all transactions are created equal in terms of system load, and thus devalues the less-intense ones in the chart so as not to overrepresent their importance.

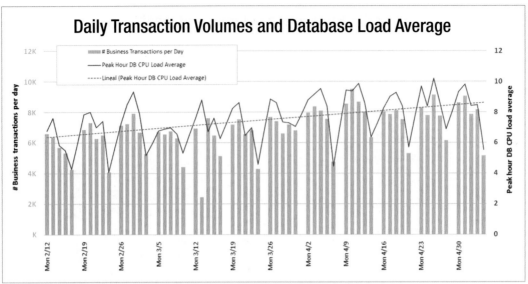

figure 8.8. CPU consumption by business transaction

Next, we move into the technical aspects of scalability. One thing that often makes sense to graph is the relationship between supply and demand. This is easiest to do when a system has a well-known Achilles heel, because then you can simply graph the subsystem in question. Otherwise you might need to graph all subsystems until you have a feel for the data.

In figure 8.8, the DB is the area of concern, and you can see with some precision how the CPU consumption rises as the number of transactions increases over time. While that ratio should be interesting to a technician, it may not be suitable for a widely distributed health status report. But it is an excellent stepping stone to figure 8.9.

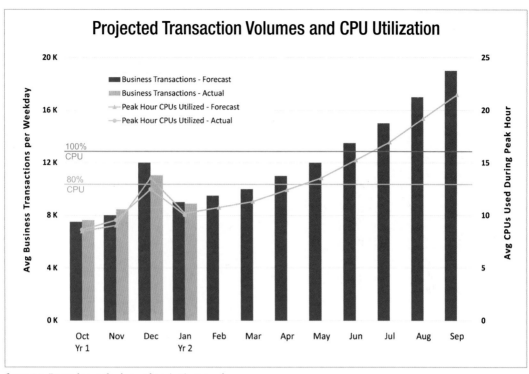

figure 8.9. Example supply-demand projections graph

In figure 8.9 we combine the growth projections with the supply and demand data. The bars are the projections of future business transactions. The moving lines use the ratio derived in the previous graph to estimate the resources needed (in this case, as in the previous example, DB resources) to complete the future transactions. And the red horizontal line shows how many resources are actually available today. So in this case, you can see that there is real concern that, starting in July, the system will be in trouble from a scalability perspective.

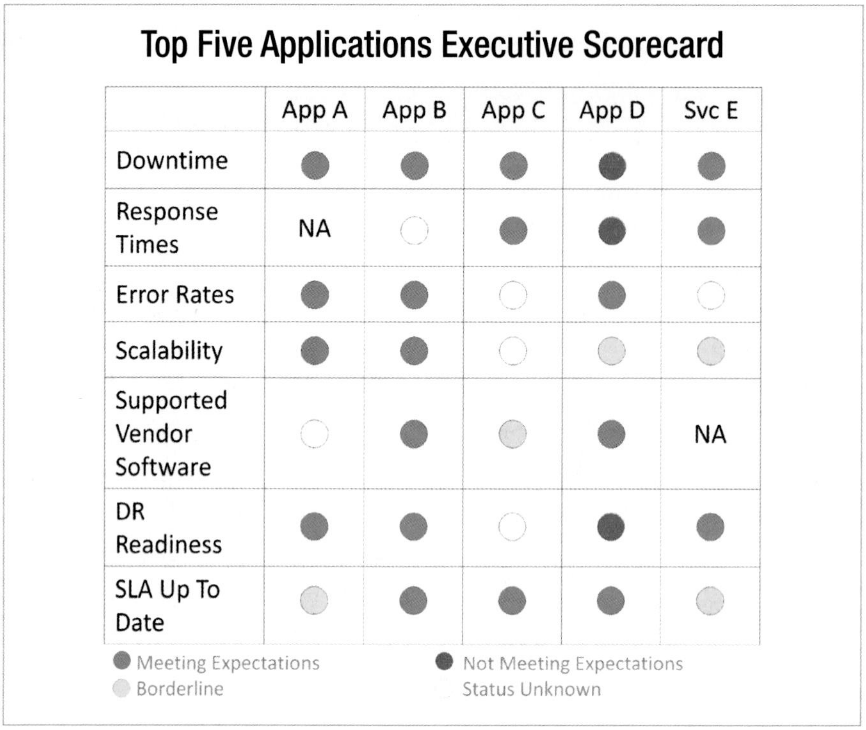

Top Five Applications Executive Scorecard

	App A	App B	App C	App D	Svc E
Downtime	●	●	●	●	●
Response Times	NA	○	●	●	●
Error Rates	●	●	○	●	○
Scalability	●	●	○	○	○
Supported Vendor Software	○	●	○	●	NA
DR Readiness	●	●	○	●	●
SLA Up To Date	○	●	●	●	○

● Meeting Expectations   ● Not Meeting Expectations
● Borderline   Status Unknown

figure 8.10. Example combined status chart

Combined Status Chart

Sometimes, for simple presentations or hallway displays, it is helpful to capture the health status of key applications along with the execution status of key projects all on a single page (fig. 8.10).

The value here is in being able to see how either a single application or a single area of concern is faring at a glance. It is also a very useful tool for the less-formal monthly quality discussion with your management team.

Bringing It All Together

In addition to all of this data, you'll want to provide context. What does the data mean? Morningstar readers don't only want to see the returns and expense ratios— they also want valuable analysis, such as an interpretation of risk, what exposure the fund has to certain sectors of the economy, and observations about the fund manager. This insight helps guide Morningstar's customers to better decisions.

Similarly, if the primary DB server only has 12% headroom, you should call out that if no action is taken it will start to fail in X months. Fill in the blanks so even semi-technical staff and managers get the point.

If you have urgent messages, make sure to put them on the front page (like a newspaper) so that people who only browse are sure to see the message. Don't just bury the good stuff on page eight, as many people will not read beyond page one. But you need to have the detail pages, because it will benefit your technicians, and it gives your publication credibility.

Here is a sample of some items you might consider putting on page one, because they resonate so well with senior management, who are least likely to read your full report:

- **Red alerts:** One or two lines at the top of the page bringing attention to key messages that require awareness (issue, risk) or attention (help from management)

- **Historical summary:** Key numbers over time, with red/yellow/green indicator for select items from the bullet list above

- **How the systems are performing relative to the goals:** Recap what the targets in each category are and what the numbers are for the period, again with red/yellow/green indicators

- **Problem management summary:** Your top 10 problem list and the status of each item in the list

If you want the report to be about more than system health, problems, or lack of problems, here are examples of other important categories you can add:

- **New capabilities:** Significant system capabilities that have business value

- **Upgrades that add value or reduce risk:** Important proactive steps that have been taken to support the business

In figure 8.11 we provide a sample of just such a front page for a status report. This one page contains just enough detail for executives. The following pages would give more granular views of what's on page one, using detailed graphs and tables, such as the ones shown in the previous pages.

Doveryai No Proveryai

Demanding these scorecards will create work for someone. But in addition to having the data available for you and your staff to utilize, it's also a way to guarantee that no stone is unturned for more than a month, because it's transparent. You and everyone

Monthly Production Quality Status Report

Monthly Production Quality Report

April 2009

- Primary DB server is predicted not to meet scalability needs by July or August

Historical Summary

	Apr 08	May 08	Jun 08	Jul 08	Aug 08	Sep 08	Oct 08	Nov 08	Dec 08	Jan 09	Feb 09	Mar 09	Apr 09
Downtime	Yellow	Red	Yellow	Yellow	Red	Yellow	Green	Yellow	Red	Yellow	Green	Yellow	Green
Response Times	Yellow	Yellow	Yellow	Yellow	Yellow	Yellow	Yellow	Yellow	Yellow	Yellow	Yellow	Green	Green
Error Rates	Yellow	Yellow	Yellow	Yellow	Green	Green	Green	Green	Yellow	Yellow	Green	Green	Green
Scalability	Green	Green	Green	Green	Green	Green	Green	Yellow	Red	Red	Yellow	Yellow	Yellow
Peak User Count	855	850	863	869	878	896	912	947	1003	1064	1068	1083	1095
Member Count	1.06M	1.06M	1.07M	1.08M	1.08M	1.10M	1.11M	1.17M	1.25M	1.26M	1.26M	1.26M	1.26M
Avg # Wkday Bus. Trans.	26,002	26,258	26,348	26,421	26,648	26,570	26,586	28,326	30,614	31,018	31,351	31,249	31,256

Production Quality Status

Quality Area	Status Color	Detailed Status			2009 Goals
Downtime	Green	*Metric*	*Result*	*Status*	• <15 BII points per month
		BII Points	6	Green	• 99.95% availability 5am-11pm in our
		Availability	99.98%	Green	core web sites
Response Times	Green	Avg page load speed	2.3 secs	Green	• Average page load speed <4 seconds
		90th % page load speed	8.1 secs	Green	• 90th percentile page load speed <10
		Order readiness avg	27 secs	Green	seconds
					• Orders ready to pick avg <5 min
Error Rates	Green	Failed orders	0.62%	Green	• Order error rate <1%
		Client app crashes	370	Green	• Client application crashes <1/user/mo
Scalability	Yellow	DB Server CPU avg peak hour	87%	Yellow	• 20% headroom available on all core
		Network bandwidth avg pk hr	45%	Green	hardware during peak hour
		Avg batch window remaining	27% (1:36)	Green	• 20% batch window free on average

Problem Management – Top 10 outstanding D-R-E-S problems

#	Action	Status	D	R	E	S
			Impacts To:			
1	CPU limitation on DB server – moving non-essential activity off-peak	In progress				Y
2	CPU limitation on DB server – plan to move to newer HW	In progress		Y		Y
3	Recent ISP instability – working with vendor	In progress	Y	Y	Y	
4	CPU limitation on DB server – Index rebuilds not completing on schedule	In progress		Y		Y
5	CPU limitation on DB server – Retest of core app with new packet size	Just started		?		Y
6	Optimization of DB Server caches. Need to study current cache behavior and try out various configurations in load test before deploying to prod	Not started		Y		Y
7	Web server logs not being archived	Not started	Y		?	
8	Batch window at end of month processing almost at limit	Not started	Y			Y
9	Audit of vendor software – several pieces no longer supported	In progress	Y	Y	Y	Y
10	Project Eureka launches in Nov – need to get in front of it from a production quality perspective	Not started	Y	Y	Y	Y

figure 8.11. Example page 1 of a production quality status report

else can see the trends for each system and subsystem. Instead of trusting that your SAs are on top of everything, you'll know. Do you think Morningstar would risk taking a month off because things will probably be the same as they were the previous month? Not a chance.

Teams must work on the assumption that the biggest problems will tend to hide out under those unturned stones. If you haven't had a close look at an important system lately, you really have no idea if it's about to blow up or not. Having that paranoia in your DNA is key.

> "I think I could sum up my position on this with the recitation of a brief Russian proverb 'Doveryai no Proveryai.' It means trust but verify."
>
> —Ronald Reagan, New York Times, Dec 4, 1987

Then there's the issue of how to manage the folks who are running your applications. President Reagan used the phrase "trust but verify" in reference to reductions of Soviet nuclear weapons at the end of the cold war. Trust but verify—it's actual managing instead of crossing your fingers. If you trust your technicians to take care of everything for you, you'd better have 100% first-rate technicians or you're going to get burned. Heck, you'll probably get burned anyway because the technicians won't have the big picture like you will. And really, what value are you adding at that point? Just approving expenses and deciding raises?

It's important to be involved in the details and know what's going on. You don't need to micromanage every decision, but if you're going to spend a million dollars, or put a system in jeopardy that does $10 million a week in revenue, you'd better know what you're doing. And that comes along with being involved.

Publishing the Monthly Health Report

You're already producing the monthly health report showing the state of Downtime, Response times, Error rates, and Scalability. So polish up the reports and start sending them out every month, like clockwork. Think of it as similar to direct marketing. Morningstar doesn't keep their information to themselves. They make sure it's available to as many people as possible in the most informative and useful formats possible. In fact, the more people who see their data and make decisions based on it, the more valuable it becomes. The power for you is in getting the DRES facts and analysis out there for people to incorporate into their system management activities.

Start by sending the monthly health report to every manager in IT who touches the products you deal with, as well as SMEs and your boss(es) up to the VP level. Sift through your e-mail to see who you think would benefit from having the information. Make this information available in centralized repositories like the intranet so even non–directly impacted parties can access it if they're so inclined. Others can see the power of the analysis techniques even if they don't work on the system in question. You'll know the concepts are taking hold when you see other groups in IT begin to adapt them based on your example.

What you're shooting for is to empower all of IT to work in the best interests of your application. People make decisions based on the information available to them. If the managers in development are not aware of the basics of what's happening in production, they are not going to consider production when they make decisions. However, if they know that you are close to having a scalability crisis, they may make sure that the next release of their product will be manageable in scope and not have any risky/untested items from a scalability perspective. And even if other groups don't take the initiative to help you out, you are armed with enough data to influence them and their bosses to do the right thing.

Also, you will become the historian for your applications. When people know that if they make a decision that negatively impacts production, it's going to come up in your report, they might think twice about taking unnecessary risks.

Few people may initially read your five-page document, but after word gets out, you're going to get a lot of requests to be added to the distribution list. I suppose that's another caveat here: once you start publishing, you really can't stop! This information's like Velcro—we didn't know we needed it, but now that we have it, we're not giving it up!

Is Your Company Political?

If you're in a political environment, you might confirm with your boss that it's okay to send production quality reports to other VPs and the CIO.

Also, be very careful of adding non-IT folks to the distribution list. We're not necessarily saying it's a bad idea; depending on the nature of your organization and the relationship between IT and the business, it can be helpful, by improving your alignment on operations-related issues, and giving more transparency to the business about what you're working on and why. But at the same time, we'd be extremely cautious about adding business leaders to the distribution list, because you are being honest about problems, and business leaders could use this data to beat up your own CIO, which will get you in hot water. One way to make sure this won't cause problems for you is to explicitly ask your boss or your boss's boss for permission to add them. Another safeguard is to ensure that the contents of your report are consistent with anything that might be included in the CIO's own scorecard that business leaders have access to.

In a perfect world, a disciplined company shouldn't have to worry about this problem. It's politically astute to watch out for the CIO, but the healthiest of companies don't behave in a way that gives IT an incentive to hide its problems. This publishing methodology is all about confessing to problems and getting them out in the open—not hiding them. You'll have to make the call on what kind of company you work in. We hope it's one that doesn't confuse accountability with blame and punitive actions.

These reports will really take on a life of their own. People will ask for new data to be added, and in some cases it makes sense, in others it doesn't. You have to know where to stop, because if your report is too long or it rambles, people might not take the time to digest your key messages. And while we are big fans of measuring, it is possible to spend too much time measuring and not enough time "doing."

Another tip we'll reiterate from the previous chapter is to make your scorecard as simple as possible via the use of straightforward graphs and charts. Take examples from everyday life, such as the weather forecast or the stock ticker (or Morningstar!). Look for ways to make your key messages so easy to understand that it only takes a minute and your audience has it, correctly, every time. Study our samples in chapters 7 and 8 and go from there.

Be Wary of Frosting

While it is important to have the data in a format that you can make use of, there is such a thing as going too far. You may be tempted to create a series of real-time dashboards on your intranet, with flashy graphics and a slick interface. Hey, there's nothing wrong with that—unless it distracts you from the core mission of gathering relevant data and acting upon it.

If you're spending 30% of your effort maintaining your web site (and customizing it to add in the new things you realize you should be tracking), you've probably misallocated your resources. Make the priority collecting the correct data and making sure it is accurate. Oftentimes, some scripts, a spreadsheet, and a rich text document will do the trick just as well. There's nothing wrong with using the web to track important operational statistics—just remember it's the frosting and not the cake.

Actions Speak Louder than Words

While Morningstar publishes financial analysis, it's the investors and the mutual fund companies themselves that actually use the data to drive change in the industry. Investors make investment decisions based on this data, and mutual fund companies like Fidelity know this, so they strive to improve their performance. Take a look at Fidelity's marketing materials and it's clear they strive to achieve Morningstar's highest ratings for everything from fees to return on investment. Morningstar data seems to be one of the important benchmarks they use to tell how well they are doing and to make adjustments and changes when needed to improve performance.

The same is true with system quality. There's more to publishing than just putting your facts, data, and analysis on paper and sending it out or placing it where folks can see it. It needs to be the data that actually informs and drives stability and scalability initiatives. Once you've got a Morningstar within IT, make sure the rest of IT starts acting like Fidelity and embraces that data and analysis, and uses it to drive system quality.

Monthly Leadership Alignment Meetings

The monthly leadership quality alignment meeting is the key next step to turning your published data into actual system quality results. This will keep all of your system stakeholders focused on what's truly important, and it is a great forum to brainstorm new ideas and forge cooperation among adjacent departments. You'll want representatives from system administration, database administration, sustainment, data sustainment, architecture, and probably others.

Why monthly?

While we have found that a monthly recurrence for the Leadership Alignment meeting is generally the right pace, we recognize that a different rhythm might be more appropriate for your organization, depending on a number of factors, such as size, culture, existing alignment, state of the systems, maturity of the organization, etc. Generally, higher-frequency meetings will cause reactionary behavior and generate too much overhead, while too low a frequency prevents you from correcting course as quickly as needed.

The desired outcome for the meeting is for everyone to have a common understanding of what the current health of production is (see the Monthly Operational Review example in the appendix), and also to support whatever projects may need to take place to shore up problem areas. If a suite of applications is healthy, this meeting can be quite short and will get poor attendance unless you keep making it worthy of everyone's time. One way to ensure this is to use the meeting as an opportunity to focus on the future. Discuss what's coming from the business, or what's going on in the marketplace and in the industry. On the other hand, if there is trouble brewing, then the meeting may need to run long and will likely feature a packed house.

Problems will be identified in these meetings, and you shouldn't tolerate much finger-pointing when they are. The tone should be, "Okay, we've got three serious problems. What are we going to do about them and in what order?" And that doesn't mean that if the SA team has a serious problem they need to pull themselves out of it alone. The entire team needs to pull together to come up with the best holistic solutions.

If you do have a team or department that is routinely not meeting expectations, meet with them on the side to help them improve, and, if necessary, make personnel changes. That is not to say that people necessarily need to be fired—rather, perhaps some people are in the wrong jobs, aren't trained well enough, are lacking resources, or don't have clear enough expectations. Having to let someone go is rare, but it does happen.

Quarterly All-Hands Alignment Meetings

As noted in later chapters, you will also want to have another formal review, quarterly, with your entire department, from the most senior manager to the most junior analyst. The discussion probably shouldn't be as detailed, but it serves a similar set of purposes.

Besides the length of the invite list, the other key difference between this meeting and the manager meeting is that you have your managers do most of the presenting—you're just an emcee here. These "all-hands, state of the union" meetings achieve the following:

1. **They energize and motivate the troops.** You formally praise them for improvements made, and conversely they know they have to report any failures in front of all of their peers. You can also impart a sense of urgency to them by translating the issues of the department into how they are affecting the business. Your staff will rightfully feel more "in the loop" and important. It's a cocktail party for geeks. They love it.

2. **They get everyone on the same page.** It makes them familiar with the DRES lexicon, and makes them aware of key issues and activities being undertaken by your department. When Jack from Team A gets a call from Suzie working on Team D that she needs help with a departmental imperative, they are much more likely to pull together than if Jack's never heard of what Suzie is talking about. Also, all members of the department are made members of your think tank, coming up with ways to improve DRES. It will also keep them from stepping on each other's toes—they'll be less likely to undertake activities that are contrary to your prime initiatives. There is a sociological aspect to this as well: IT people are often introverts. True problem solving begins to happen when people are acquainted and interacting. We used to joke that all of the best cross-functional IT partnering happens in the smoking area—because the biggest cross-functional team of all is smokers![18]

3. **You will build up useful capital.** When you generate enough buzz about what your department is up to, that you are organized and have a plan and are executing that plan, word is going to get out. Your guests and guest speakers are going to spread the word that you know what you are doing. While good for the ego, more importantly, this translates to leadership capital. When you are seen as a positive force in IT, and you need to ask for something, you are more likely to get a favorable answer. Can we slide release Z for one week to make sure the quality is there? Can I have $200,000 for a new test environment? Can I break the hiring freeze to bring on these two key personnel? This is not to say you should ask for the moon every time the opportunity arises, but when spent carefully, your leadership capital can make a world of difference in the success of your endeavors.

So could you do all of these things if you kept your data limited to your direct reports? We didn't think so!

---

18 Note: The authors are not endorsing smoking in any way, shape, or form.

Tri-level communication is a powerful way to align the different layers of management to accomplish key objectives.

Your VPs and CIO may wish to have a regular review as well. This three-tier approach, simultaneously cementing your message at the line level, manager level, and senior leadership level, can be extremely effective. In a manner of speaking, it becomes a positive form of propaganda, wherein your message becomes the dominant production message in IT, and, to a certain extent, activities revolve around it. Assuming you're making informed decisions from the best data possible, this is a good place to be.

Get Off of My Cloud

There is a final benefit to mention when it comes to being organized: choosing what you are going to work on based on facts and data and goals, and then telling the world about it. Remember, you are setting the agenda!

Your boss is not going to worry that you don't know what you are doing. She may have input on how you do your work, but she also knows that all of your cards are on the table, and you are operating in the best interests of the company, and she will be updated as things progress. Most of the time, this will make your boss very satisfied, and she will not consume too much of your time with extraneous requests. The bottom line is that employees who are clearly doing good work are more likely to be left alone.

If, however, you are in the unfortunate position of having a boss who doesn't get it, then at least you are in a defensible position. If she wants you to summit Mt. Wastemore for no discernable reason, you can ask how that's going to improve DRES, and also ask which folks you should pull off of DRES-centric activities in order to make it happen. Good times.

Switzerland

In your published reports and leadership meetings, you'll want to be careful to remain as objective and neutral as possible. Remember, if Morningstar's reports had significant issues with accuracy, or if they were perceived to be playing politics, the harm to their credibility would put them out of business in a heartbeat. They know that their reputation for neutrality, accuracy, and objectivity is their most valuable asset. If a mutual fund's performance underperforms its benchmark, has the highest fees in its class of funds, and is, in general, a dog, they don't say the fund manager should be fired; they just report the facts.

If you name names, you are going to make the offenders mad and start a war. The reports should be as objective as possible, and when events are necessary for context, the passive voice should be used. Instead of "Team X accidentally brought down the server again," say, "The server was accidentally brought down during the online window." You'll also want to give the manager of the offending team an apologetic heads-up about the mention in the report so he doesn't get blindsided. Focus on the problem—not the offender. Everyone knows who the offender is anyway.

Since you are being vague in the reports about "whodunit," you are probably going to get called with questions. This is not your time to burn bridges, either. If it's the clear responsibility of one team, do feel free to say so, but if your own folks were even a 10% contributor to the problem, stand in there with them and take some of the heat. You need to err on the side of taking blame (perhaps even using the Perkins Maneuver from chapter 4), so that everyone can move on and start focusing on solving the problem at hand. The political capital you build by doing everything else right will weigh much more than the mistakes you must admit to. You also need to be perceived as being fair, even overly fair, so that people will take you seriously and not just think you are playing political games. If you get caught in just one act of skullduggery, it will tarnish your next 100 statements. So don't—just be neutral and fair when it comes to blame, and move on to solutions as quickly as possible.

This advice on office politics may seem like minutiae, but it is terribly important. To be an effective manager in a large IT organization, political awareness has to be part of your skill set.

Conclusion

Just as companies like Morningstar fill the need of reporting facts, data, and useful analysis about mutual fund performance, your IT organization needs to provide the very same service with regards to your major IT system(s). You need to be publishing and actively communicating your technical teams' analysis so that it becomes an institution within IT. You also need to be tailoring the reporting to communicate the information in the most useful ways possible, being careful never to compromise your objectivity or even your perceived objectivity.

Mutual fund companies frequently use Morningstar's data to market their funds and boast of their success. You'll know you've created a Morningstar within IT when you see various teams referencing DRES data (like Fidelity does with Morningstar's data) to track their own progress and accomplishments. When this happens, you're nearing the top of the pyramid.

Summary Checklist

Create the equivalent of a Morningstar in your group to improve your organization's focus.

- ✓ **Transparency:** Openly publishing key facts and data (good *and* bad) about your systems and services will benefit you and the entire organization.

- ✓ **Trust but verify:** Rigorously publishing DRES data ensures you don't have to hope that all important metrics are being tracked and reviewed regularly.

- ✓ **Publish** summary DRES results for your key systems to a wide audience to give broad transparency into your system, its challenges, and upcoming plans.

- ✓ **Leverage:** Over time, more transparency will result in increased leverage; all who have an impact on the data published will exhibit more and more positive behaviors.

- ✓ **Reinforce** these positive behaviors by taking the following actions:

  - ○ Run regular leadership alignment meetings to discuss and act upon the data published with key stakeholders

  - ○ Host quarterly all hands alignment meetings with the entire department to motivate the teams, get everyone aligned, and build organizational capital

- ✓ **Neutrality:** In publishing data, remain neutral and focus on problems, avoiding finger-pointing.

- ✓ **There's more!** A nice side benefit of doing all this is that it's great for career building and upward managing.

Perpetual Motion

What do we mean by perpetual motion? Well, we've layered dozens of techniques on top of each other to help you and your business succeed. Apply these techniques consistently, and you'll do great things.

The problem is, there's a lot to keep track of. It can be exhausting, especially for the leaders. So this level of the pyramid is all about how to achieve momentum, giving your quality program a life of its own (like a snowball rolling downhill), but make sure it's targeted toward the things that will make the biggest difference to your business (we don't want your snowball randomly rolling over anything in its path!).

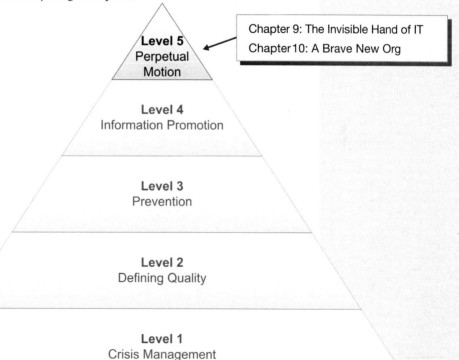

Chapter 9: The Invisible Hand of IT
Chapter 10: A Brave New Org

Level 5
Perpetual
Motion

Level 4
Information Promotion

Level 3
Prevention

Level 2
Defining Quality

Level 1
Crisis Management

CHAPTER 9

The Invisible Hand of IT

Get All of IT to Work for You

Chapter Overview

If your job involves leading individuals, teams, or organizations, effective goal setting is critical for unleashing the creativity and resourcefulness of your entire staff, enabling you to leverage them on a wide scale in ways you never imagined possible.

In order to achieve aggressive and highly beneficial IT production quality targets, you need to formalize departmental quality goals. These goals should be very specific, measurable, and oriented around DRES. They should also be rolled out as part of a formal program so that they will be taken seriously. Doing so enables everyone in your organization to make decisions on a daily basis that will get you closer to where you want to be. People will do things that you didn't know were relevant or even possible to improve quality. This chapter gives guidance on how to make it all happen, including innovative IT-specific tips.

The Value of Quality Goals

In a special address to Congress on May 25, 1961, President Kennedy challenged the nation to send a man to the moon and return him safely to the earth by the end of the decade. It was a bold and lofty aspiration, and it was also clearly and concisely communicated: only a sentence was needed. It was immediately comprehendible, measurable, and highly relevant—not to mention inspiring. As a result of this remarkable challenge, NASA created the Apollo program. The Apollo program used a series of clearly defined and measured incremental objectives (Apollo missions 1 to 10), which led to that momentous day on July 20, 1969, when Neil Armstrong, as part of Apollo 11, took that first step on the moon, more than 226,000 miles away from the earth.

Cont. →

Before it became a reality, this staggering achievement had to first be a goal. A clearly understood objective that thousands of people in the space program, the associated private sector contractors, Congress, and the entire American public could rally behind and use to focus their collective energies. Both quantifiable and measurable, Kennedy's throwing down the gauntlet made it unequivocally clear how we would know if we had succeeded. Not only was it understandable, quantifiable, and measurable, it was also relevant and meaningful to the country that saw the space race as a critical battlefront in the Cold War and a spectacular achievement in the advancement of all mankind.

A Goal for the Ages

"I believe that this nation should commit itself to achieving the goal, before this decade is out, of landing a man on the Moon and returning him safely to the Earth."

–*John F. Kennedy*, May 24, 1961

We believe that one of the best things we have going for us when managing large IT systems is that they are easily quantifiable and measurable. This allows us to leverage the power of managing to tangible, objective goals. A goal is an objective goal if there is a straightforward way to determine whether you are making progress or not and there is no talking your way out of it—you either succeeded or you didn't.

This is a huge benefit; don't squander it. Clearly defined and quantifiable system quality goals provide the finish line toward which to point all of your strategic and tactical efforts. In fact, they become the rallying cry for your entire organization. Goals did this for NASA's Apollo program, and they can do the same for you. The power of goals is compelling and has been proven over and over again both empirically and anecdotally. A good goal is the first step toward any remarkable achievement. Well-defined goals

- **Set and reinforce priorities.** Rather than having your people work on whatever they judge to be of importance, you can establish a global view of what the top things are to help the business succeed. NASA could have engaged in thousands of different types of space exploration, but Kennedy's challenge forced them to zero in on manned space travel.

- **Demonstrate leadership commitment.** Written, clear, formal goals provide sustained alignment of your group's activities, whereas a speech may have less lasting effect. Employees may be skeptical whether you are serious or not if it's all verbal—because verbal directives often change quickly.

- **Encourage alignment of teams**—particularly when common goals are shared across multiple departments.

- **Provide motivation.** You should not have a single staff member who doesn't know what your group is aiming for and why. Smart people like to work for leaders who have a clear view of where the organization is headed.

- **Drive management alignment.** Whether your organization uses status reports, dashboards, or scorecards, your goals will be the foundation for the metrics you'll use for upward status communication. Who's more likely to be in the good graces of management, the team that is making great progress against highly meaningful and clearly defined objectives, or a mystery team on which no one is quite sure what their focus is or how well they're doing?

> ### The Invisible Hand
>
> Your staff will undertake dozens of actions every day in order to keep things running. You can't micromanage them all, and even if you could, you wouldn't want to, because you don't have the detailed knowledge that they do. By setting system quality goals and letting your people figure out some of the ways to hit them on their own, you are empowering them, and those hundreds of decisions will mostly be made in your favor.
>
> Employees hate being micromanaged, but they like being managed.

- **Drive customer alignment and trust.** The business sees you charging hard on the things that matter to them the most.

- **Enable more informed decision making.** When your managers and staff are faced with tough decisions, they can ask themselves "what is going to best help us achieve our goals?"

- **Allow achievers to productively exercise initiative.** By setting the end goal and not necessarily figuring out all the details, your folks will exercise their own resourcefulness, innovating new ways to achieve them. With a nod to Adam Smith,[19] we refer to this action as the invisible hand of IT.

What Is a Good Goal?

It's clear that you need goals, but creating them effectively is the real challenge. We've found that effective system quality goals always meet four important criteria. They must be:

Quantifiable

We're called computer *scientists*, and we should act like scientists. Too often, IT teams act on spotty empirical evidence and anecdotal information. That's not science; that's guesswork *pretending* to be science. Goals such as "Have the best system quality" or "Achieve world-class quality" are not very useful goals because they are

---

19 Adam Smith, 1723–1790, Scottish philosopher and political economist, noted in several of his written works that the "invisible hand" of economic supply and demand encouraged people to take actions that were in their own best interest, and coincidentally those same actions would be good for society as a whole. While not perfect, we find it to be a useful analogy.

qualitative; how are you to know if you've gotten there or are on track? What would have happened if President Kennedy had said something like, "We should endeavor in the future to achieve great things in our space program"? Do you think we would have ever actually achieved something like the moon landing in less than 10 years?

It's the same for system quality goals. Quantifiable system goals state specific, tangible targets like "Meet or exceed 99.96% system availability" or "Reduce outages 50% over the previous year." Most system quality goals should center 100% on empirical data—the more objective and quantifiable, the better and more useful the goal is. Unquantifiable system quality goals tend to be for superficial purposes only, wasting time and burning up credibility with your customers, peers, and staff.

Measurable

We define measuring as being able to capture system behavior data to show if things are getting better, getting worse, or staying the same. If you can't measure it, it's generally not a real goal (although if you can't measure it today and have an intermediary goal to start measuring it in the future, then that can work just fine). Not only must it be theoretically quantifiable, you must also be able to effectively capture the results you're getting to prove how well you're doing.

Significant (Yet Achievable)

The holy grail of mountains to climb is Everest. Why? Because it's the highest peak in the world[20] and incredibly difficult to summit. We know how hard it is to climb because of the countless unfortunate souls who have perished in that thin air. Jim Collins cleverly refers to these overarching goals as Big Hairy Audacious Goals, or BHAGs.[21]

The flip side of being significant is being achievable. We talk later about making sure your goals are difficult yet reasonable. Goals that are perceived to be impossible will de-motivate your troops and encourage them to give up before they even get started. You need complete buy-in to be successful.

System quality goals don't have to be the equivalent of scaling Everest or going to the moon, but they must be relevant or nobody will care. Would you work long hours or put forth extra effort to achieve a goal that doesn't matter to anyone? Management support, budget support, and resource support are all the more likely to come your way if you're working to solve the problems that are the most relevant to your company.

---

20 We know that K2 and some other peaks are technically harder to climb, but you hear the most about Everest, which is 29,028 feet, or 5.5 miles above sea level.

21 Jim Collins, *Built to Last*, p. 9.

Understandable

Goals have to be intuitively understandable if they're going to reach people, take hold with them, and get you to where you need to go. Breaking the four-minute mile, wiping out smallpox, sending a man to the moon and returning him safely to the earth, or achieving the unconditional surrender of Nazi Germany in WWII are just a few examples of goals that were intuitively clear in a single, concise statement. The ability to communicate a goal so that others can understand it is essential to putting in motion the actions necessary to achieve the goal.

A fairly well-known variant on our philosophy of what a good goal looks like is SMART. While the origin of the SMART acronym is unknown,[22] most commonly SMART refers to goals that are:

- Specific

- Measurable

- Attainable

- Relevant

- Time-bound

Are your goals SMART?

Align System-Quality Goals with Business Objectives

One of the keys to choosing significant system quality goals is to align them with the most pressing needs of the business. Management visionary Peter Drucker was among the first to point out the danger of workers who endeavor to do the work that matters to them rather than what is needed to make the enterprise succeed. He correctly observed that when employees don't understand how their work impacts the business, "Their efforts are wasted. Instead of teamwork, there is friction, frustration, and conflict."[23] Don't let your system goals be seemingly arbitrary technical objectives independent of the business. Whenever possible, your system quality goals should contribute directly to critical business objectives. The more critical the business objective, the better the system quality goal that helps achieve it should be. Doing this helps ensure proper IT alignment with the

> ### Motivation Tip
>
> People want to know how what they do matters. If you can relate to them how their actions are important to the success of the company as a whole, that will go a long way to keeping them engaged and motivated.

---

22 Good information on SMART can be found at both http://edis.ifas.ufl.edu/FE577 and http://www. projectsmart.co.uk/ smart_goals.html

23 Peter Drucker, *The Practice of Management* (Harper and Row, Publishers, Inc., 1954) 121.

business and also reinforces the relevance of your goals themselves. Resources will be the most focused and motivated when they know their work is contributing directly to the success of the company.

The four categories of quality (DRES) are by definition the most critical areas of system quality, and we always advise working all four simultaneously to ensure overall system health. Align your DRES goals directly with objectives of the business function your system supports. Most companies spend a great deal of time and energy defining annual strategic objectives. Leverage these wherever possible.

Business Problem	Production Quality Priority
Cutting costs	Improving **response times**, which can result in a significant cost savings if you currently have a large number of customer service representatives (CSRs) because you won't need as many CSRs to handle the same workload.
Increasing business volumes	Improving **scalability** in advance of the increased business volume. Otherwise your systems might not work.
Improving customer satisfaction	Aggressively addressing **downtime**, **response times**, and/or **errors**, depending on how well your systems are performing today.

table 9.1. Examples of aligning IT with business goals

Work with your business customers to ensure that your own IT quality goals align with their business goals. Document this and present it to your teams in the annual kickoff town hall meeting described later in this chapter. Include these associations on team goal documents and individual performance plans.

It will often be necessary to emphasize some quality categories over others depending on the business need, so don't feel obligated to weigh each of the four quality categories equally. "Scratch where it itches" is the concept to keep in mind here. If the enterprise is suffering mightily because of system downtime, it makes good sense to stress the availability goal (as long as scalability, performance, and error rates continue to be measured and managed). If scalability is what's hurting the most, focus there as long as the other three categories aren't forgotten.

You can add emphasis by making the goals in that area more challenging or by lining up more projects in support of that area. It's perfectly alright to de-emphasize one or more quality categories, but never exclude one altogether or else you risk being blindsided by problems in those areas somewhere down the road.

Overarching Moon-Shot Goals for the Four Categories of Quality

We've discussed how every goal should be quantifiable, measurable, meaningful, and understandable and that each of these should be aligned with a key business objective. The centerpiece of your system quality program should be a single, intuitive, overarching goal for each category of quality. It's your Moon-Shot goal for each. Here's an example of an effective set of high-level quality goals:

Example A

Downtime

- X% or better system availability

Response Times

- All key system transactions must be X seconds or faster

  or

- X% of system transactions must be within their SLA

Error Rate

- Less than X% error rate for all transactions

Scalability

- Less than X scalability-related outages (in other words, no system outages where root cause is related to capacity planning issues)

  or

- Meet the three DRE goals above while scaling to X users and/or Y transactions

---

All that we've done here is focus each goal in a manner consistent with our previous guidance. It's completely reasonable that you could create somewhat different overarching goals from these that are consistent with our guidance but based on different business needs. Here's another example:

Example B

Downtime

- X Business Impact Index points or less/month

Response Times

- Consistent transaction performance—transaction speeds at peak usage less than X% slower than off peak

Error Rate

- Less than X% error rate for key business-impacting transactions (e.g., revenue-related transactions)

Scalability

- Maintain no less than X% "headroom" for key scalability indicators: storage, memory, throughput, CPU, etc.

Defining Your Targets

Once you've identified your overarching goals, you should next define the specific targets for each. You'll notice that in our example goals, the targets are typically "X." This is because targets can never be universal values. Different systems in different companies demand unique targets based on the specific circumstances. For example, a system supporting emergency services for a large city might require an availability target of 100% or 99.999%. A customer service system for a software company (for which lives aren't at stake if the system goes down) may have a target of 99.9% or even lower depending on the business priorities that balance cost versus the customer needs (fig. 9.1). Again, aligning the goals with the business need helps drive the targets.

Whenever possible, a target should be defined taking into consideration the desired business result and the estimated cost to achieve the goal. A good target must be meaningful, and it also must be achievable. Ideally, you look for targets that

- meet the business requirements;

- stretch your teams to excel and overachieve;

- are reasonably achievable so they aren't seen as an impossible cause.

How Deep Are Your Pockets?

The incremental cost of many nines is exponential. Only you and your business can determine how high it makes sense to aim...and how much you are willing to spend on IT versus other business priorities.

One way to stretch your IT dollar is, instead of setting a firm goal across the board, to set tiered targets depending on how important it is to the business for each tier of applications or services to be up—more on this in chapter 11, "Where to Start."

Historical data should also be considered when formulating targets. It's important to measure current results and to factor that information into the creation of the targets. In cases in which the current state is very bad, it will often be necessary to create incremental milestones that lead to the ultimate target. We once led a turnaround effort on a major CRM system for which the availability target in the first year was 99.5% but was increased each year for several years after, until the ultimate target of 99.95% was achieved. Breaking the goal up into challenging but achievable incremental targets allowed the teams to focus on something within reach. Had we made the ultimate goal the initial and only goal, it would have felt impossible, and it would have been harder for the teams to engage. Instead, the incremental targets created focus and generated a feeling of momentum and progress.

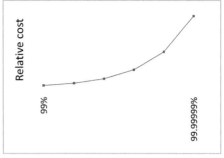

figure 9.1. Availability-cost relationship

Even though it's ideal to understand the desired end state you're shooting for, it's not mandatory in order to define meaningful incremental targets. We once worked on a system scalability crisis in which it was not clear what the ultimate error rate should be, due to the immaturity of the business processes and the system itself. It was, however, well understood that the current rate was too high and was negatively impacting business. In this case, our error reduction target was completely based on incremental improvement. We challenged the organization to reduce the error rate by half within the next six months. When that goal was accomplished, we challenged the team to reduce it by half again in the following six months. During that time, the business processes matured, and it became clear that business would be optimized with a specific error rate target percentage. That number became the annual target for each year afterward.

Contributory Incremental Goals

Before Apollo 11 went to the moon, there first had to be a series of incremental achievement that led to the ultimate achievement. Apollo Missions 1–10 accomplished numerous smaller but nonetheless essential goals, such as unmanned orbiting of the earth, manned orbiting of the moon, separating and re-docking the command module and lunar module, and numerous others. It's the same with system quality. Once the overarching high-level quality goals and targets have been defined, it's necessary to establish detailed intermediate goals that lead to the overarching goal. These lower-level goals should always point to one or more of the overarching goals and should be more granular and detailed. They can then be assigned to a specific team or individual. Every overarching goal should have multiple lower-level goals that contribute to its achievement.

These goals can be harvested from your very own team. It is fair to say to your own line-level managers, "Here's where we need to get to. How do you all feel we can best get there?" They in turn can seek input from their own personnel. You don't have to accept everyone's suggestions, but listening and selectively harvesting the best ideas will (rightfully) make them feel involved in the decision-making process, and they will be more likely to work hard to achieve success.

Getting the Right Skin in the Game

> If the act of choosing and communicating these goals and sub-goals seems daunting, fear not, as there are examples and tools to help out in chapter 11, "Where to Start."

In order to go to the moon, many companies partnered with NASA to design and build all of the complex vehicles and systems. Given the limitations of time and the complexity of the mission, it was simply too much for the government to attempt on its own or for the work to be shared only by a few firms. It was a team effort of epic proportions that was worked on by literally hundreds of thousands of people.[24] For example, the defense contractor North American Rockwell built the command module that took the astronauts into space, while their competitor Grumman built the lunar module that was used for the actual moon landing.

How could two separate companies, located in different parts of the country with different corporate cultures and processes, who normally are ruthless competitors, come together successfully? The answer is they first had to share the same overarching goal given to them by President Kennedy. Without that unifying objective, they're simply two separate organizations—both trying to perfect their individual contributions without the alignment needed to achieve the ultimate objective. This was exemplified in the movie *Apollo 13* in which, after an explosion crippled the spacecraft, you saw the various contractors rallying together at Mission Control in Houston to safely bring back the astronauts.

In most medium- to large-sized IT organizations, it's common for system quality to depend on the contribution of numerous teams who often fall under separate management chains. The DRES goals are higher level and often span these multiple organizations.

However, we often see the quality goals, where they exist, heaped 100% on the production-oriented teams. This creates two significant problems. For one, the production teams may be hesitant to buy into a goal that requires the contribution of other teams who do not share that goal or sometimes even have conflicting goals, because they feel that they do not have sufficient control over the outcome. Secondly, the other teams that do not share the production quality goals are not motivated properly. We've consistently found over the years that division-level quality goals shared across key teams can be a powerful unifying factor that facilitates partnership and teamwork.

---

24 See *Team Moon: How 400,000 People Landed Apollo 11 on the Moon*, Catherine Thimmesh, 2006.

We once observed a situation in an IT organization in which the production operations team had a well-defined and well-measured availability target of 99.95% for a large-scale system that had been recently deployed. The development organization, however, was primarily driven by goals related to implementing releases by certain dates with specific functionality. The development teams had no stake in the availability goals at all. In fact, they were only vaguely aware of how the production system performed except via hallway conversations and other word of mouth. The system was in crisis with frequent outages.

Our analysis revealed that in this case the primary source of instability was related to numerous code issues. We also found development almost exclusively focused on releases containing new functionality rather than bug fixes for these problems. This is a classic example of how unaligned goals lead to an undesirable system result. Once the system was stabilized, we implemented new and more sweeping goals that were shared across departments, including development. These shared goals addressed downtime and the other three categories of quality, in addition to their important functionality and delivery date goals. Once the development managers shared the same quality goals as operations, a remarkable thing happened: the two groups aligned their problem-solving efforts and quality rapidly improved.

Once stability improved, an interesting thing happened: code releases of new functionality began moving into production even faster than when the development had been completely date driven. The improved system stability created a more predicable production and work environment that ultimately allowed for more frequent deployments.

Goal Weighting

Once you've defined your goals, it's time to get skin in the game by formalizing them with your people. In order to achieve accountability and cross-functional alignment, all teams with a significant contribution to your system's quality should own the quality goals. Normally, these would be teams such as production operations, systems administration, production support, development, architecture, and possibly more.

However, based on their respective contributions, you may want to use percentage weighting as a way of ra-

---

The Development Divide

If your development/engineering teams are significant sources of production quality problems, there are four main approaches that can be used to improve things:

1. Ensure that the senior managers of the production/operations department have good, open, two-way communication with the senior managers of the development/engineering groups.

2. Share the exact same production quality goals across both sets of departments.

3. Dedicate a fixed percentage (perhaps 10 or 20 percent, depending on how well production is faring) of each new software release to addressing production problems.

4. Strictly enforce the quality requirements that must be met before allowing deployment of a new release.

tionalizing it effectively. Teams that work exclusively on production should have a higher percentage ownership stake than those who have other responsibilities. The specific percentage is not important as long as it drives the accountability needed to achieve the focus and ownership required to succeed. For example, a development team that is responsible for new functional releases may have production quality goals that constitute 25% of their overall targets, while a production support team that works exclusively on managing the production system might have a significantly higher percentage related to quality goals—like 80%. The important thing is to get all teams who have an impact on quality sharing the same goals even if the weights vary.

Repeated Broadcasting

In order to align your virtual quality team, whether it's made up of ten people or one thousand, it's best to formally announce these goals in an annual all-hands-style town meeting. Assemble everyone who will share these goals and present them formally and in detail. Have your managers make these presentations to demonstrate their ownership of the goals to reinforce that you're holding them directly accountable. Take questions and work through the issues that are brought up. Make sure everyone understands how the goals tie to the business results and why the goals are important. Welcome dissent, since dealing with those questions and concerns ultimately leads to stronger goals and wider buy-in. Don't fear initial conflict as it is an essential step toward achieving understanding and ultimately trust.

As noted in other chapters, to achieve focus and follow-through, hold formal quarterly follow-up meetings throughout the year to track progress, chart success, and adjust for areas that require improvement or a fresh approach. Use these quarterly meetings to revisit the purpose of the goals and to continuously educate new and old team members alike about them.

Between these meetings and the regular quality reports from chapter 8, you will have a consistent flow of relevant information that will keep your people focused. If you think there is a chance that not everyone is aware of the new mode, consider adding posters in the hallways (that specifically show both the high-level goals and the progress to date) or other advertising to drive the point home.

Linking Pay to Performance

Finally, in order to achieve the quality results you desire and to drive accountability at the individual level, it's best to explicitly put your quality goals onto the performance plans of managers and individual contributors. This directly aligns their success with the system quality results you desire. For instance, if your employees receive a performance-based annual bonus, your production quality goals are an ideal measure to leverage for at least part of the bonus. Unexpected smaller bonuses or non-cash awards for stellar quarterly or yearly results can also be effective.

There are numerous models for giving your teams extra incentive to achieve, and we have not tried them all. But if you leverage any types of bonus or recognition program, production quality should be the key driver for a significant portion of the rewards.

We have seen a program in a large company that sent the top 1% of individual performers and the most influential team on an all-expenses paid trip to a tropical resort. While not inexpensive, as long as the winners were carefully chosen based on merit, this was a tremendous motivator. Other non-cash possibilities include formally presented trophies, fancy team dinners for meeting quarterly milestones, and signed congratulatory cards from the CIO. Numerous programs can even be used in combination, giving you a rich set of options.

No matter what type of reward program you choose, you will be putting your money where your mouth is, giving production quality extra urgency and focus.

Evolving to a Culture of Goals

Goals are a good thing. They exist to tell us what's most important and to help us know how we're doing. Goals should be used to reward success and reinforce accountability. They are not something to be feared. In our experience, when goals are defined as we've indicated, and measured in a fair and objective way, a culture of achievement develops, in which individuals and teams have the incentive to use their resourcefulness, ingenuity, and determination to achieve the required quality results.

Conversely, there are some who don't like quantifiable goals because they make it clear where success is happening and where it isn't. Those resistant to goals in our experience tend to be underachievers who fear that focus on goals will reveal their lack of contribution toward goal achievement. When implementing a goal-oriented culture, don't kowtow to the resistance of the poor performers.

A Caution About Bonuses

If you plan on utilizing cash bonuses to provide extra motivation, be extremely careful. Money accelerates behaviors and can sometimes have unintended consequences. If you bonus against the wrong objective, you will likely get the wrong result. If you bonus on some right objectives but not others, the ones left out may not happen. So definitely spend some time thinking things through.

Can Very Skilled Technicians Also Be Underperformers?

Yes. Don't assume that just because an employee has deep technical skills they are delivering the most value for your company. Very technical employees, even if they are well-intentioned, can get caught up in low-business-value side projects or stir up intense debate about minutiae. To be sure, many skilled technicians are hitting home runs for you every day, but don't presume that's the case just because they are highly technical.

Summary Checklist (Splashdown!)

Goals are a terrific tool for the IT manager that over time can help you solve your department's biggest problems and achieve great advances. Carefully select them and then leverage them to drive success. Here is a summary of how:

- ✓ **Goals:** Goals define priorities, drive alignment, and provide the best measuring stick. IT goals should always align with what matters most to the business.

- ✓ **The right goals:** The way to do that is to carefully set goals that make sense and are easy to gauge progress against:

  - ◦ They must cover the four areas of Downtime, Response times, Error rates, and Scalability.

  - ◦ They must be clear and simple to understand.

  - ◦ They can't be too easy—they should challenge your people.

  - ◦ They can't be impossible.

- ✓ **Good goals** are quantifiable, measurable, significant, and easily understood.

- ✓ **Broadcast goals:** This will help your personnel take actions and make decisions that align with the desired end result.

  - ◦ Repeat them at regular intervals so that they will be taken seriously and not forgotten.

- ✓ **Shared goals:** Your goals program can be turbocharged by having shared goals across departments where it makes sense. That way, adjacent departments are more likely to cooperate with each other.

- ✓ **DRES alignment:** Define at least one overarching goal for each category of quality (DRES). Define multiple lower-level goals that contribute directly to one or more of the overarching goals.

- ✓ **Skin in the game:** Get everyone's skin in the game. Formally assign your goals to all relevant parties and hold them accountable—even if this means spanning multiple functions. Announce the goals in public forums and hold quarterly review meetings to reinforce them and track progress. This can be reinforced by having regular public checkpoints and aligning your compensation model with goal achievement.

- ✓ **Culture of performance:** Strong performers thrive in a goal-oriented culture. Poor performers resist being measured and graded. Use goals to create a culture of performance and achievement.

## CHAPTER 10

A Brave New Org

Organize for Quality

Chapter Overview

Many IT organizations struggle with system and service quality because they aren't organized effectively. Large systems and organizations demand a new organizational approach to address these challenges. In this chapter, we will introduce the new and innovative concepts of the production excellence leader (PEL) and the DRES team. Together they form an independent entity with the expertise, focus, and influence to ensure the broader IT organization achieves the necessary quality results.

Why You Need a Symphony Conductor

Considering all the things that have to be done right for a large IT system to run optimally from a DRES perspective, it's no surprise that so few IT shops excel at it. And depending on an organization's level of maturity and self-awareness, the IT department might not even know how far from excellence it is, or it might be seeking ways to get closer to world-class levels. The recent increasing interest in ITIL, CMMI, Six Sigma, and other similar frameworks is an indication of a growing awareness, and a realization that improving the quality of IT service levels requires a disciplined approach.

In this chapter, we acknowledge that implementing all the concepts covered thus far requires not only a disciplined approach, but also clarity on organizational roles and responsibilities, and ultimately, clear ownership of and accountability for quality. What we recommend here is intended to address the complexity of large systems and large organizations and may not be appropriate for smaller IT shops.

Cont. →

In some cases, organizational accountability is obvious. For example, a disk failure is 100% the responsibility of the infrastructure group or an identified code bug is 100% the responsibility of development. But where it gets tricky is identifying ownership of the quality of the user experience holistically. There are three main reasons for this:

1. Today's IT systems are rarely self contained, but are a complex web of interrelated subsystems.

2. Many different organizations play a role in the big picture.

3. Certain functions necessary for system quality require a very specialized skill set that is unlikely to be present throughout the organization.

It's as if you have an orchestra and you want to figure out how to get it to play beautiful music! Let's take a closer look at each one of these concepts.

The Evolution of Modern Systems

There was a time in IT when systems tended to stand alone; ownership of problems was often clear. "Is the problem on the mainframe? Oh, yeah, that's Steve's group." However, over the past decade, the level of system integration has skyrocketed. Rarely do we have isolated systems. Rather, we have multiple series of interconnected systems that rely on each other for various related pieces of business functionality. There are now many more failure points, and the sheer complexity of highly integrated systems makes the management of quality much more complex.

When you look at a diagram of your systems, it is likely they are such an intricate mesh of interaction that it is difficult to keep it all straight. The hardware implementations alone can be enormous, spanning multiple data centers and countless work locations; a partial driver for this is that as disk, memory, and CPU continue to become more and more affordable, it's all the more easy to throw hardware at your scalability challenges and increase the scale and complexity of hardware implementation. Multiple network paths can be involved. In addition, multiple data stores are used. Evolving from mainframes to partially integrated client/server architectures to highly integrated, multi-tiered, web-oriented applications has moved us from the jazz combo era to the orchestra era, and as a result we must change our behaviors accordingly.

Musical Factoids

A **jazz combo** is a small musical group. One performer will often provide the tempo, while the others play off of one another. The group takes advantage of their close proximity, small size, and familiarity with each other. Improvisation is an expected and appreciated element.

A **symphony orchestra** usually has about 104 players and consists of four proportionate groups of similar instruments: woodwinds, brass, percussion, and strings. Given the size and complexity of the group, the performers look to the conductor for tempo and overall direction.

The success of the overall system is completely dependent on all of the various IT component functions coming together to deliver the desired result. If the code is working, but the hardware is down, the user sees a down system. If the hardware is up, but the code won't run, the user sees a down system. If the hardware and software are both up but not configured properly to work together, the user sees—you guessed it—a down system. In all cases, the system is just plain down, and your customer likely doesn't care why; he just wants it back up. Clearly the business looks at the system result holistically.

Synergy

Not only are the systems complex these days—so are the roles to support them. We discussed earlier how your systems need to be well defined, architected, designed, tested, and deployed; how you need to have instrumentation and monitoring in place; how you need to be able to accurately report on the health of your systems; how your organization needs to be good at troubleshooting, crisis management, change management, and capacity planning; and how alignment to a common set of goals needs to happen at a cross-functional level.

Because of this complexity, responsibility for DRES is shared across many functions—each making a significant contribution that can help ensure success when done optimally, or drive failure when not done well. Achieving the results you want for the four categories of quality requires good code, the right hardware, good network performance, all of the right production configurations, proper capacity planning, and much more. All of these functional areas within IT have to be firing on all cylinders to maximize your DRES results.

However, the functional areas can't maximize their contribution in a vacuum. It would be nice if every group in IT could just do their own thing in their own space and all of that would add up to a quality system experience. But you have numerous teams in multiple organizations that must be in sync and working together to achieve results, and each team can only see its isolated contribution. If you took a symphony orchestra and separated the strings, woodwinds, brass, and percussion into separate soundproof recording rooms with no common reference, and had them play Brahms' Symphony #3 in E flat, how do you think it would sound when you tried to mix it all together to create a CD? There's little chance that the isolated performances would meld together harmoniously the same as they would if the players had all been playing together.

> **Another Musical Factoid**
>
> A **conductorless orchestra**: The First Symphonic Ensemble was formed in the USSR in 1922. Since the government believed Marxism did not allow for one person to be above any other, it was thought there was no need to be led by a conductor. A committee was formed to lead the orchestra, which eventually disbanded in chaos. A failed experiment.

This is a challenging problem to address, but doing so is essential to achieving your quality results. Without some sort of holistic quality oversight, it's highly unlikely all of these different technical groups will end up making beautiful music together. Without some amount of overt cohesion, at best you'll get suboptimal quality results, and at worst will suffer a quality crisis or catastrophe.

Specialized Shared Functions

In IT, there are some functions that benefit from having dedicated resources. For instance, each system team can take a shot at doing capacity planning, but the quality from one team to another will likely vary, or even worse, be mediocre for all teams. In addition, even if the results were acceptable, it is unlikely that the deliverables would look at all alike across systems, making reconciliation difficult. Imagine if sheet music were not standard around the world. What would the extra burden on the conductor be if the sheet music for each type of instrument were significantly different in layout and style? "Okay, let's take that from the top of page 23. Make that page 26 for the trumpets, 5A for the strings, and 2-12 for the percussion."

Capacity planning is just one function that has become a discipline of its own that requires a certain level of expertise and experience to master. Furthermore, it is a function that lends itself well to being shared across teams. Capacity planning is not an activity that needs to be performed daily, so it would make sense to consider having a team that specializes in capacity planning and does it very well for all IT systems.

A shared model also warrants consideration for other functions, such as collecting and presenting system health data, performing root cause analysis, or managing crises. Trying to have all system teams in IT be experts at these things is one strategy, but not necessarily the best one. From efficiency, specialization, and standardization standpoints, it makes more sense to centralize these functions as a shared service for all organizations.

There's another advantage of placing ownership of some of the functions that support system quality separately from ownership of particular systems. It is the benefit of having a third party act as a neutral agent that will have less incentive to make skewed decisions, or downplay and even hide negative news. It's similar to the concept of having independent financial accounting auditors to ensure no conflict of interests when balancing the books.

Where Does the Buck Stop, Anyway?

Given the need for cross-functional teaming, the high integration of systems, and the specialization requirements of today's IT environment, where does ownership and accountability for the end-user or customer experience lie? Chances are that in your IT department, as in many others, the ownership is distributed functionally in the organization, and the CIO is the single point of convergence for all of the pieces that need to come together for the business to enjoy high-quality systems.

There's nothing wrong with the ultimate accountability being with the CIO for this. In fact, running systems at a level that enables the business to be competitive and grow should be one of the primary concerns of the CIO. This is pretty much what an orchestra conductor does—but then again, the conductor probably doesn't have to worry as much about budget, regulatory compliance, and other IT-specific issues.

So how does the CIO ensure that all of the efforts of the different teams involved lead to the desired quality results? If the CIO is the first point of integration for these cross-functional quality issues, then he's either spending a tremendous amount of time managing them or, more likely, some problems are languishing out there, being awkwardly worked around by the business or being addressed very slowly because of ownership and leadership challenges. You might see this manifested in the outage response when all of the groups report they've done their diagnostic work and have found their component to be fully functional, yet the user is still unable to work. In these instances, the various teams seem more interested in proving the problem isn't theirs than in actually getting service restored.

Typically the organizational layout of such IT departments is as follows: The CIO holds her leader of infrastructure accountable for the system hardware, her leader of development accountable for the application code, her leader of production support accountable for production management, her leader of architecture accountable for the design, etc. And the CIO is responsible for ensuring all of these different functions are working together to achieve the four categories of quality.

But how does she hold them accountable? Do they all share accountability for the four categories of quality? Do they have quantifiable quality goals specific to the major IT system on their performance objectives? Or are they all working to achieve quality goals specific to just their component of the solution, and the assumption is that the four categories of quality numbers will naturally fall into place? The CIO is the one who's on the hook for ensuring that the necessary cross-functional management is occurring, but does that mean she's the one and only person responsible for making it happen?

While overarching quality goals can certainly help, in large IT organizations, we would offer that a CIO simply can't successfully manage the complexities and fulfill her other responsibilities. It's simply too much. It's a full-time job for a senior IT leader with a highly specialized skill set devoted to delivering the system results that are needed. The four categories of quality need to be clearly and explicitly owned and managed by one or more people with the bandwidth, expertise, and clout to be effective. What you need is a conductor who can focus on making the music as good as it can be without having to book concerts or purchase advertising. The exception might be in a small organization or for a small system implementation, where this person can be the CIO. This can work and is probably preferable in smaller IT organizations with smaller and less complex major IT systems—sort of like a string quartet!

For large organizations, however, we are not advocating a one-size-fits-all recipe for organization design. How an IT department implements the function that will own production system quality must take into account the existing organizational structure and culture. But the key point is that such a function is necessary. In the following pages, we will outline one possible organizational design that has proven to be effective.

Sidebar: Would You Benefit from Having a Deputy CIO?

While not a panacea for production quality, in large IT organizations, one thing that can help significantly is the institution of the deputy CIO position. The deputy CIO typically complements the CIO by taking responsibility for overseeing operations, delivery, compliance, and/or architecture, freeing up the CIO to focus on strategy, budget, and interacting with senior leadership. In addition to being able to back each other up and use each other as a sounding board, the deputy CIO provides for sustained focus in key areas that otherwise might not be possible because the standalone CIO is spread too thin.

The deputy CIO in many ways is like the COO to the CIO. Or in the Navy, the XO to the captain. The football defensive coordinator to the head coach. It is not a unique concept by any means.[25]

Does this completely address leadership in operations? Unless the IT organization is medium-to-small, the likely answer is no, so keep reading on!

The Production Excellence Leader

The production excellence leader (PEL) is your single point of responsibility for system quality. The PEL has to be on-task for optimizing the DRES of the applications within his portfolio. With rare exception, it's the only thing he does. He's the go-to person and your expert, and he keeps sustained focus.

Recognizing the need for the PEL role is recognizing that the development/solution delivery organization is usually purely focused on delivering functionality to the business, and the operations organization is purely focused on running the system day in and day out, with little time for proactively managing DRES. The PEL is the necessary link between the two worlds. He's the person who understands that production is where the rubber meets the road, where the customer experience is being lived, but who also understands that focusing only on the daily operational aspects

---

25 For more information on the deputy CIO concept, read Polly Schneider Traylor's article in *CIO Magazine* at http://www.cio.com/archive/111501/two.html.

of production support in a tactical way is not sufficient to reach the quality levels needed by the business.

The production excellence leader owns the system quality result. He is on the hook for ensuring that overall IT efforts are achieving the quality objectives. Most of the various IT functions, such as requirements gathering, architecting, coding, testing, and even in some cases operating, don't report to him—they remain under the direction of their own leadership. But he is responsible for ensuring that these groups are working together to achieve the desired system result. Since he doesn't have to worry about creating non-production deliverables, this gives him the latitude and focus to execute on a pure production quality agenda. Further, this individual becomes an expert at virtually all the topics covered in this book, and can be a great resource for anyone in the organization seeking best practices and advice in those areas.

One way to think about this role is to make a parallel with the manufacturing process. If a company is in the business of building widgets, it likely has an engineering department that designs blueprints and builds prototypes for the widgets that the company has identified a need for in the marketplace. While the engineers should keep the manufacturing process in mind in their design, they are not the ones most preoccupied with how that process will consistently produce the widgets with high quality and low defects.

On the other hand, in the factory, there are people who come to work every day to get on the production line and build the widgets that will be used by the company's customers. Their role is just as important as the engineers' because how good a job they do will have a direct effect on the quality of the product. But the factory line workers and even the managers supervising them are not always in the best position to guarantee that customers will be happy with the overall quality of the product. They might manufacture the widgets according to the specifications, but the demands of their job (e.g., production line A must produce 7,000 widgets per day) do not allow them to take a step back and look for opportunities to make quality the top priority.

That's why so many companies from Honda to Boeing have teams dedicated to ensuring high quality throughout the manufacturing process. Those teams analyze data, report on the status of quality to senior management, identify the quality goals, implement quality improvement programs, and communicate the importance of quality to all involved in the manufacturing process. To be sure, these quality teams rely heavily on input from the folks working the line, but they have the luxury of taking a step back and being strategic—and that is a function every significant operation dearly needs.

> ### Wacky Thought
>
> If the PEL had a motto, it could adapt BASF's famous advertising slogan: "We don't make a lot of the products you buy. We make a lot of the products you buy better."®

The PEL is akin to the person owning the quality assurance program of a firm's manufacturing operations. It's not necessarily the person to whom the engineers or the people on the factory floor report, but it's the person the CEO will want some answers from if the company is faced with a situation in which a batch of products with significant defects made it into the hands of paying customers.

The Right Type of Person for the Job

So how do you find this uniquely qualified person, your quality conductor? Here are some traits to screen for. To be effective, a PEL must have the following qualities:

1. **An effective PEL must be organized** in order to keep track of all of the significant activities happening to systems in her purview. Change requests, releases, and maintenance activities must be actively scrutinized and monitored to make sure that they do not negatively impact DRES. The PEL also needs to know the current health of her systems at all times. Spreadsheets and scorecards are a PEL's best friends! (This is the only one of the four criteria that could potentially be supplemented by a PEL's staffer. If you find a great PEL who's strong in points two through four, you might still be in business.)

2. **An effective PEL must be goal-oriented**, not so much in terms of his own personal career goals, but rather in terms of his departmental goals. The PEL must be able to create tangible, specific IT goals (with substantial input from all stakeholders) that will directly improve life for your business customer. All of the people who directly and indirectly work for him must understand the criticality of goals impacting DRES, and know that the PEL takes them seriously and is going to stand by them, quarter after quarter, year after year. Ultimately, this leads to building a culture of objective, measurable quality.

3. **An effective PEL must be able to manage laterally**. Most managers can direct their own folks with reasonable success, but here the PEL has to ensure that peer teams (generally this means upstream teams, too) are all on the same page, because if not, they can cause significant harm to production. There are a variety of techniques to do this, but it boils down to being proactive in partnering with your peer management. This includes managing vendors as well. PELs will only have limited success in isolation. Depending on the political environment, the PEL must be politically savvy as well. This can be a very tough job if the various IT teams don't get along and trust each other.

4. **An effective PEL must be able to understand technology**. Over and over, decisions will have to be made regarding technology. With rare exception, a nontechnical manager will be limited in her ability to contribute to difficult technical decisions, and in some cases, even if she is a good manager otherwise, will have a hard time winning over key staff (or, for that matter,

the CIO). While a PEL needn't be an amazing technologist, ideally she will have previously been a software tester, developer, administrator, or operator at some point during her career.

PELs can have a variety of backgrounds, leadership styles, and ways they go about their business. But without the four key criteria above, you'll be hard-pressed to make great gains.

Does this sound like a tall order? Perhaps. But the PEL is a key role that can turbo-charge your production implementations. You can't just grab your nearest idle PM and expect him to make it happen, but once you find the right resource, things will evolve from being at risk to being within plan.

The Balance of Power

There's another role that the PEL plays. In IT, there is often an issue with balance of power between development/engineering/release management and production/operations management. In many cases, releases are pushed out with varying levels of quality, and the production managers are expected to install the software that they receive, cope, and make it all work. Oftentimes, decisions are made that harm the enterprise, while the correct risk-reward decision is not made. In part, this is because the production team is underrepresented in the decision-making levels of IT. Sufficiently empowered, the PEL helps remedy that deficiency, restoring the balance of power.

Note also that if you have a very large number of systems, it may be appropriate to have multiple PELs, who can divide up the systems to shoulder the load. Three hundred systems may call for five or ten PELs, depending on the size and complexity of the systems.

The DRES Team

The PEL needn't have a large direct headcount, but there is one especially key team that must be under his direct purview. This team can of course be given many suitable names, but for the remainder of the book, we will call it the DRES team. Many IT organizations don't have a DRES team, but most of them should.

Your mainline production teams are often strapped for resources to perform their core jobs. They are often too heads-down loading tapes and responding to requests and alerts to take the time required to determine the most beneficial improvement ideas, and then lobby to get those things done. That is where the DRES team steps in.

The DRES team's purpose is to focus exclusively on the four quality goals and track (and sometimes lead) the strategic efforts in place to ensure you hit those quality targets across all of IT. The DRES team doesn't have to be large, and the frontline production technical resources typically aren't on it. In support of the PEL, the team needs to be empowered by management to work the goals and set the direction needed to achieve them. They contribute to and execute on the strategy to achieve the quality goals and track and publish the overall progress. The DRES team has to have strong technical acumen, excellent communication ability, and above all, outstanding judgment. After all, they determine if IT leaders should sleep soundly, be very nervous, or something in between.

DRES Team Tasks and Deliverables

It is ultimately the production excellence leader's call as to how much scope he wants to undertake on his DRES team. This will partly depend on whether other parts of the organization already have ownership of some of these functions. We will list here all the functions that are great candidates for being owned by a team with no direct affiliation to a given system.

- **Monitoring:** Establish best practices, provide expertise about monitoring solutions, perform proof of concepts. In some cases, perform actual monitoring.

- **Root Cause Analysis:** Analyzing, researching, investigating issues, and recommending fixes. Authoring, educating, and implementing best practices to prevent future occurrences.

- **Subject Matter Expertise** on the biggest and most common causes of poor production quality. For example: SQL tuning or network round-trip analysis. Working with peer groups to improve problem areas. This includes working with upstream architecture, development, and test groups to help them address current production issues that impact DRES.

- **Diagramming:** In chapter 7, we pointed out the importance of having diagrams that depict various aspects of your systems and organization. The DRES team is well suited to create those. They not only have the skill set, it is also a great way for them to further their expertise in the systems they support.

- **Capacity and Scalability Planning:** Includes publishing past and forecasting future user and transaction volumes, predicting future load-related failure points, and recommending actions to ensure the systems will scale to meet demand.

- **Performance and Scalability Testing Methodology:** Few IT organizations are really good at performance and scalability testing. Even those with big quality assurance departments often focus mostly on functional testing, or just don't know how to make performance and scalability testing truly useful. The DRES team can add value by establishing a common lexicon and approach to performance and scalability testing.

- **Quality Tracking and Planning:** Analysis and trending of previously captured data related to the four quality categories. Steering activities designed to shore up deficiencies. They can even be on the lookout for ways to make DRES improvements when there isn't even a problem per se.

- **Regular Status Reports:** For all of the above. Relaying historical and current data on the state of your top systems in regard to the four quality categories.

- **Firefighting Assistance:** If the teams who own various systems are having trouble resolving a difficult incident, DRES team members can step in to assist.

The DRES team is the production excellence leader's eyes and ears, arms and legs. Essentially, it drives all the things discussed in previous chapters. What the DRES team doesn't do are all of the day-to-day activities necessary to build and run your systems. The DRES team doesn't do that work, but rather ensures that all of that work is leading to the right quality results.

While the DRES team is the key execution branch of the PEL, other functions may roll up to the PEL as well. This will in part depend on who the PEL reports to himself. For example, if the PEL reports to the person who has the highest level of ownership of a system, that system owner might want all things related to production to report to the PEL, including database administrators, system administrators, support analysts, etc. If the PEL reports to the CIO and oversees multiple systems, owning the DRES team for multiple systems may be plenty of scope.

The Various Roles on a DRES Team

Staffing your DRES team is as much an art as it is a science. You certainly need clearly defined skills, but you also need some intangible qualities. The conductor's job of selecting musicians for the various chairs is a tough one! In the case of DRES, above all else you require smart people who are technically curious—the kind who want to know how things work and why they don't when they're broken. The kind of people who will take apart a watch just to see how it works, but who also have the skill to put it back together again in working order. Or the kind of people who are content to spend their entire day hunting for forensic evidence. Not people who just try to randomly find a needle in a haystack, but those who use technical astuteness to invent useful needle-finding devices like metal detectors or x-ray machines. To be sure, these folks all are classical music enthusiasts, yet they play a wide variety of instruments. Here are the common types of roles you'll need to fill.

Thinkers, Researchers: Here you need people who are technically skilled, who love to solve complex problems and get their hands dirty. They need to obsess over the problem that is hurting you that nobody else can figure out. They need to scour logs, keep track of various hypotheses, and test them in a lab. They need to belong to user groups on the web to share ideas, and they need to bounce things off of architects and senior developers. They love having access to large data sets and enjoy sifting through them to draw conclusions.

In this category, you may need some folks with deep skills in some areas, but you also want your collective team, if not some individuals, to cover all the tiers of a typical IT system architecture (client, network, web servers, application servers, database servers, and storage). Some of them also need to understand the software development process enough to be able to discuss technical issues with architects and developers.

Ideally, a certain percentage of these folks will feel comfortable working with other teams to turn their discoveries into actionable outcomes. Not all of them need to be able to do this, but some of them do. There is certainly room for a fair amount of introverted personality types on the DRES team, but if it starts to go far north of 50%, you may have trouble getting certain types of activities done.

Firefighters: Similar to above, except these people thrive on pressure, have good instincts, and can get you out of a serious jam in a hurry (without being reckless). These folks need to know production intimately and be very detail oriented. These people aren't necessarily good at managing their own time or long-term projects. But when fire strikes, they are there and in charge, and you sleep easier because of it.

Measurers/Trenders: These folks are moderately technical, and are in charge of monitoring, measuring, trending, and synthesizing key technical data to help your department effectively run their systems. They are the analytical types who pore over logs and comb through mountains of data, looking for trends and problems, and who can take that data and convert it into useful charts and graphs. These resources need to have strong technical ingenuity for gathering and manipulating data.

They alert you and your relevant staff when there is a danger sign, they produce regular summaries of key health indicator data, and can create projections that help you decide when to order new gear or be concerned of a software scalability bottleneck. These folks have to be able to leverage third-party tools, write custom automated scripts, and be careful about double-checking their results to eliminate mistakes before the larger community leverages their work.

Project Managers (PMs): You will find over time that your technicians will uncover great projects that need to be done on the production side to achieve your objectives. Perhaps indexes need to be standardized across many homogeneous databases. Maybe server permissions need to be reduced from where they are today. Or maybe several third-party monitoring tools need to be evaluated.

Some of these projects will cross various departments, and a PM from the DRES team is ideally suited to execute them. A good DRES team requires effective project managers to drive initiatives cross-functionally to completion. It's worth noting that production-oriented PMs are significantly different than development PMs, because the environments they have to navigate (engineering vs. operations) work much differently than each other. You can certainly convert one PM type to the other, but not instantaneously.

This role is critical to the DRES team success; if you try to go with 100% technical resources, you are going to have challenges making big changes happen. These PMs are the ideal complement to your technical resources, which may have the skill to find problems and propose solutions, but are like a bull in a china shop when it comes time to actually drive that solution. These are also the folks who have the communication skills to help produce your critical written status communications.

Documenters/Publishers: Most of the folks above will not be skilled at creating quality reports for general consumption in IT and for senior management. You are going to have a lot of great data at your fingertips that they are going to be thirsty for. You need someone to create these high-value reports. Accurate, intuitive reports increase your team's credibility and enhance your group's ability to hit quality goals because the group will easily be able to measure their progress. Don't skimp here! Sometimes you can find a PM who enjoys doubling as your production writer.

Manager(s): The DRES manager has a tough job. The peer teams don't always voluntarily cooperate with DRES, so a lot of lateral managerial skill is involved. Also, the DRES team tends to attract a very diverse set of individuals who bring a lot of high-value skills to the table but are also harder to manage, in part due to the heterogeneous tasks involved. In a way, the DRES manager is the strategic arm of the PEL, and a logical choice for succession to the PEL role.

So you're looking for a Level 5 leader. Someone who leads from the front but with confidence that comes from having the right ideas, not using intimidation or scare tactics. In this book, we elaborated on "the power of the problem." That's the power you have when you're focused on solving the problems that really matter. When you're working to resolve the most critical problems is when you can amass the greatest organizational momentum. Your DRES team leader must have the self-confidence and humility to put aside petty politics and just care about getting the problem solved. He doesn't seek glory for himself, but takes great satisfaction in hitting the quality targets and giving all of the credit for doing so to the technical teams. Objectivity and the use of facts and data are essential to his success.

> ### Level 5 Leader
>
> In Jim Collins's fine book, *Good To Great*, Level 5 Leadership is the most effective level, distinguished by the ability to blend humility with professional will.

Staffing Tips

Assembling such a team will take time. However, you can actually start with just a clarinet, a violin, a harp, and a percussionist. You needn't have all the roles filled to be able to make an impact. You may actually want to start small and have a few victories before you take it to the next level. One benefit of this approach is that you will build a reputation that will attract talented individuals, which will make your job easier when trying to convince candidates of the value of your team.

Recruiting a diverse team from across IT yields two further benefits: you diversify the technical skill set of your team, and you also gain political insight/leverage from each department that you've successfully recruited from.

> **TIP**
>
> Allow a certain number of introverted types onto the DRES team, but don't go overboard—the team has to be able to work with peer teams to get certain things done!

Also, the DRES team should customize its staffing skill set requirements where necessary to address the specific challenges the systems face. For this reason, it's often advantageous to leverage at least some contract labor to supplement your core team with specific contractors who possess the skill to address the particular technical problems that are most pressing at any given time. When the system in question is third-party software or looks like it might be hardware related, it's usually a good idea for the DRES team to have at least one professional services person from that vendor, even if only on a part-time basis.

DRES team members need to be of the mind-set that their job is to make others more successful in the technical teams actually out there on the front lines. These teams should see them as friends, not foes. You need folks who will be assertive but not come across as threatening to these core teams.

Lastly, keep in mind that even if unsuccessful in your initial employee recruiting efforts, the DRES team can have great leverage by utilizing non-DRES resources across the organization—that's right, people who aren't even directly on your team! And come budget time, you don't have to pay for them either. Sometimes team managers will be caught up in how much headcount they have, and meanwhile, you'll be borrowing resources to do great things. It's not an altogether bad setup.

Who the PEL and the DRES Team Should Report To

The PEL will usually be most effective as either a peer of the most senior person designated as the system owner, or reporting to that person. For instance, if a VP owned both operations and development of a suite of 50 applications, the PEL should probably report directly to her. Usually, this is the person who also owns application development, but it can vary greatly in different IT shops.

Keep in mind while figuring out where to place this role that neutrality can be of great benefit to the DRES team. This is particularly true in political environments. It is possible to have situations in which DRES comes from the development side of the house and, as a result, operations distrusts it, and vice versa. (If your conductor also plays the tuba, will the clarinets take her advice seriously?) One possible solution to this is to position the DRES team in a neutral department outside of development and operations. For instance, in a "gray area" group that contains deployment and conversion, which are also teams that require extensive interaction with both development and operations to succeed.

To build on the manufacturing analogy used earlier in the chapter, some companies have the quality program leader report to the product group leader; some have that person report to the person in charge of manufacturing, while others make it a direct report to the COO or CEO.

All that said, the key to the success of the PEL and the DRES team isn't so much reporting relationships as it is sponsorship from IT senior management. If the leadership of IT is clearly committed to PEL/DRES, and everyone knows this, then they will be best positioned for success. What's important is that the function exists and has the endorsement of, and strong support from, the top.

The Perfect Concerto

Production excellence also requires organization and clear responsibilities. While many things discussed in previous chapters can be leveraged sporadically throughout IT teams, the best way for large organizations to see measurable improvement for all of the critical systems, and to increase the whole organization's maturity level, is to have a PEL focused on the quality goals and a DRES team specialized in executing them.

A small jazz band doesn't need a conductor. They can rely on the drummer to provide enough leadership that they can just improvise and be successful. But for extremely complex systems with large numbers of teams to support them, you need a solid quality plan to thrive. And you need a specialized form of leadership to execute that plan—the conductor and his helpers.

When you consistently leverage the material in these last few chapters, you're in PMM Level 5 territory. Congratulations, and enjoy the beautiful music.

Summary Checklist

✓ **Organizational challenge:** Large, intertwined systems have numerous teams to support their various parts, which has made comprehensive quality management complicated.

✓ **PEL:** Just as a symphony requires a conductor to ensure a successful musical performance, large IT systems may need a production excellence leader (PEL) to deliver holistic system quality results.

✓ **Accountability:** The PEL is your single point of accountability for system quality.

✓ **Matrix management:** The PEL owns the quality results but not all of the teams who support the system(s). Just as the conductor owns the musical result yet doesn't personally play all of the instruments.

✓ **PEL qualities:** The PEL role is highly challenging and requires a highly effective leader who is the following:

- Well organized

- Goal-oriented

- Agile working across boundaries

- Technically adept

- Politically independent

✓ **DRES team functions:** The PEL leads the DRES team, which has the specialized skills and roles intended to make all of IT more effective:

- Monitoring

- Root cause analysis

- Subject matter expertise

- Capacity and scalability planning

- Performance and scalability testing methodology

- Quality tracking and planning

- Quality status reporting

- Firefighting assistance

✓ **Roles:** The types of resources needed for the DRES team are the following:

- Thinkers/researchers
- Firefighters
- Measurers/trenders
- Project Managers
- Documenters/Publishers
- Managers

✓ **Executive support:** It's not so important who the PEL reports to, as long as there is the proper endorsement from the CIO.

Where to Start

How to Get Impressive Results Quickly

Chapter Overview

Taking all of the guidance in this book and applying it to your application portfolio may seem like a gargantuan task—like walking up a giant pyramid. The key to making it manageable is to prioritize. The best factors to prioritize on are

- relative application importance;

- relative importance of D vs. R vs. E vs. S for your most important applications;

- what is most broken in terms of production quality.

In this chapter, we offer a few simple frameworks to help get your IT improvement initiative successfully off the ground. This information will be particularly helpful to leaders in very large IT organizations, though smaller IT shops will benefit as well.

Targeted Improvements to Your Portfolio

In the preceding chapters, we have discussed numerous concepts you can use to improve the production quality of your applications in IT. But assuming you have a large portfolio of applications to take care of, it can certainly seem overwhelming. Level 5 (Perpetual Motion) might appear to be a very long way away.

Table of Contents

If you've ever been involved with remodeling a house, you also know that such a project isn't completed in a day,[26] or even a month. Why? Because it's very unlikely that you can work on all of the fixes at once.

Assuming you don't have unlimited funds at your disposal, you might have to live in the house while you remodel it. Or you might choose to continue to live in it during the process just to avoid the inconvenience of moving. If you're living in it, how can you do work in every room at once? Where would you put your stuff? Where would you spend your free time?

And even if you were willing to move, would you have the bandwidth to effectively manage all of the various projects at the same time? Probably not. Will any of the projects conflict with each other? In the same room, can you replace plumbing at the same time as you paint the interior and refinish the flooring? Not really.

But wait, it gets better. Now imagine you were a landlord of 30 buildings, and they all needed remodeling. What would you do?

This is a conundrum that we share in IT, yet it's a solvable one. What if instead of buildings, you had 30 applications in various states of disrepair? What would you do then? The short answer on how to make the most of your limited resources is to:

- Prioritize by application

- Prioritize by goal family

- Take it one step at a time

Relative Application Importance

The first way to make the task of ascending the Production Maturity Model (PMM) pyramid more manageable is to cut scope. You probably have over 30 applications in IT for your business, and you may well have several hundred. If you tried to get all of them to PMM 5 within the same short timeframe, you'd need an army of DRES team members. And even if you had them, your IT department probably couldn't absorb that much change rapidly.

If you were a landlord of 30 buildings, and they all needed remodeling, could you decide which ones to work on first? You probably could. One way to take a first cut would be to examine the business value of the buildings. For instance, which ones provide the most rent? Which ones have leases that are coming up? Or which do you think would provide the most rent after the remodel? Perhaps you are able to divide the buildings into categories, with rents of over $10,000 per month, rents between $2,000 and $10,000 per month, and rents less than $2,000 per month. The

---

26 Except on TV.

top category may only be four of your buildings, but what if it represented 60% of your rental income? That's income you'd want to protect, but if you could do it by only upgrading 13% of your properties, then you've already cut down the complexity a great deal.

Money might not be the only deciding factor. Maybe the city is on your case because three of your mid-tier buildings don't meet code. It would probably be worthwhile to add them to the list of properties you care the most about also. Maybe one has the mayor's office in it, or a school. Maybe one houses a restaurant, which brings its own set of health and safety requirements.

IT is a similar animal. Our applications and systems vary a great deal in what they do. Some are so critical that the business would cease to function without them. Some are so noncritical that when they break, nobody notices for hours or even days. And there are loads of applications somewhere in the middle. As in the landlord example, depending on your business, it might be possible to know the dollar value, to the business, of your key applications and to use that data for stack ranking. Or you may have a very clear sense from years of exposure to your applications of what is truly important. But more likely, you'll need to gather some information and make some judgment calls.

Beware of using your gut too much here. If your classifications are based more on art than science, you will open yourself up to skepticism and possibly resistance. Where possible, try to identify and leverage the key criteria that make a system important. Below is an example of a simple classification mechanism you may use:

- Sustains the life or well-being of people (e.g., operating room systems)

- Ensures the security of people or assets (e.g., cardkey entry systems)

- Generates revenue for the organization (e.g., point of sales systems)

- Is used to manage customer relationships or customer satisfaction (e.g., product registration systems)

- Supports internal back-office or administrative functions (e.g., HR, accounting, etc.)

Such a classification approach is simple and shouldn't be too controversial. People can usually agree under which category applications should fall. However, in a large portfolio of applications (some IT shops have thousands), this is not granular enough. Too many applications may fall in too few buckets. In that case, additional criteria can be used to refine the classification mechanism. Here are some examples of such criteria:

- Number of concurrent users

- Number of business transactions per hour or per day

  ◦ Dollar value of business transactions per hour or per day

- Internal use only vs. customer facing

- Supports business-to-business functions

- Supports business-to-consumer functions

Depending on your own situation, you might think of other useful criteria. The key is to boil the list down to the criteria that best serve as indicators of a system's level of criticality to the business. The next step is to assign a score to each criterion and then rate each of your systems on all these attributes. Totaling up the scores gives you a grand total that then can be used to stack rank all of your applications.

It may be possible to leverage the insight of an existing governance board or IT steering team to improve the validity of your ranking. In addition to making the ranking more accurate, it will take negativity and political pressure away from your efforts; after all, it wasn't your choice but that of the board. If, however, such a board doesn't exist at your company, then be cautious when asking business people which applications are most important, because they will often indicate that theirs are.

Also, when asking the business to help gauge relative application importance, it is useful to ask very specific questions in order to get a consistent and meaningful result, such as "Which applications, if they were completely unavailable for four hours, would cause irreparable harm to the business?" Perhaps if you were performing research for disaster recovery (DR) purposes, the interval would be 12 or 36 hours instead of four.

One other thing that sometimes gets confusing is the difference between an application and a subsystem. If there is an application that is deemed to be very important, then all of the layers of systems underneath that application that are required in order for it to run are very important as well, by implication. So as long as you know what supports what, you only have to rate the applications that are used by the business and not the subsystems underneath. Often a systems dependency diagram is handy to illustrate this; see chapter 7 for an example.

Keeping It Simple: Application Tiers

Depending on the method used above, you may have spreadsheets full of useful yet cryptic information. Here's how to simplify it into something really useful over the long term: group your applications into categories that everybody can easily understand. A popular approach is to use the medals system from the Olympics: bronze, silver, and gold. Some feel compelled to add a platinum level as well.

This application categorization can be useful in several ways. First and foremost, it will help you know what applications you should focus your energy on when it comes to improving production quality. If you and your team are getting solicited from many directions (e.g., by dissatisfied users of many different systems), and you need to make some tough choices as to who you're going to help and who you're going to have to politely send to the back of the line, it will be a much easier call to make once you know if a given issue is related to a gold or a bronze system. Few people will argue with your sense of priorities if you focus more on the golds and platinums of the world.

This application classification approach is also useful in negotiating service levels both within IT and with the business. When talking with the business, having the applications classified by level of criticality will aid in determining the allocation of funds to where they are needed the most. Instead of trying to explain how shooting for 99.9% availability for all applications in IT is not cost effective, the discussion can be about identifying the right target for availability in each category (e.g., 99.5% for bronze, 99.9% for silver and 99.95% for gold). This, in turn, will facilitate the establishment of service levels within IT.

For instance, you might have a different operating level agreement (OLA) with the hosting group for each application category. If your overall availability target for gold is 99.95%, then you want availability of the hardware to be higher (say, 99.97% or 99.99%) to allow room for non-hardware issues without affecting your overall goal. That way, the data center people will know which applications require more fault tolerance or on-site spare parts in order to meet the more stringent requirements.

It is also very helpful for DR purposes to have such a list. If your system is gold, perhaps it requires a fully duplicate copy in another data center with real-time data replication. If it's silver, perhaps the data replication can be nightly, and bronze means you ship tapes off-site every night and in the event of a problem, you procure hardware afterward and load the tapes. The appendix contains a basic example of a master systems list.

Once your application classification is well communicated and adopted, it can help you in one more important way: getting to PMM Level 5 by making certain best practices mandatory for higher-tier applications. One approach to this is to leverage whatever software development lifecycle (SDLC) methodology your company utilizes and bake a series of quality checks into it that may be required for higher-tier applications but optional for others. For instance, if you use the gold/silver/bronze taxonomy, you might make performance testing required for gold applications but optional for bronze. Throughout each step of the SDLC, you could incorporate required/optional practices that will ensure the most important applications get the most rigorous treatment, while not making the SDLC process overly complicated for lower-tier applications.

Now, we strongly believe that for shops with a large number of applications, this is great stuff. But sometimes there's resistance in organizations to prioritizing and creating a hierarchy of systems. People involved either on the business side or the IT side who own the silver and bronze systems resist because they feel this permanently relegates them to second-class citizenship status. They see a system hierarchy as a statement that they don't matter. They don't realize it, but these folks are diluting your focus across all systems because they insist all systems be treated equally, regardless of importance. This is why discipline is required in order to make the objective and data-driven choices that go into defining your system hierarchy. Ultimately, when everything is considered important, nothing ends up being important!

Are we advocating that silver and bronze systems never get worked on? Of course not. Once all the gold systems are under control, focus can be shifted down into silver. But you have to start somewhere, and working on the gold systems first gives you better return on investment. Surely, as a landlord, after you've addressed all of the important issues in your gold buildings, you would move on to take care of the rest. To ignore them indefinitely is a recipe for disaster.

Choosing the Right DRES

Now that you know which applications in your portfolio are most worthy of your investment, you are able to focus on them. It's a helpful step in the right direction, but if your list of gold applications has been pared down to nine, that's still a big list.

The next step is to decide what exactly to work on in those nine applications. You could direct your staff to work on everything in this book: Downtime, Response times, Error rates, and Scalability. But if your resources are finite, you still won't get a great result.

If you decided to approach your nine buildings with a "fix everything" approach, you'd still have a mountain of work in front of you, and you'd still have issues with plumbers, electricians, and painters tripping over each other. Plus, you'd have a huge cash outlay all at once. What you'd probably do instead is try to narrow down what really needs attention and focus on that.

To refine the focus further, we need to prioritize DRES for each application. And to get there is either a one-step process or a three-step process.

The one-step process is to handle the blindingly obvious. If the business is extremely unhappy with some aspect of IT, and they have clearly and consistently voiced their concerns—for instance, the application is so slow that it is hurting sales—then it may be as easy as starting there. If four of your nine "gold" buildings have had flooding issues in the last year due to faulty plumbing, you'd probably want to focus on plumbing above all else without needing any fancy analysis to tell you so.

The longer, three-step process is for all other production issues, and takes some resources to make happen.

Step One is to define specific quality goals for all gold applications within D, R, E, and S. These goals should make business sense, so don't feel like you need the same level of strict goals for each category. Perhaps your business is very sensitive to availability and performance, but doesn't care about errors and hasn't grown in five years, so scalability is not a concern.

Then devise very thorough and challenging goals for downtime and response times, and lighter goals for error rates and scalability. Do what makes sense. If you know that your commercial buildings all need top-rate air conditioning to be desirable, then make it a priority to make sure it's working right.

This is a flexible framework, to be sure. IT systems have similar alignment issues depending on their function as well. Depending on the type of business process, the relative importance of each of the four DRES areas may vary considerably.

For example, the accuracy of an ATM system when a customer needs cash is probably of higher importance than the availability of that ATM. It is more important to take the right amount out of the right account than it is for that particular ATM station to be online 24x7, especially if the ATM is in a large city where another one may be found nearby. In contrast, the availability of a Wi-Fi Internet access point at an airport may be more crucial than its performance. A traveler might be willing to accept a mediocre performance if all he needs to do is check e-mail. But if the access point is unavailable, there is no opportunity to charge a traveler for the service. For other systems, speed of transactions is paramount. Some online stock brokers base their whole marketing campaigns around speed of execution. A batch system that processes health care claims, on the other hand, will usually allow more flexibility in terms of availability, but in some cases will have a critical need to be able to scale because the company may be expanding into new markets rapidly. Making these decisions requires strategic thinking and is where you will earn your keep as a manager!

Step Two is to audit all of your gold applications against the goals set forth in Step One. This measuring process might take some time to implement for the first iteration, but it generally takes much less effort for subsequent cycles. Typically, this measuring is performed constantly, though the analysis of the data will more likely be monthly. This is where you get key insight to guide your decisions.

Step Three is to compare the data in Step Two against your goals, looking for variances: places where your applications missed one or more goals. Make a list of these variances, sorted by how big the variance is. This is where you start to apply focused effort to make improvements.

If you have standards for all of your nine gold buildings regarding heating and cooling, lighting, plumbing, security, and appearance, you would likewise want to audit against those standards on a regular basis (although for most buildings a longer interval than monthly probably makes sense) to make sure things are up to snuff. Then you would know where to apply your resources.

Also, keep in mind it is possible and appropriate to blend the one-step and three-step processes. You can vigorously work on the plumbing issues while keeping an eye on everything else. Perhaps for your IT shop you know availability problems are public enemy number one, but for R, E, and S, nobody is really sure. Feel free to attack availability issues immediately, and at the same time start to work RES in a more conventional way in the background.

In fact, you may desire two levels of goals—universal goals that apply across all of your gold applications, and application-specific goals that only apply to selected applications. Maybe only three of your nine gold applications are performance sensitive. And maybe only the 6 applications that support your new division are really growing much, so they are the ones you are concerned about from a scalability perspective. It's all up to you, but be thorough and clear here, because all of your staff are going to start reacting to your direction in a very powerful way.

Planning and Executing with MPIP

MPIP is a tool we've been using for several years to make sure that when we're attacking DRES, we're covering all of our bases. This is a key takeaway from the book that we highly encourage you to use. MPIP stands for the following:

- **Measure:** Measure, store, and trend everything related to the area of DRES you are working on.

- **Prevent:** In most cases, the IT equivalent of the Hippocratic Oath applies: "Do no harm." If you are making improvements in one area, and you or another team is also accidentally making things worse, you'll be both confused and unhappy. Get out in front of negative changes so that the rest of your program can roll out smoothly.

- **Improve:** This is where you are actively making changes to stabilize the systems in question.

- **Publish:** Share information on a routine basis with all shareholders so that they can assist you (or at least stay out of the way).

Using MPIP is a great way to ensure the success of your production quality initiatives.

The MPIP/DRES Grid

Table 11.1 is a handy device to keep track of your quality goals, along with the projects you undertake to support them. You could either have one of these grids for each of your gold applications, or you could have a large grid and, for each initiative, list which applications they apply to. By ensuring that you are taking specific actions to measure key indicators, prevent new problems, improve the current situation, and publish on all of the above (MPIP), you will be covered. If you start to fill out this grid and see a lot of blank spots, there is probably more you can be doing.

MPIP vs. DMAIC

If you are familiar with Six Sigma, you probably know of DMAIC, which in our opinion is the Six Sigma equivalent of MPIP. DMAIC stands for "define, measure, analyze, improve, and control." We came up with MPIP on our own, and it has worked great. DMAIC makes a lot of sense, too (though we enjoy the emphasis MPIP places on prevention and publishing). No matter your preference on the particulars, you can get a lot of mileage by using a simple, repeatable framework for planning your actions to achieve your quality goals. So we advise that you choose one (or make up your own!) and run with it.

Goal Family	Specific Quality Goals	Projects to Support Goals			
		Measure	Prevent	Improve	Publish
Downtime	99.XX% weighted availability <XX BII pts/month	Project A	Project C Project D Project E	Project C Project D Project E	Project H
Response Times	<X sec average page loads	Project A	Project F	Project F Project G	Project H
Error Rate	<.XX% page error rate	Project A	None	None	Project H
Scalability	Able to handle XX,000 business transactions per hour	Project B	Project B	Project B	Project H

table 11.1. Sample production goals sheet for one or more applications

In essence, for each quality area, you should have specific goals. Each improvement goal should have one or more projects in place to help achieve the goal. If the goal is just a "maintain the status quo" goal, then a corresponding project may not be required.

Are you unsure which projects will help you achieve your goals? You'll probably be surprised that, once the goals are made known, people will flood you with improvement ideas, probably whether you ask for them or not! If you communicate your important objectives widely, relevant projects just seem to have a way of making themselves evident organically. See "Goal Setting" in the appendix for an additional example of the grid.

Of course, in all the examples in this chapter, the point can be made that all four areas of DRES are important. And we wholeheartedly agree! But again, for the purposes of giving attention to the areas in need of it most, you must force yourself to determine the relative value of each area for each system.

Biting Off the Right Amount

How do you know if you're being aggressive enough while at the same time setting yourself up for success? That's a judgment call that you will have to make, but take the following factors into account.

- Make sure that the goals for your most important gold-system problems are meaningful. Ten percent improvement over a year is generally not all that impressive; aim higher in places so everyone can see the value of what you are trying to do.

- In a best-case scenario, you'd have a difficult time moving from PMM Level 1 to PMM Level 5 in the same year. Trying to jump so far in one fell swoop is fraught with peril. Whether it is in deploying large systems or implementing ambitious programs, the "big bang" approach often fails. Sometimes it's because the organization has only so much appetite for change, and other times it's because it simply takes too long for improvements to be seen, so the program loses steam and support. Set your yearly goals for less than that (perhaps shooting for PMM Level 3). If you make excellent progress, you can always ratchet up the goals at the mid-year progress check.

- Your ability to make change will be impacted by how you arrange your staff. If your current staff is already busy, and you don't free any of them up to work in a dedicated or semi-dedicated fashion on DRES, then you are going to have a difficult time making much progress.

While in an ideal world you would want all of your systems to be top-notch, the reality is that you have limited time and resources that you must use judiciously. You need a way to maximize the business's investment in IT by giving them the most bang for their buck. So you must first prioritize the importance of your systems and then assess the relative urgency of addressing and preventing their quality problems. It takes real discipline to create a hierarchy of systems based on business importance, but you'll never get to the top of the pyramid treating everything the same or pretending all systems are equal.

Confirm Your Approach with the Business

A recurring theme of this chapter is that you must have a good sense of what the business needs to be more successful. In a very small business, you probably already know this like the back of your hand. But as a business grows, separate business functions become more distant, and sometimes the lines of communication break down. With companies that have over 1,000 employees, this is a real danger.

So don't guess that response times are the most important thing. As landlord, if you worked extensively on your properties to upgrade the windows, but many of your tenants are fed up with outdated water fixtures and didn't care about the windows, the misalignment would result in a missed opportunity. Likewise, it'd be a shame for you to implement a very successful project to improve response times by 50%, only to find out that the business is getting killed by error rates. Do your homework.

Conversely, as noted in previous chapters, if the business has formalized key business goals, scrutinize them to see if IT can directly or indirectly help them succeed. Run your ideas by the business to make certain that, if implemented, your plans will truly be of value, and if so, then run with them.

It can be helpful to have a standing meeting with key business partners, in which you can share what you are working on and they can give you feedback on how they perceive things are going. It doesn't have to be all that often; a monthly or even quarterly breakfast may do the trick. And then you'll be armed with supplemental opinion to go along with all of your great data and statistics.

Prioritization and Communication Tools

Your approach for deciding and communicating priorities needn't be cumbersome. A simple assignment of one of the following relative values of each goal may suffice: very high, high, medium, low. Do this with significant input from the business. Acknowledge that all these goals are important, but ask what they would do if they were confronted with tough choices. For example, would they prefer an application that is always available, even if it sometimes doesn't perform well, or an application that may occasionally be unavailable but performs very well when it is?

Once you know what quality areas are more or less valuable to the business, determine whether you are already performing well in each area or not. Then summarize the two concepts in a table, like in table 11.2.

	Business Value of Goal	Meeting Goal?
Downtime	Very High	No
Response Times	High	Partially
Error Rates	Medium	No
Scalability	High	Yes

table 11.2. Simple DRES prioritization table

A glance at this table quickly indicates the area to focus on first: Downtime!

If plugging in your own data doesn't really make it as obvious as in table 11.2, a quick and easy technique is to plot the two dimensions in a grid as shown in figure 11.1.

The upper-right quadrant reflects the most important and urgent areas needing attention. In this simple example, there are just four circles, but you can use the same grid to overlay importance and compliance for your other top-tier systems and, at a glance, get a view of your roadmap to reaching higher system quality and satisfaction of the business. An even more advanced technique is to plot all gold systems on the same grid, using a different color for each application. Then you can easily see where your attention is most needed in the enterprise. It may be so obvious to everyone that this graph is not needed. But if it's not clear, this can be a useful tool.

How much you bite off is up to you, but at least with this you know where to start. Knowing where to start is not only good for you and your team, it's also good for the business. If the business has had input in the relative value of the goals, they will buy in to your approach to prioritizing execution, try to help you wherever they can, and be confident you're on the right track.

Making Your Own Luck

If you owned one or two homes and needed to do some remodeling, you might not feel the need to get out spreadsheets to figure out what to work on first. It's probably self-evident. But as you scale up to dozens or hundreds of properties, things get much more complex and thus more rigor is called for. If you just worked on things that were called in as complaints, you wouldn't be spending your time on the highest-value items. Unless you got lucky.

Likewise, if you're responsible for a small system with few moving parts and interfaces, perhaps you can get away with winging it. But if you're accountable for the health of one or more large enterprise systems, you'd have to be very lucky to just guess what your improvement plan should look like. And even if you are lucky once, luck won't help you execute the plan.

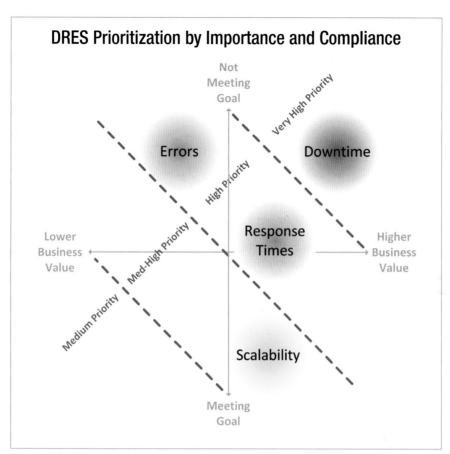

figure 11.1. DRES prioritization by importance and compliance

The only way we have been able to consistently execute with success is by applying the methods and techniques outlined in this book. None of which rely on dice, Ouija boards, or Magic 8-Balls.

Summary Checklist

✓ **Prioritize:** Trying to start doing everything in this book at once, particularly for large shops, is nearly impossible.

✓ **Prioritization methods:** There are numerous ways to prioritize, including the following:

  ○ Moving up the pyramid one level at a time

  ○ Focusing initially only on your most important business applications

  ○ Focusing initially on the parts of DRES that will have the most impact for your particular business or specific business application

  ○ Focusing on what is most broken—though doing this alone might not result in the most impact being made

✓ **Application tiers:** Dividing groups of applications into gold/silver/bronze tiers can be a helpful activity.

✓ **Governance:** You may be able to leverage an existing IT governance board or IT steering committee to help make some of the calls on what is most important.

✓ **MPIP:** Utilizing the MPIP framework (measure, prevent, improve, publish) to organize your goals can cover your bases in a way that increases your chances of making significant improvements.

  ○ The MPIP/DRES grid is a useful planning tool.

✓ **Partner:** Deal closely with the business to confirm you are working on the right stuff.

Conclusion

Scope

Above all else, we have attempted to make this a practical book about management. Regardless of what platforms you use, what industry your business is in, or how large your shop is, we have tried to give select insight that is valuable to management of IT, and specifically IT operations.

Putting the priority on practicality has freed us up to move laterally more than most other works in this genre—you won't find many books that mix discussions of CPU measurement with C-level communication with organization design. Yet here it is.

The Menu

Please recall that in the introduction, we advised you to keep an open mind and selectively pick and choose what you think will add the most value to your organization. Here is a brief recap of the material covered, sorted by Production Maturity Model level. Definitely be choosy here, and don't try to order everything off the menu at once!

PMM Level 1: Crisis Management

Level 1
Crisis Management

Chapter 1: In Case of Emergency Break Glass – *How to Manage a Crisis in IT*

✓ **Recognize a crisis**: If your solution or service is impacting the business in a highly negative way for an extended period of time, it's in crisis.

- ✓ **Deal with the crisis**: The purpose of this book is to avoid crises altogether, but when they do happen, you must stabilize your service or solution before you can start building a culture of quality.

- ✓ **SWAT Teams**: Create a SWAT team to resolve crises.

  - ◦ **Leadership in times of crisis**: It's critical to assign the appropriate leader or leaders of the SWAT team effort. The leader must be both sufficiently skilled and empowered to take the actions needed to resolve problems.

  - ◦ **The right SWAT team**: Your SWAT team must consist of skilled resources from all key teams, including vendor and business representation.

  - ◦ **SWAT team location**: The SWAT team is ideally colocated in a single room whenever possible.

- ✓ **Exit criteria**: Set objective quality targets that define what stability means and when the SWAT team effort ends.

  - ◦ Use technical monitoring to assess progress.

  - ◦ Understand the end-user experience to ensure technical improvements are translating into the needed business benefits.

- ✓ **Change management**: Use disciplined change management to effectively balance the risk of changes against the intended rewards and to understand the specific impacts of changes.

  - ◦ Make one change at a time whenever possible.

- ✓ **Too much of a good thing**: It's important to be good at crisis management, but it's dangerous and costly to become exclusively reliant on it. The best IT organizations do crisis management very well but very infrequently.

PMM Level 2: Defining Quality

Level 2
Defining Quality

Chapter 2: The Four Cornerstones of Production Quality – *Introduction to DRES*

- ✓ **Complexity:** Large IT systems are, by definition, highly complex and consequently difficult to manage.

✓ **Prevention:** If we don't prevent problems, they can have disastrous consequences for the business.

✓ **DRES:** The four key cornerstones of production quality, collectively known as DRES, are:

- Downtime

- Response times

- Error rates

- Scalability

✓ **Full picture:** No single metric actually captures overall production quality. Ignoring any of these four vital signs creates a situation in which IT is not aware of how a system is actually performing.

- All four must be monitored and measured concurrently in order to fully assess overall systems health.

✓ **Predictable results:** By proactively focusing on the four key quality areas for your mission-critical applications, you are much more likely to provide a predictable quality result and help the business succeed.

✓ **There's more:** While DRES covers the vital signs of production quality, there are other aspects of quality that shouldn't be ignored, such as security and usability.

Chapter 3: IT Orienteering – *Key Measurements for DRES*

✓ **Monitoring, measuring, and trending** are essential activities for managing IT quality.

✓ **Four essential measurements:** You must measure all four of the cornerstones of quality (downtime, transaction response times, error rates, and scalability) to ensure you're delivering and will continue to deliver the level of service your customers expect.

✓ **Downtime:** Measuring availability is a critical but also very basic and somewhat limited quality metric.

- **BII:** To truly understand the ramifications of outages, you need a metric that translates downtime into a quantifiable measurement of damage done to the enterprise. We call this the Business Impact Index, or BII.

✓ **Response times:** If you aren't measuring transaction response times, you may be delivering a poor customer or user experience and not even know it.

- Monitoring transaction responses can be done by active monitoring, whereby dummy transactions are created solely for the purpose of timing them, and passive monitoring, whereby actual business transactions are tracked as they happen.

- These are the four main methods of monitoring transaction response times:

    1. Stopwatch timings

    2. Instrumentation of custom code

    3. Installed monitoring software

    4. Third-party monitoring as a service

✓ **Errors** are the manifestation of single transactions or jobs that don't produce the expected result. Even when a system or service has high uptime and good response times, you can have serious quality issues if errors are happening.

- Errors are the hidden killer because they are not obvious like transaction slowness or a full-blown outage. They often go unreported and untracked, resulting in user frustration, increased costs, and customer dissatisfaction.

- Errors must be identified and categorized, and you must implement a system to track them.

- You need to understand the business impact of errors to rally the focus needed to eliminate them by fixing the broken technology or process that allowed them to be created in the first place.

✓ **Scalability** is the hardest of the four cornerstones to quantify and measure.

- Supply – Contention = Net Supply

- Net Supply – Technical Demand = True Spare Capacity

Chapter 4: Turning Problems into Opportunities – *Why Problem Management Is Your Best Friend*

✓ **Incident:** An incident is a single event that disrupts service to your production system or service.

✓ **Problem:** A problem is the issue that allows one or more incidents to happen.

✓ **Resolving problems:** By focusing on resolving all known problems, rather than just quickly closing incidents, you will be practicing a simple yet effective form of prevention that will improve quality over time.

- ○ If known problems are not worked, more incidents will occur from them.

- ○ A surplus of known problems that are not being worked can create an environment where quality is not valued, both because people can see that problems are acceptable and also because the "clutter" from having many open problems makes it more difficult to ascertain which problem caused a particular incident.

✓ **Attitude** is important. Every time an incident happens, treat it as an opportunity to make your systems better.

✓ **Tracking:** For trending purposes, carefully track the particulars of each incident in a database.

✓ **Band-Aids** are temporary solutions that mask problems but don't resolve the true root cause.

✓ **Keep asking why:** If you are unsure that you are getting to the true root cause, use the "keep asking why" technique to get to the bottom of things.

✓ **Prioritize:** If there are many open problems to pursue, prioritize them based on the business benefit of solving them. Always have a prioritized list handy, because it can be used for several things.

✓ **Culture:** Ingrain the culture of transparency and openness about problems into your group. Public criticism, blame, and heavy punishments will yield a culture of hiding problems, which doesn't serve your best interests.

✓ **Perseverance:** Problem management takes time and numerous actions to be successful. Work your prioritized list, and over the weeks, see your system quality trend in the right direction.

Chapter 5: Hands-On Problem Solving – *Powerful Problem Management Techniques*

✓ **Evidence and expertise:** Like a detective investigating a crime, an effective IT problem troubleshooter leverages evidence and expertise to get to the bottom of the problem.

✓ **Facts and data:** Systematically gather data and collect the facts of an incident.

✓ **Forensics:** When resolving an incident, while it is important to restore service as quickly as possible, it is essential to ensure forensic data, such as logs and dumps, are not lost.

✓ **Enlist** the help of all relevant technical experts.

- ✓ **No limits:** Obtain the appropriate permissions to cross organizational boundaries as part of your troubleshooting efforts to enable capture of all technical data you may need, no matter which organization the system or subsystem in question may lie in.

- ✓ **Circumstantial evidence:** Although factual evidence is most effective, circumstantial evidence can often be helpful in driving to root cause.

- ✓ **Proof:** Recreating an incident in a safe and controlled manner can be an effective way of achieving a high level of proof.

- ✓ **Use testing and validation** to ensure your hypothesis was correct and that the fix adequately addressed the problem.

PMM Level 3: Prevention

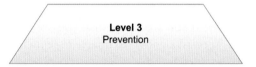

Chapter 6: Cut Your Incidents in Half! – *Prevention, Prevention, Prevention*

- ✓ **Preventive Care:** As in health care, preventive care of your IT systems creates a more stable environment and better longevity.

  - ○ There's no substitute for leading a healthy IT lifestyle.

- ✓ **Monitoring:** Effective systems monitoring makes you aware of problems before serious business impact occurs, allowing preventive actions to be taken.

- ✓ **Maintenance:** Routine systems maintenance is essential to good systems health and must always remain a priority. It may feel like you can get away with not doing it in the short run, but ultimately neglecting it leads to costly problems.

- ✓ **Tuning:** In order to perform well over time, system tuning is necessary, particularly for highly dynamic environments.

- ✓ **Audits:** It is vital to track in detail what you are running in production and do regular audits to ensure everything is still configured as it should be.

- ✓ **Change Control:** Rigorous change control is important and allows you to improve service quality by reducing incidents related to system changes; it also improves your time to restore when incidents happen.

- At a minimum, a good change control process should include change tracking, change review and approval, and risk assessment and mitigation.

- All changes involve different degrees of risk. Sometimes it makes sense to take risks, and sometimes it doesn't. Good change control allows you to make change decisions in an informed manner.

✓ **Access:** Be particularly judicious in allowing production access to non-operations personnel. Also ensure software programs all have unique database logins.

✓ **Upstream Influence:** IT operations must have influence in the software development process to ensure the needed quality in releases.

- Establish clear quality guidelines for development groups.

- Have operations participate in architectural decisions and design reviews.

✓ **Disaster Recovery:** A solid disaster recovery plan is needed in case unforeseen events cause your primary systems to become unavailable for a long period of time.

PMM Level 4: Information Promotion

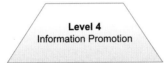

Level 4
Information Promotion

Chapter 7: The Power of Pictures – *How to Take Advantage of the Data You Already Have*

✓ **Diagram:** Most IT systems are complex. Not diagramming and visualizing them can cost you in several ways:

- Time wasted speaking a thousand words instead of looking at a single picture

- Time to train new hires

- Bad decisions based on insufficient understanding of how systems work or are interrelated

- Dependency on key staff or consultants who have all the information in their heads

- Lower service quality due to poor understanding of the health of the systems

- ✓ **Share:** Big organizations are more effective if all their members have access to the same, easily comprehended information about complex things. Then they can focus on higher-value tasks rather than simply trying to re-collect and re-comprehend vast amounts of information.

- ✓ **Value:** Envisioning information effectively does come at a cost, but it's a small investment when compared to the benefits.

- ✓ **Invest** in diagramming in situations that are *important* and/or *complex*.

- ✓ **Must-haves:** Typically, IT organizations benefit from the following diagrams (at minimum):

  - System interaction diagrams

  - System ownership diagrams

  - Data store diagrams

  - Data flow diagrams

  - Application dependency diagrams

  - Infrastructure diagrams

  - Geo-diagrams

  - Combination diagrams

- ✓ **Be creative:** Invent your own diagram that combines the various things that will make it useful.

- ✓ **Balance:** A good diagram is not too complex, yet not overly simple.

- ✓ **Expertise:** System subject matter experts need to be involved in creating or reviewing any system diagram, or the diagram is not likely to be used.

- ✓ **Combine:** Make diagrams come to life by combining static information (e.g., how a system works) with status information (e.g., health status of the system).

- ✓ **Quality** of data presented is more important than how fancy the representation of the data is.

- ✓ **Start simple:** It's perfectly fine to start with simple diagrams and enhance them as you go.

- ✓ **Pace:** Having high-quality information less frequently is better than having poor quality data in real time.

Create the equivalent of a Morningstar in your group to improve your organization's focus.

✓ **Transparency:** Openly publishing key facts and data (good *and* bad) about your systems and services will benefit you and the entire organization.

✓ **Trust but verify:** Rigorously publishing DRES data ensures you don't have to hope that all important metrics are being tracked and reviewed regularly.

✓ **Publish** summary DRES results for your key systems to a wide audience to give broad transparency into your system, its challenges, and upcoming plans.

✓ **Leverage:** Over time, more transparency will result in increased leverage; all who have an impact on the data published will exhibit more and more positive behaviors.

✓ **Reinforce** these positive behaviors by taking the following actions:

○ Run regular leadership alignment meetings to discuss and act upon the data published with key stakeholders

○ Host quarterly all hands alignment meetings with the entire department to motivate the teams, get everyone aligned, and build organizational capital

✓ **Neutrality:** In publishing data, remain neutral and focus on problems, avoiding finger-pointing.

✓ **There's more!** A nice side benefit of doing all this is that it's great for career building and upward managing.

PMM Level 5: Perpetual Motion

Chapter 9: The Invisible Hand of IT – *Get All of IT to Work for You*

Goals are a terrific tool for the IT manager that over time can help you solve your department's biggest problems and achieve great advances. Carefully select them and then leverage them to drive success. Here is a summary of how:

✓ **Goals:** Goals define priorities, drive alignment, and provide the best measuring stick. IT goals should always align with what matters most to the business.

✓ **The right goals:** The way to do that is to carefully set goals that make sense and are easy to gauge progress against:

- They must cover the four areas of Downtime, Response times, Error rates, and Scalability.

- They must be clear and simple to understand.

- They can't be too easy—they should challenge your people.

- They can't be impossible.

✓ **Good goals** are quantifiable, measurable, significant, and easily understood.

✓ **Broadcast goals:** This will help your personnel take actions and make decisions that align with the desired end result.

- Repeat them at regular intervals so that they will be taken seriously and not forgotten.

✓ **Shared goals:** Your goals program can be turbocharged by having shared goals across departments where it makes sense. That way, adjacent departments are more likely to cooperate with each other.

✓ **DRES alignment:** Define at least one overarching goal for each category of quality (DRES). Define multiple lower-level goals that contribute directly to one or more of the overarching goals.

✓ **Skin in the game:** Get everyone's skin in the game. Formally assign your goals to all relevant parties and hold them accountable—even if this means spanning multiple functions. Announce the goals in public forums and hold quarterly review meetings to reinforce them and track progress. This can be reinforced by having regular public checkpoints and aligning your compensation model with goal achievement.

✓ **Culture of performance:** Strong performers thrive in a goal-oriented culture. Poor performers resist being measured and graded. Use goals to create a culture of performance and achievement.

Chapter 10: A Brave New Org – *Organize for Quality*

✓ **Organizational challenge:** Large, intertwined systems have numerous teams to support their various parts, which has made comprehensive quality management complicated.

✓ **PEL:** Just as a symphony requires a conductor to ensure a successful musical performance, large IT systems may need a production excellence leader (PEL) to deliver holistic system quality results.

- ✓ **Accountability:** The PEL is your single point of accountability for system quality.

- ✓ **Matrix management:** The PEL owns the quality results but not all of the teams who support the system(s). Just as the conductor owns the musical result yet doesn't personally play all of the instruments.

- ✓ **PEL qualities:** The PEL role is highly challenging and requires a highly effective leader who is the following:

  - ○ Well organized

  - ○ Goal-oriented

  - ○ Agile working across boundaries

  - ○ Technically adept

  - ○ Politically independent

- ✓ **DRES team functions:** The PEL leads the DRES team, which has the specialized skills and roles intended to make all of IT more effective:

  - ○ Monitoring

  - ○ Root cause analysis

  - ○ Subject matter expertise

  - ○ Capacity and scalability planning

  - ○ Performance and scalability testing methodology

  - ○ Quality tracking and planning

  - ○ Quality status reporting

  - ○ Firefighting assistance

- ✓ **Roles:** The types of resources needed for the DRES team are the following:

  - ○ Thinkers/researchers

  - ○ Firefighters

  - ○ Measurers/trenders

  - ○ Project Managers

- ◦ Documenters/Publishers

- ◦ Managers

✓ **Executive support:** It's not so important who the PEL reports to, as long as there is the proper endorsement from the CIO.

Chapter 11: Where to Start – *How to Get Impressive Results Quickly*

✓ **Prioritize:** Trying to start doing everything in this book at once, particularly for large shops, is nearly impossible.

✓ **Prioritization methods:** There are numerous ways to prioritize, including the following:

- ◦ Moving up the pyramid one level at a time

- ◦ Focusing initially only on your most important business applications

- ◦ Focusing initially on the parts of DRES that will have the most impact for your particular business or specific business application

- ◦ Focusing on what is most broken—though doing this alone might not result in the most impact being made

✓ **Application tiers:** Dividing groups of applications into gold/silver/bronze tiers can be a helpful activity.

✓ **Governance:** You may be able to leverage an existing IT governance board or IT steering committee to help make some of the calls on what is most important.

✓ **MPIP:** Utilizing the MPIP framework (measure, prevent, improve, publish) to organize your goals can cover your bases in a way that increases your chances of making significant improvements.

- ◦ The MPIP/DRES grid is a useful planning tool.

✓ **Partner:** Deal closely with the business to confirm you are working on the right stuff.

Have Fun With It!

In IT operations, the mood can often turn sour, particularly when there has been a series of serious problems. You can implement these teachings in a harsh, cold way, or in a positive, encouraging way. For the most part, it will work either way, but the latter makes for much more rewarding careers.

We strongly recommend a balanced approach that seizes the opportunities to focus on the positives. Be inventive. Cook a fancy pancake breakfast for your folks (or shave your head or wash their cars, etc.) if they hit a certain target. Give awards when they are merited. Place at least as much focus on improvement as the bad news.

Seriousness has its place. Just use it judiciously. Remember, half the fun is getting there.

The Summit

We are firm believers that the contents of this book can lead you down the path to high levels of production IT quality and success. Doing these things is "The Opposite of Luck" and is the best way we know to begin your journey toward consistent quality. The advice is tried and true. We wish we'd had access to this information many years ago.

Yet this book does not contain all of the answers. An effective IT manager constantly looks for improvement opportunities wherever she might find them. So keep reading other books, study other methodologies, and participate in professional organizations in order to keep on the higher path of learning.

Appendix

This appendix holds a few examples of documents to help you manage and plan in such a way as to get upstream of your IT quality problems. These deliverables won't do all the work for you, but they will give you a head start.

Example: Goal Setting

When it comes to managing your department, you often get what you ask for. And if, above all else, you want high production quality, you have to explicitly ask for it!

Example figure A.1, utilizing the simple framework initially shown in chapter 11, puts strong emphasis on the different families of production quality. The strategic objectives are the outcomes you are seeking. The tactical goals are the how—what activities are you going to perform in order to meet your strategic goals?

Lastly, if you have your people involved in the creation of the goals, they will buy in more and work harder to achieve them.

2009 IT Production Quality Objectives (Strategic Goals)			
30% Improved Stability over 2008	**Good Client Response Times**	**Low Client Error Rates**	**Scale in Advance of Business Growth**
For all applications in IT: 27 Business Impact Index points per month or less	For applications A, B and C: • 95% of end-user page loads <4 seconds (broadband N. America) • 90% of end-user page loads <8 seconds (broadband rest of world)	For applications A, B and C: • .05% client error rate or less (broadband N. America) • .15% client error rate or less (broadband rest of world)	For top-10 customer-facing applications: Scale in advance of projected business growth with at least 20% headroom

	Underlying Tactical Goals in Support of the Quality Objectives			
Measure	Implement the Business Impact Index.	Utilize a 3rd-party internet performance monitoring service to perform a formal monthly deep dive on response time data.	• Utilize 3rd-party internet performance monitoring service to perform a formal monthly deep dive on error rate data. • Determine how to measure error rates for all back-end processing, including but not limited to middleware.	• Obtain business growth projections for next year from the business. • Create complementary projections in IT based on historical figures. • Take regular utilization measurements at the client, server, DB and network levels.
Prevent	• Perform a monthly scalability health check on all top-tier servers. • Build out DR phase 2 to improve our flexibility in the event of a disaster. • Continue to utilize a rigorous yet fair change control process that differentiates the level of control needed for high/ medium/low risk changes.	Performance test all new major releases before allowing into production.	During load and performance test of all new releases, inspect all layers of the application/ system for errors.	• Load test all major new releases before allowing into production. • Create and/or validate formal scalability plans for each system. • Audit all patch levels to make sure we are on suitable versions.
Improve	Host monthly incident trend analysis & action meeting.	Utilize 3rd-party internet performance monitoring service to fine-tune application response times.	Put team X in charge of monitoring, measuring and addressing errors in production.	Perform tuning audits, potentially involving vendors, to make sure we are getting the most out of our platforms.
Publish	• Create and publish a monthly production systems health report that covers all of the above. • Hold a formal monthly review with selected technicians and management for all of the above.			

figure A.1. Example of a yearly DRES goals table.

Example: Monthly Operational Review (MOR)

The spreadsheet in figure A.2 provides a summary of the quality results achieved for a family of applications. Ideally the categories would line up well with the yearly goals. This type of table is useful for walking through during a monthly review of group progress.

Enterprise Customer-Facing Applications Goals Matrix
Actual Results May 2009

#	Goal	Customer Care	Home Page	Order Entry	Billing Engine	Order Fulfillment	Sales Tool
	peak concurrent users	875	500	350	300	125	75
1a	Gold: 99.95% Availability		99.91%	100%			
1b	Silver: 99.9% Availability	100%			99.76%		100%
1c	Bronze: 99.8% Availability					99.85%	
2	Baseline Client Response Times for apps w/ >300 users	Put hooks into custom code to capture response times. Mining logs and generating monthly reports.	Implemented 3rd party monitoring tool.	NA - already in place.	Not started.	NA	NA
3a	Error Rate	Client crash rate .02% per day. Other errors under investigation.	.31% (mostly timeouts)	.84%	2.6%	Unknown	Unknown
3b	Error Resolution	94% <5 business days	Not tracked	97% <1 hour	83% <5 business days	Not tracked	Not tracked
4a	Annual Growth Rate	7%	29%	-4%	9%	2%	Unknown
4b	Scalability Headroom	25% DB CPU except NJ, 12%	55% DB CPU can add web servers in 3 weeks	Not a concern	15% peak, mainframe cycles limited	Not a concern	Unknown
5	Audit DR System & Procedure Effectiveness by EOY	Complete	Complete	On track	Complete	Not started	Not started
6	Audit: 3rd party hardware & software supported	Found 3 exceptions – creating plan to resolve	Clear	Found 1 exception – will live with until v6 (Aug)	Clear	Clear	Clear
7	Audit: Customer SLA current	2.5 years old. Meeting with key customers to refresh.	Does not exist.	Current.	4 years old.	Current.	Does not exist.
8	Detailed system health report published each month	Yes	Yes	Yes	Yes	Yes	Yes, but quarterly

figure A.2. Example of a monthly operating review template

#	Acronym	Name	Description	System Type	Service Level	PEL	Engineering Owner	Notes
1	ISW	International Shopping Web	Customer-facing sales front end through which 78% of company revenue comes	Customer Facing App	Gold	Li	Patel	
2		Global Network Infrastructure	Network for all internal, partner, and internet traffic	Infrastructure	Gold	Dubois	Gardov	
3		Big-IO	Web site load balancers	Infrastructure	Gold	Dubois	Patel	Project under way to upgrade to web-acceleration enabled load balancers
4	CI	CustInfo DB	Holds nearly all customer information	Subsystem	Gold	Dubois	Gardov	Active-Passive across 2 data centers
5	MK	Mid-Knight	Middleware used for the movement, processing, and recording of assets, and much of the back-end processing	Subsystem	Gold	Li	Patel	
6	SAN	Storage Area Network	Central storage for almost every gold application	Infrastructure	Gold	Dubois	Gardov	
7		WebCat	Product catalog	Subsystem	Silver	Li	Patel	Only silver because ISW caches product data on a daily basis
8	UPS	UPS	Uninterruptible Power Supply	Infrastructure	n/a	Dubois	Gardov	
9	CSMC	Customer Service Management Center	Section of the web site that customers use to interact with care reps	Customer Facing App	Silver	Li	Patel	Live chat going live in November
10	CP	Commission Plus	Calculates commission	Back office		Li	Patel	
11		Exchange	E-mail and shared calendars for all employees	Back office	Silver	Dubois	Gardov	
12	CMS	Coupon Management System	Initially just managed the ability for shoppers to use coupons. Now supports web promotions.		Silver	Li	Patel	
13		Sales Brain	BI system for sales data	Back office	Bonze	Li	Patel	Switches to Silver support in last 15 days of the quarter
14		FTP demo	Legacy download FTP site	Customer Facing App	Plastic	Dubois	Gardov	To be retired by end of year

figure A.3. Example of a simple list to track all systems within a company or operating unit.

Example: Master Systems List

The basic spreadsheet in figure A.3 is a central repository containing a line for every system and application supported by IT. While a larger company may implement a formal service catalog, perhaps even a purchased vendor product, a smaller company may not have the resources available to do so. This simple alternative is far better than nothing.

As with many of the charts we recommend, the Master Systems List has many uses. It can be used to track ownership so that when problems come up the right people can be contacted. It can be used for DR planning. It can be used for SLA management. It can be used to train new IT staff. And so on.

For most companies, it makes sense to put each entry into one of four categories: customer facing systems, back office, subsystems (systems that support other systems without their own front end), or infrastructure.

It can be useful to augment the above information with some basic load statistics, such as number of users, number of transactions, number of servers, and size of data store for each application. It can also be helpful to track what platforms are used by the various systems.

Example: Business Impact Index (BII)

The Business Impact Index allows you to quantify the business impact of one or more IT incidents. It allows you to compare the harm of incidents to one another, even if they are not in the same application. This can be very useful to see if you are doing better over time or not, or to take specific action for very large incidents.

To determine figures for the various incidents, you have to build a formula that is specific to your business. This is only an example—the specific implementation is up to you. For usability, we recommend making the scale such that all incidents achieve one of a small number of levels (perhaps three, four, or five), and that the point value for the levels is somewhat exponential. Here are two sample formulas, one for OLTP and the other for batch.

OLTP

Step 1: Determine Raw Downtime (DT)

Raw Downtime = Number of minutes that the system was unexpectedly unavailable.

Do not count approved, planned downtime in this formula.

If multiple applications are impacted by the same incident, perform each step separately for them and add the total at the end.

Step 2: Calculate End-User Downtime (EUDT)

If the user base is known, multiply typical user base at time of the incident by the number of raw downtime minutes.

If the user base is not known, estimate.

For web applications, estimate based on typical usage (visits per hour divided by average length of visit) at that time. Web traffic tracking software can be very handy for this.

Step 3: Adjustments

Adjustment A: Adjust Based on Business Function

Some applications are more important than others, and thus cause more or less business pain when they become unavailable (you will need to assign a level of criticality to all of your business applications and store them in a table or spreadsheet).

We will categorize discounts based on the criticality of the business functionality that is unavailable.

If multiple categories are impacted, assign the highest impact category (lowest discount).

- Extremely time critical or contract-critical - - - - no adjustment

- Highly Critical - discount EUDT by 25%

- Moderately Critical - - - - - - - - - - - - - - - - - discount EUDT by 50%

- Somewhat Critical - - - - - - - - - - - - - - - - - - discount EUDT by 75%

Adjustment B: Partial Outage Discounting

If an application is partly available during a timeframe, discount by the amount the application was working properly:

- Partial functionality: We could still sell gadgets but not widgets. Gadgets make up 80% of sales. So discount by 80%.

- Partial geography: We couldn't create bills for European customers, who make up 37% of sales. So discount by 63%.

- Partial response time: The app is working, but is 200% slower than normal. Since it's working 33% as fast as normal, discount by 33%.

Normally, we wouldn't recommend officially calling an outage if the response time degradation is minor to moderate, say, less than 50% slower than normal, though it depends on your business sensitivity to this category of quality.

Step 4: Apply Business Impact Level

Add the Discounted EUDT together for all the applications impacted by the incident.

Using that number, choose the incident level based on a table (that you create) such as the example in table A.1.

Discounted EUDT (minutes)	Discounted EUDT (hours)	Level Name	Incident Level	Points
<18,000	<300	Small	1	1
18,000–60,000	300–1,000	Medium	2	3
60,000–300,000	1,000–5,000	Large	3	10
300,000–1.5m	5,000–25,000	Extra Large	4	50
>1.5m	>25,000	Catastrophic	5	250

table A.1. Incident business impact level table

Creating this table in such a manner that it works properly is tricky business, to be sure. Generally, we recommend devising a scenario that would truly be a catastrophe for your business, such that you make the newspapers or lose customers—for instance, if your primary sales application stays down for two full days. Then work backward from there to fill out your table.

Batch/Other

Since batch applications don't have user bases that reflect their business importance, use specific formulas based only on the amount of time each batch app was down (table A.2).

Downtime	Level	Points
0–60 minutes	1	1
60–240 minutes	2	3
4–12 hours	3	10
12–48 hours	4	50
2+ days	5	250

table A.2. Batch application X

And some applications, especially financial applications, are more sensitive at the beginning or end of the month. So it is entirely appropriate to have dual scales for such a situation (tables A.3 and A.4).

Downtime	Level	Points
0–60 minutes	1	1
60–240 minutes	2	3
4–12 hours	3	10
12–48 hours	4	50
2+ days	5	250

table A.3. Batch application Y from 5th–25th of each month

Downtime	Level	Points
0–15 minutes	1	1
15–60 minutes	2	3
1–4 hours	3	10
4–12 hours	4	50
12+ hours	5	250

table A.4. Batch application Y from 26th–4th of each month

At the end of the day, these scales and formulas need to work for you, so don't feel constrained by what you see here. A good way to validate whether your scale does what you think it needs to is to apply the formula to historical incident data to see what happens. And even after you launch, it's okay to tinker, as long as you keep the tinkering to a minimum and only do it to make the result as accurate as possible.

Example: Production Release Guidelines

As a production manager, if you aren't involved in the creation of new software releases, you should be. You can add tremendous value by making clear to the release team what is important regarding your ability to operate the software they deliver. You can give them a target to aim at. Furthermore, you can check their progress to ensure that the quality is up to snuff. And in the undesirable and unlikely event that they are trying to toss software over the wall that isn't operationally sound, you'll have the ammunition you need to prevent the release until changes are made.

Generally speaking for large enterprises, we recommend creating a reasonably short formal requirements document that gives the development team a clear idea of what you expect of them. Then you can take that document and meet with each release team early on to make sure they are clear on what you need to succeed.

Here we have listed out examples of several categories of quality to consider when creating your own guidelines. Note that this level of rigor is likely only appropriate for your largest and most high-profile applications.

Requirements Relating to SDLC

Name	Description
Technical Design Review	The development team should host one or more formal technical design review meetings for the operations team to understand the technical design and be able to comment on any operations-specific design issues early enough in the process that they can be addressed.
Load Testing (a.k.a. Scalability Testing)	The application must be tested to demonstrate that it can handle the business load that will be placed on it, plus a comfortable margin for growth (at least X%). Detailed results must be made available for all utilization, including CPU, memory, storage, and network, on all tiers of the system (client, server, middleware, etc.) Any warning conditions (such as memory contention or disk contention) must be flagged in the report. It may be reasonable to request that operations provide limited personnel to assist in this activity.
Performance Testing	The application should be tested to demonstrate that it can provide adequate response times while under the business load that will be placed on it (on realistic data sizes as well). Detailed results should be made available for all frequently used business transactions. Any response times in excess of what is specified in the business SLA (or over eight seconds in lieu of an SLA) should be flagged.
Test Scope Review	The test plans for system test, load test, and performance test should all be formally reviewed with operations in a meeting before beginning execution, so that operations can comment on the plans.
Test Results Review	The results of system test, load test, and performance test should all be formally reviewed with operations in a meeting.

Requirements Relating to Production Quality

Name	Description
Response Times	The application's client response times while under load and using production data sizes should be acceptable to the business. At a minimum, this means no button clicks that take longer than eight seconds to respond. Any exceptions should be addressed. Any more-stringent business requirements would trump this simple threshold (and, in fact, it is preferable for the business to provide requirements in this area rather than operations).
Recovery From Network Blip	In the event of a short network incident, the system as a whole should recover gracefully and not need to be restarted.
DB Connections	For applications that access a database, the application should not utilize a prohibitively high number of database connections, such that the database cannot provide enough connections to all of the requesting applications.
Stability/Crashes/ Hanging/Fatal Errors	The application and all of its components should not crash, hang, or produce fatal errors. If any whatsoever are detected during load test, they should be flagged and addressed before go-live. This is particularly true on the server side. If one client out of a very large number of clients crashes one time only, this may be acceptable.
Error Rates	The error rates for the application should be within acceptable thresholds. Any errors identified during load test from any subsystem (client, server, middleware, network, etc.) should be flagged and addressed prior to deployment.
Single-Threaded Processes	Any server-side designs that incorporate single-threaded processes should be analyzed from a scalability perspective. If there is any question whether such components will scale to meet demand, every effort should be made to make them multi-threaded.
Database Coding Guidelines	All custom code written for the application should adhere to efficient database coding best practices.

Requirements Relating to Operability

Name	Description
Error Capture	All errors captured by the application should be written to a log for troubleshooting purposes (at all levels of the application, including client, server, and middleware). The detail in the log should be sufficient to allow the troubleshooter to diagnose the problem.
Memory Leaks	The application should not leak significant amounts of memory, if any. If an application needs to be restarted more than once a month to clear a memory leak issue, that is far too much.
Operations Training Session	Before deployment, there should be a formal meeting in which key operations personnel are walked through the procedures required to operate the application.
Simple Cycle	The process to start or shut down the application should be as straightforward as possible, reducing the chance of error by the operations team. Where possible, the process should be scripted, and any associated manual procedures should have written guidelines and be extremely clear and unambiguous.
Log Levels	The level of logging should be configurable such that if production personnel need more data to diagnose a problem, they can increase the level of detail, yet if so much data is being logged that it is difficult to accommodate the file sizes, the level of detail can be decreased. Ideally, the configuration would be dynamic so that the application would not need to be restarted to recognize the change, though this may not be feasible.
Application-Level Monitoring	If any application-specific values (as opposed to standard infrastructure monitoring, which is assumed to be automatically covered by operations) need to be monitored to ensure the smooth running of the application, they need to be formally documented. If the values are large in number or otherwise complex, a utility should be provided to assist with the monitoring of the values.

Requirements Relating to Formal Documents

Name	Description
Infrastructure Request Document	If new infrastructure is needed for this release, it should be formally requested of operations in advance. The timeline for the requests is dependent on the nature of the infrastructure—new gear requiring floor space in the data center or an enormous amount of network bandwidth may require months, while a small to moderate amount of additional disk may only require weeks. If insufficient lead time is given, the infrastructure may be provisioned suboptimally, at higher cost, or not at all.
Deployment Plan (Includes Rollback Plan)	The deployment itself should have a formal, written plan along with a timeline of activities. The plan should also include the timeline for support handoffs and make clear at what point the application will begin following the standard formal change review process. Also, if the application is an upgrade or replaces an existing application, the deployment plan should contain a formal, detailed rollback plan in the event that the deployment needs to be rolled back. Depending on the criticality of the application, it may be desirable to test the rollback plan as well.
System Administration (SA) Guide (SAG)	Development should provide a formal system administration guide for production personnel to use. This should include, at a minimum, installation and uninstallation procedures, startup and shutdown procedures, key application statistics to monitor, troubleshooting guidelines, and escalation contacts. For each release after the initial launch, the existing guides should be updated.
Batch Administration Guide (BAG)	If the application has one or more batch components, detailed directions on how to operate batch should be provided. In addition to day-to-day operations, this should include guidelines on data archival and deletion.
Scalability Plan	The development and operations teams should jointly produce a detailed, formal scalability plan for the application as it grows. For instance, this plan could assume that the application will need to quadruple in terms of users and business volume over the next four years (the desired rates of growth could vary greatly depending upon your business). The plan should address how to add bandwidth at every level.

Disaster Recovery (DR) Plan	Development and operations should jointly produce a detailed, formal disaster recovery plan before deployment. This plan would detail the steps to recover the application from a severe incident, such as destruction of a data center.
Business Customer Service Level Agreement (SLA)	The main business customers of the application, along with development and operations, should negotiate and sign off on a service level agreement (SLA) that details the expectations of the user experience. This should include, at a minimum, the hours of operation, availability target, client response time targets, error rate targets, data archival and deletion timeframes, and supported business growth levels of the application.
System Interaction Diagram	The development team should provide a detailed yet straightforward diagram that shows how all of the key components and external systems interact with each other. Ideally, this would be delivered at the operations training session.
Deferred Defects Document	Any defects that are agreed to be allowed to enter production should be formally documented in a list prioritized by severity and made available to the operations team before deployment.

Once you've determined what requirements are important to you, you should probably categorize them as high/medium/low, and assign owners to each specific requirement from the development and operations teams. These requirements are primarily designed to address the concerns of the operations team. There may be other parties in addition to the business who have requirements (e.g., security, compliance, etc.), so you may want to consider taking their input into account as well.

Requirements Document Usage

Use of this document is a game, or a dance if you will. It is difficult to be successful by being hostile. Rather, there are two general pieces of advice that will get you the best results:

1. Engage development as early as reasonably possible. This will give them the most time to plan and prepare to adapt to your requirements.

2. Whether you are organized as a PEL team or any other production group, truly partner with development to get what you need to succeed. If development doesn't fully understand your requirements, offer up one to two of your people on a part-time basis to interpret them. If development doesn't have the deep database skills to completely fulfill your requirements, have one of your skilled production DBAs pitch in to investigate. With your help-

ful participation, you are demonstrating that you want the overall effort to succeed, and you will be taken much more seriously.

Near the end of a release cycle, you may also have to do some negotiating. Perhaps there is a severe business need to cut a release quickly. Perhaps a release is on the small side and can't afford all the rigor from a budgeting perspective. Rather than handcuff the business with your requirements, you may have to pick and choose what is truly important to you. It is an interesting part of the game to determine when to put your foot down and when to cave in.

There may be other reasons to feel comfortable with negotiating away requirements. For instance, if a release is going to utilize a long pilot in order to assure quality before a full cutover, then some other risk mitigation techniques may be reduced or eliminated entirely. Or if a release is tiny and thus the risk is small to begin with, these may not apply at all.

Ah, so many judgment calls. That's why you make the big bucks.